ADVANCE PRAISE

"In *Radical Self-Care for Helpers, Healers, and Changemakers*, Nicole Steward translates her gifts to the book we have all been waiting for. It's a rare gem when you come across a book that helps you feel deeply seen amid the throes of burnout. Every page is written with undeniable compassion and points to the systemic structures that keep us in cycles of overwhelm. Instead of offering a checklist of quick tips, Steward instead is a close companion, holding up the mirror and allowing us to finally see the truth and return home to ourselves with deep care. A true recalibration for the spirit. You won't be the same when you finish this book."

—**Zahabiyah Yamasaki, MEd, RYT,** trauma-informed educator, consultant, and author of *Trauma-Informed Yoga for Survivors of Sexual Assault: Practices for Healing and Teaching with Compassion*

"*Radical Self-Care for Helpers, Healers, and Changemakers* is an incredibly useful resource for those who have committed their lives and professions to helping and healing others, especially those furthest from justice. Recognizing the immense importance of helping and healing others, individually and collectively, Nicole Steward highlights the need for self-care among those doing this important work and outlines skills and tools to make this a reality. Each chapter culminates with a list of cultural and ancestral practices readers may consider for their self-care. This book is a gem of a resource brimming with practical tools and ideas."

—**Parvin Ahmadi,** school superintendent and president of the Association of California Administrators, 2023–2024

"Steward draws from her years of experience as a social worker to lay the foundation for her book on radical self-care. She introduces the reader to the definition of radical self-care, discusses historical and societal influences around it, and shares her personal journey with examples from her own lived experiences and self-reflections. Her book serves as an instruction on how and why to embark on a journey of deep and meaningful self-reflection, and provides the reader with the next steps and tools in achieving more impactful and workable self-care practices. This book emphasizes the important balance of taking care of self—and why and how we can do so—as we continue to care for and serve others within our professional capacities."

—**Michelle A. Jorden, MD,** practicing forensic pathologist and neuropathologist

RADICAL SELF-CARE FOR HELPERS, HEALERS, AND CHANGEMAKERS

Note to Readers: This book is intended as a general information resource for social workers, teachers, healthcare professionals, caregivers, and other professionals whose jobs regularly involve working with people in crisis. In certain cases, the gender of the people described has been changed. The author is not a neuroscientist or other healthcare professional, a sleep specialist, or a cold immersion therapist. Please do not do any yoga exercises without consulting a healthcare professional to make sure it is safe for you to do so, especially if you have diabetes or any other condition that may affect your circulation. If you feel severely depressed or you have any doubt or concern about your own physical or emotional health or well-being, consult a healthcare professional. Do not hesitate to seek emergency care for yourself if you think it may be needed.

Products or service providers recommended in this book are preferences of the author. Please conduct research and utilize professional advice to find the services that are best for you.

Any URLs displayed in this book link or refer to websites that existed as of press time. The publisher is not responsible for, and should not be deemed to endorse or recommend, any website other than its own or any content that it did not create. The author, also, is not responsible for any third-party material.

Printed in the United States of America
First Edition

For information about permission to reproduce selections from this book, write to Permissions, W. W. Norton & Company, Inc., 500 Fifth Avenue, New York, NY 10110

For information about special discounts for bulk purchases, please contact W. W. Norton Special Sales at specialsales@wwnorton.com or 800-233-4830

Manufacturing by Lake Book Manufacturing
Production managers: Gwen Cullen and Ramona Wilkes

ISBN: 978-1-324-03017-1 (pbk)

W. W. Norton & Company, Inc., 500 Fifth Avenue, New York, NY 10110
www.wwnorton.com
W. W. Norton & Company Ltd., 15 Carlisle Street, London W1D 3BS

1 2 3 4 5 6 7 8 9 0

radical self-care

FOR HELPERS, HEALERS, AND CHANGEMAKERS

NICOLE STEWARD

An Imprint of W. W. Norton & Company
Independent Publishers Since 1923

This book is dedicated to all the youth and families I've served throughout my career. Thank you for trusting me to hold space for your stories, your struggles, and your successes. Thank you for sharing your courage and resilience with me. May you be happy, may you be safe, may you be at peace.

This book is also dedicated to all the helpers, healers, and changemakers who came before and especially to those who did not survive this work. My radical self-care practice is a dedication to you, honoring the sacrifices you made to create a more just, healed world. Thank you.

And for Yasmine and Kenya. Auntie Niki loves you to the moon and back.

CONTENTS

ACKNOWLEDGMENTS

Writing this book has been one of the biggest challenges I've taken on so far in my life, second only to being a foster parent. It would not have been possible without the love and support of my amazing husband, Dr. William T. Armaline (Bill), who picked up *all the slack* while I labored on this manuscript (even as he wrote his own book, *Human Rights Praxis and the Struggle for Survival*). He has healed me in so many ways over our 28+ years together and is absolutely my person.

Asa Archibald, thank you for letting me come into your life almost 15 years ago. I am so incredibly proud of the man and father you are and are constantly becoming. Thank you for your unconditional love and support over the years. I can't wait to read the book I know you will write!

I also have to thank the people who made me who I am . . .

My parents, who made education a priority in our home. My dad, Jefferey Steward, worked hard so we could live in a good school district, and my mom, Julie Steward, worked hard to make our house a love-filled home. My mom was my first example of what helping others looked like and provided invaluable input into the writing of this book. Thank you for your unconditional support, Mom.

My sisters December and Rosalyn are also a huge part of who I am. I loved being a middle child and being the negotiator of the family . . . is it any shock that I became a social worker!? I am so lucky to have these two wonderful women as my confidants and partners in crime. And my brother Joel, Jr., who I just reconnected with recently—thank you for seeing me and for being the same kind of weird as me.

I have many aunts, uncles, and cousins, but I need to acknowledge my Aunt Carrie and Uncle John Boerio who let me live with them after undergrad and while I was working for CASA. Thank you for putting up with my messes and my crafts, and for being my surrogate family. I love all my cousins too, but my cousins, Tony Boerio, Michelle Boerio, and Jennifer Lacey Keller specifically have been very active in cheering me on with this book. Thank you for your love and support.

My wonderful in-laws, Bill Armaline and Kathy Farber, for their love and support. Special LOVE to my mother-in-law for giving me honest feedback on this manuscript and for reminding me (very gently with lots of love) to stay in my lane when writing about topics beyond my scope of expertise. Kathy, thank you for your firm but loving guidance. I am truly grateful for you. My sister-in-law Abby Griffith, a fellow social worker, also provided invaluable guidance and support for this book. Thank you, Abby.

I am very lucky to have an amazing group of friends who have been an integral part of my becoming, who have held me up, and cheered me on. My best friend from middle school, Stephanie Schollenberger Gundogdu, has been my ride-or-die for more than 30 years. (We're old!) Though we're on different ends of the country, we have a connection that cannot be broken. My friends from undergrad and the University of Toledo's Leadership UT program helped make me the leader I am today. My MSW cohort and friends from the University of Connecticut School of Social Work shaped who I am as a social worker and social justice warrior.

My mentors from the University of Connecticut School of Social Work, Dr. Eleanor Lyon, Dr. Robin Spath, and the late Dr. Barbara Pine. Each of these amazing women encouraged my academic pursuits and supported me as I entered the field. If I am any good as a social worker, it is because of what I learned from these amazing, intelligent, powerful women.

I have also been very blessed to have some amazing colleagues, my emotional support coworkers. While I can't name everyone, I want to thank my coworkers and bosses from the various agencies I've worked: executive directors Rita Soronen and Kathy Bartlett from CASA of Franklin County; Gail Burns-Smith, Nancy Kushins, Joanne Zannoni, and Laura Cordes from the Connecticut Sexual Assault Crisis Services (CONNSACS, which is now the Connecticut Alliance to End Sexual Violence); Mary Lynn Fitton from the Art of Yoga Project and Taraneh Sarrafzadeh from Be The Change Yoga & Wellness; superintendents Doug Gephart, Parvin Ahmadi, Cary Matsuoka, Cheryl Jordan, and my colleagues from Fremont Unified, Pleasanton, and Milpitas schools districts. Each of these folks hired me and supported my growth as an employee. I am grateful for the experiences, good and challenging, that I had in each of these agencies and for the great work we got to do together on behalf of survivors, clients, and students.

When I moved from Connecticut to California, Pam Lozoff, MSW was the first person I ever mentioned my idea of radical self-care to and she instantly encouraged me to share it with the world. This book is a testament to the power of Pam's belief in my work from the start. My "OG Yoni Crew": Revia Romberg, Laura Damian, and Gali McClure, and my girls Noel Clark and Shandara Gil for their unconditional encouragement and constant reminders that I can do great things in the world. I also have to mention Jenna Alderton and Sara Stockinger, both social workers I met on Instagram, but who have become confidants and trusted advisors and who hold space for me in my darkest moments. This book wouldn't have seen the light of day without their persistent urging that my work is needed. Love you ladies!

A HUGE thank you to Deborah Malmud, Mariah Eppes, Jamie Vincent, Julie HawkOwl, Olivia Guarnieri, McKenna Tanner, and the amazing team at W. W. Norton who helped this overwhelmed social worker write a book. After many, many deadline extensions (over three years . . .), I am eternally grateful for their patience and understanding through this process.

And this book would still be an idea in my heart without Zabie Yamasaki. Zabie hired me to teach her Trauma-Informed Yoga for Survivors of Sexual Trauma at Stanford University and at UC Berkeley over a decade ago and encouraged my radical self-care workshops. After finishing her book with W. W. Norton, Zabie spoke my name in rooms I wasn't in and connected me with Deborah Malmud, so I could bring this book into existence. Zabie, from the bottom of my heart, THANK YOU.

There are many more wonderful humans who have poured into me, motivated me, mentored me, encouraged me, and supported me along this crazy journey. Too many to name here, but know that your contribution has not gone unnoticed or unappreciated. THANK YOU to anyone who has crossed my path and helped me learn how to be a more present, grounded, radical voice in the world.

PREFACE

As I started my social work career, more than 20 years ago, I began noticing the heaviness of the work and looked for ways to hold it. I knew it would be challenging work, but no one told me being a social worker would break my heart. And certainly no one told me being a social worker might harm my health. There was no guidance on caring for myself amid the heaviness and heartbreak of this work, even in my graduate program. Once, I asked a professor how to handle the heaviness of working with child abuse, and the response was, "Well, occasionally when I get really overwhelmed, I take myself to the opera."

That's cool, but that wasn't a helpful response for a broke graduate student who was seeing the devastating reality of child abuse and the lack of prevention, resources, or political will to protect children. I entered my career with solid social work skills but without a foundation of support or a real understanding of the kind of care I needed, as a social worker, to hold the weight of the work that would become my life's calling.

My work as a rape crisis counselor at the height of the Catholic church abuse scandal in New England in the early 2000s left me facing my first real burnout. I found myself sacrificing my health and well-being to serve survivors with an internal sense of urgency I couldn't control. *I had to save the world from child sexual abuse!* This meant working long hours, being on call, and ignoring my own needs for food, sleep, bathroom breaks, etc. to be available for the deeply sensitive needs of victims/survivors. I was in a constant state of hypervigilance to meet the urgency of the work.

Soon, I began experiencing health issues. My hair started falling out in clumps, rashes broke out all over my body; I had insomnia, caused by intrusive nightmares about survivors and their stories; and

I alternated between lacking an appetite and binge eating comfort food. Most insidiously, a triggering of my own trauma history caused a shift in my world view, causing me to see every man as a threat to the safety of women and children. I even jumped whenever my boyfriend (now husband), one of the safest men I know, touched me. I wasn't "in" my body and when I spent time with loved ones, they would often tell me I "wasn't there." I dissociated from myself as a form of protection from what I now know was vicarious trauma.

In an effort to engage in self-care, I adopted the "treat yo self" ethos of self-care, spending money I didn't have on manicures, happy hours, massages, vacations, books, and random things that made me feel better in the moment but did nothing to alleviate the stress and trauma I was absorbing from my work. Buying into the commercialized, capitalistic version of self-care only exacerbated my health issues toward addictions and unhealthy habits that landed me deep in credit card debt.

And I was *still* burned-out.

It would take two more major burnouts, including being tested for lupus and getting shingles in my 30s, for me to realize that my attempts at self-care were not working and that I needed something more sustaining. I needed something that truly supported my mind, body, spirit, and heart in this work without draining my bank account, negatively impacting my health, or stimulating the need to chase adrenaline/dopamine hits or the latest wellness trend. I needed to get out of survival mode, out of fight-or-flight mode.

The result of my search for *deeply rooted healing* to support my body, mind, and spirit, is the book you're reading now.

I read and reread books by activists, feminists, therapists, and revolutionaries which prompted the cultivation of radical self-care practices to counter the constant dysregulation I experienced as a social worker. I began to research compassion fatigue and vicarious trauma, which allowed me to understand what was happening in my brain and body. I gave myself permission to center caring for myself amid my work, which felt all-encompassing. I found communities of fellow social workers, advocates, and other child welfare professionals—my allies, and accomplices—who were also searching for answers to their dysregulation.

I started by listening to and coming back into my body, which I had abandoned and dissociated from for the sake of serving others. On my yoga mat, the connection between movement and breath brought me back to myself. Yoga brought me individual healing on my mat and introduced me to a global community of yogis to support my healing journey. The poses helped me stand in my power both on the mat and at work. My experience with yoga prompted my exploration of meditation, breathwork, mindfulness, restorative practices, and sound healing practices (and their respective communities) as additional supports for my healing and nervous system regulation.

I reclaimed myself, my passion, and my purpose, but I did not do it alone.

This is the essence of radical self-care.

We must initiate and actively engage in our own care, but *we do not have to do it alone.*

This book is the culmination of many conversations I've had with fellow helpers, healers, and changemakers over the past 20 years. While I had to be the one to initiate and do the work, there was—and is—an entire community behind me, supporting me every step of the way.

This is the book I needed 20 years ago when I started my social work career. This book is a gift, an offering of love, and a respectful nudge to my fellow helpers, healers, and changemakers—especially for those who have served through the pandemic (my fellow essential workers, I see you!), for those who are returning to or staying in the work, and for those who are considering these professions in the future. May this book be a reminder of the transformative work you do, a declaration of worthiness, and a communal offering of deep, courageous support as you continue to be the change we need in this world.

Thank you for the work you do and for how you show up for those you serve. It's time for us to show up for ourselves and each other. I see you, I love you, I love us. Now let's get to it!

The world is filled with way too many bright people for us to still have all the problems we have in the world. . . . We have the answers. We have the technology, we have the wealth, we just have to be willing to share it. And in order for us to do that, we have to do the work in and on ourselves so that we can be conduits of change and improvement for other people.

—Lauryn Hill, The London Hotel, 2018 NBA All-Star Weekend (Edwards, 2018, 5:05; 7:11)

INTRODUCTION

> If we have no peace, it is because we have forgotten that we belong to each other.
>
> —Mother Teresa, *Where There is Love, There is God*

Things are off.

The past few years have dysregulated, disconnected, and dislocated us in ways we are still feeling and just beginning to measure. The rhythm and cadence of our lives have been continuously interrupted by unrelenting streams of social, political, and economic challenges: recessions, mass shootings, police brutality, homelessness, an insurrection, natural disasters, climate change, the pandemic. The pace of our work, the manipulation of information, the dishonest use of data, the lack of resources, the intrusion of politics, and the purposeful destruction of social supports are meant to keep us off center. If we're honest, we've been a little off for a while. It just took a pandemic to shake everything loose and to expose systemic inequalities and crumbling infrastructure.

While the COVID-19 pandemic shed light on the broken systems we work within, none of these issues are surprising to those of us who have been helpers, healers, and changemakers for a long time. We have been working through long shifts, high caseloads, and constant budget cuts. We have been critiquing our professions and pushing for more funding. We have been moving systems toward change and more meaningful outcomes. We are standing on soap boxes, screaming from rooftops, doing the hard work, and having our hearts broken. Over and over again.

The dysregulation we are all feeling in the helping professions is not new, nor is it accidental. Our systems are set up in silos which keeps us from collaborating in meaningful ways that would disrupt many of the systemic inequalities impacting those we serve. The lack of collaboration keeps us from taking care of ourselves and supporting each other. The lack of care keeps us in these cycles of crisis, unable to change anything because we're all just surviving and bracing for the next tragedy. The lack of change keeps us stuck in this dysregulation. This dysregulation is the result of holding the heartbreak of our work in our bodies.

> *As a first responder your heart breaks each tour and a new heart grows in its place. Then that one breaks too.*
>
> —Jennifer Murphy, *First Responder*

Heartbreak is an unavoidable occupational hazard for helpers, healers, and changemakers. We are subject to heartbreak because our hearts are exposed to the same atrocities we work to protect others from and because we hold the weight of others' heartbreaks (their traumas, abuses, violations, assaults, etc.). Our hearts break when we lose a student, client, or patient to death or to matriculation as they cycle through the time-limited supports we and our organizations or institutions offer. Sometimes our hearts break because of the way society treats our students, clients, or patients, or because of the apathetic or negative responses we receive when we advocate for those we serve on an organizational, institutional, or societal level. Sometimes our hearts break because we have reached the limit to the resources we can offer, and we recognize that we haven't even begun to touch the root cause of their suffering. Our hearts hold the stress, the anxiety, the worry, and the fears of and for those we serve.

And still we show up, ready to serve others, regardless of the cost to ourselves.

None of us would be doing this work of helping, healing, and change-making if it didn't tug at our hearts. We love those we serve, we love the work we do (for the most part), and we show up whole-heartedly to do this work. But what happens when that heartbreak is continuously denied, excused, or exploited? What happens when the love we bring to our work is used to silence us and maintain the status quo? What can we do when we begin to see that our work is upholding the very systemic issues we work to address? How do we continue this work when our hearts are broken?

A heartbreaking reality of the COVID-19 pandemic were the deep systemic inequities and the utter lack of solutions (or at least the will to carry them out in good faith) exposed by the pandemic. Education, healthcare, housing, and the economy were all impacted. We watched the education and healthcare systems practically collapse onto the backs of teachers and medical workers; we saw how inequalities in housing became deeper and more permanent.

My hope was that these events would galvanize our policymakers and legislators to act on changing the inequities and injustices that have been exposed in education, housing, and healthcare, but that hasn't been the case. My hope was that the public would recognize the challenging work of teachers, medical professionals, social workers, and others who were on the front lines, protecting them and their children, but that didn't stick for long. My hope was that our systems and employers would see the critical value of childcare, medical benefits, and a living wage to support helpers, healers, and changemakers, but that never materialized. Even as we've witnessed a global pandemic, more mass shootings, and horrifically damaging weather events that impact the health and well-being of everyone (regardless of political affiliation or class), universal healthcare, sensible gun control, and climate change action are still considered radical ideas.

For a brief period of time, when the pandemic exposed our failing infrastructures, there was a surge of energy to make things work better, a window of opportunity to create new, more just, and equitable structures. Funds became available, bureaucracies moved more quickly, and there was a feeling of possibility for real change. Sadly (and very much intentionally) that change never materialized. Instead, we witnessed political division and increased inequality, and those of us in the helping professions were exploited. This impacted our mental health and exposed the lack of care in our work, which, along with the squandering of opportunity for change, gave rise to the cynicism, hopelessness, burnout, and turnover that is decimating our helping professions at alarming rates. We are seeing a mass exodus of current practitioners and students who no longer have the bandwidth for the work they were once passionate about.

The heartbreak is real and impacts our health in tangible ways. We start to feel "off" or have a sense of general unease in our bodies that may start with small symptoms that we write off . . . we're just tired, we're just clumsy or forgetful, we're just under the weather, we're just busy. But then those symptoms pile up or get worse and we find ourselves in a physical or mental health crisis. I know teachers who have had strokes, social workers who have developed Bell's palsy (partial paralysis of the face), and first responders who have suffered heart attacks. Many folks in the helping, healing, and change-making fields end up with autoimmune diseases and cancer diagnoses later in life. Much of this is caused by the stress-induced inflammation from our work. The needs of society are so great that it is easy for us to minimize our own needs; but working to complete exhaustion without support or resources is simply not cutting it anymore.

> *I've been tired so long, now I am sick and tired of being sick and tired, and we want a change. We want a change in this society in America because, you see, we can no longer ignore the facts. . . . The truth is the only thing going to free us.*
>
> —Fannie Lou Hamer, *The Speeches of Fannie Lou Hamer*

We are tired and we want radical change. For some folks, the change they need may be to leave the work. I've had many half-joking conversations with folks in these professions about quitting their jobs to live in the jungle in Costa Rica or to establish a homestead far away from other humans. I get it. While that may be possible for some, I also know many brilliant social workers, teachers, therapists, lawyers, and others who love their work and want to continue to push for change in their respective professions.

If we want radical change, we need a radical shift in how we do our work. This shift must honor and protect our hearts so we can courageously create the world we all want and *the world we know is possible.* What an incredible opportunity we have to tell the truth about our current reality, see clearly what is no longer working, acknowledge the work that needs to be done, create the cultures of care we need, and imagine a new future. When we radically prioritize care in our helping, healing, and change-making professions, we feel more connected and resourced, and the weight of the work becomes a bit lighter. We are able to center care for ourselves, each other, and our work. We have the bravery to challenge harmful systemic practices and the capacity to imagine new healing ones in their place.

Radical self-care is the shift we need to produce real change.

Radical self-care is a way of being, a fundamental way of showing up in our work that gives us the courage to see clearly what no longer works, to speak confidently about the impact of our caregiving in the world, to collaborate with others, and to creatively address the inequalities and harm in our world without being swallowed whole by the weight of the work. Radical self-care allows us to stand in our power as passionate professionals and reclaim our work as helpers, healers, and changemakers. Radical self-care creates a safe, solid foundation from which we can challenge systemic bullshit and topple systemic barriers, which keep our professions separate, so we can better connect with each other, collaborate on programs, blend and braid resources (funding, space, supplies, etc.), act in solidarity, and facilitate progress.

There is a sense of urgency to address the dysregulation and heartbreak in the world. We all know what isn't working and what needs to change, but we wait for someone else to do it. It has to start somewhere, and I propose *change must start with those of us in the helping, healing and change-making professions.* This is the work we know how to do when we are well-resourced and supported. I humbly—but with confidence, determination, and unshakable knowing—believe that radical self-care is required for the work ahead.

We are the ones we've been waiting for.

WHO ARE HELPERS, HEALERS, AND CHANGEMAKERS?

> *We each have to create a culture, a new story, in which we shoulder the weight together, growing ever more powerful and whole in the process. We can't wait for our culture to become whole so we can heal. We must become the people resilient, creative, and courageous enough to bring healing to ourselves and others from within a fractured culture.*
>
> —Langston Kahn, *Deep Liberation*

I am the only social worker in my school district, but I do not serve students alone. I work within a community of educators, counselors, administrators, community organizations, faith communities, and local governments to serve students. Because I serve youth experiencing homelessness, foster care, or who are system-involved, I work with probation officers, foster parents, Court Appointed Special Advocates (CASA), homeless shelter staff, judges, lawyers, school resource officers, social services staff, and more. The people I work with are highly educated professionals or volunteers, who dedicate their lives to serve their students, clients, patients, constituents, congregations, or communities.

Anyone who does high-touch, face-to-face, one-way, trauma-focused, intense-content work with other beings (human, animal, plant, etc.) to relieve suffering is a helper, healer, or changemaker: The people who show up in the chaos, the trauma, the darkness and bring calm, healing, and light. The people upon whose labor society depends to fix massive, systemic, global, intersectional, generational issues. The people who stand in the gap, act as a bridge, and push systems to action.

Only a relative few care to be confronted daily with the concerns of others. . . . It must be a special breed of person who chooses as his life's work the daily confrontation with some of humanity's most fundamental polarities: adjustment/maladjustment, social success/social failure, mental health/mental sickness.

—Adolf Guggenbühl-Craig, *Power in the Helping Profession*

Helpers, healers, and changemakers are a special breed. We have a strong, intrinsic sense of responsibility to do good in the world. We can get things done with few resources and through bureaucratic red tape. We are passionate and proud of the work we are privileged to do. We tend to have a high pain tolerance, a low bullshit threshold, and a sense of humor that would make those outside of our professions blush.

Helpers, healers, and changemakers are social workers in schools, medical/psychiatric hospitals, forensic/court settings, the military, substance use treatment facilities, and child welfare organizations. We are educators in public schools, continuation schools, adult schools, charter/private schools, colleges and universities, special education, court schools, juvenile halls, and in other settings. We are attorneys working in civil rights, juvenile justice, public defense, public education, tenant law, and public policy. We are in the medical field as nurses, doctors, physician assistants, clinicians, coroner/medical examiners, patient transporters, dentists, and veterinarians. We are first responders, such as firefighters, peace officers, homicide detectives, EMS/EMT/paramedics, LifeFlight operators, and community street outreach.

Helpers, healers, and changemakers are counselors, therapists, childcare workers, foster parents, academics, journalists, activists, psychologists, climate scientists, human rights advocates, 911 dispatchers, agriculturists, epidemiologists, refugee case managers, military and prison chaplains, nursing home employees, hospice carers, massage therapists, physical/occupational therapists. We are yoga teachers, reiki masters, herbalists, curanderas, midwives, doulas, caretakers, sound healers, restorative justice practitioners, circle-keepers, etc. We are also librarians, animal control/animal carers, digital first responders, cosmetologists, dental hygienists, hair stylists, and other occupations that are, more and more, coming in direct contact with suffering. This is not an exhaustive list, of course. There are many more helpers, healers, and changemakers I didn't name and there are many specialty roles under each of the professions listed.

Our work is intersectional and interdependent; however, because of the nature of our work and the confidentiality required to protect those we serve, it can be challenging to work across systems, agencies, and organizations. The beauty is that we often move between our helping professions when our passion is truly helping others. I know police officers who became teachers or principals; I know teachers who became lawyers; I know public defenders who became politicians; I know prison guards who became social workers; I know nurses who became activists; and I know social workers who became firefighters. I also know folks in all these professions who became mentors, foster parents, or Court Appointed Special Advocates. This is such a beautiful cross pollination in our work that allows us to deeply understand each other's professions and that we must keep in mind as we move forward toward cocreating collective change.

These people are my fellow helpers, healers, and changemakers.

WHAT IS RADICAL SELF-CARE?

> *Radical self-care involves embracing practices that keep us physically and psychologically healthy and fit, making time to reflect on what matters to us, challenging ourselves to grow, and checking ourselves to ensure that what we are doing aligns with what matters to us.*
>
> —Donna J. Nicol and Jennifer A. Yee, *Feminist Teacher*

Radical self-care is not a new concept. My framework of radical self-care is influenced by ancestors, authors, academics, and activists such as Fannie Lou Hamer, W. E. B. Dubois, Audre Lorde, Ella Baker,

Martin Luther King Jr., Bertha Capen Reynolds, Ida B. Wells, Toni Cade Bambara, Paulo Freire, bell hooks, Erica Huggins, Angela Davis, Grace Lee Boggs, Reverend angel Kyodo williams, adrienne marie brown, and many others who are just starting to make their presence known.

The foundation of radical self-care comes from the roots of social justice activism and, more specifically, from Black, queer, feminist, liberation pedagogies of resistance and healing. These lineages encourage us to embrace our agency and authority as revolutionary helpers, healers, and changemakers to empower ourselves and others. These lineages are unapologetic about the revolutionary work we must do and the radical care we must practice to do this work.

These folks were rooted in self-determination, self-preservation, and self-restoration. They didn't just want to survive, they wanted to thrive. Their contribution to revolutionary action was to use writing, singing, nature, yoga, art, protest, meditation, poetry, and/or journaling to help them hold the weight of their work. They may not have known much about regulating the nervous system, vagal nerve toning, earthing, or sound healing, but they engaged in these practices as an intuitive means of survival. Their bodies knew what they needed.

When Fannie Lou Hamer was threatened and beaten during marches for voting rights and when she was jailed, she would practice sound healing and vagal nerve toning by humming or singing "This Little Light of Mine." "Singing . . . is one of the main things that can keep us going. When you're in a brick cell, locked up, and haven't done anything to anybody but still you're locked up there and sometimes words just begin to come to you and you begin to sing" (Mills, 2007, p. 21). Erica Huggins and Angela Davis, both Black Panther Party members in the 1970s, practiced yoga and meditation to regulate their nervous systems while in jail and awaiting trial for their activism. Audre Lorde and Ella Baker enjoyed resting in nature and connecting with friends as a way of reenergizing themselves during their own activism work. They all engaged in radical self-care while working to change the world.

In reading the work of these amazing helpers, healers, and changemakers, a few things stood out.

1. They engaged unapologetically in individual and collective practices as part of their radical self-care, knowing that they are not mutually exclusive.
2. They recognized that the work of revolution requires accomplices, allies, and coconspirators to help carry the work inside and outside of systems of oppression, and they were *radically inclusive* in who they worked with to achieve that liberation.
3. None of these folks knew exactly where they were going, if they would ever see the change they fought for, or what the outcome of their efforts would ultimately be, but nevertheless, *they persisted.*

More importantly, they all persevered during times of intense crisis and global change in our country. They showed up amid economic depressions, wars, racism, sexism, genocide, and political upheaval. They took up space in places where they weren't welcome. They spoke up for themselves and for others who were very different from themselves. They stood up for the rights of others even as their own rights were being violently threatened. They paid the price for thinking outside the box and disrupting the status quo, both from folks outside their movements *and from within.* They didn't shy away from prioritizing themselves, though many of them died from cancer or other inflammation-based diseases that may have been a direct result of their activism due to late nights, long days, exposure to violence, and delayed medical care. Each of them gave something—some giving their lives—toward the awareness of the need for radical self-care. So, what *is* radical self-care?

Radical self-care is a deeply rooted way of being. Being able to stand in our power as professionals; being willing to look directly in the face of what's coming toward us; being able to tell the truth about what's happening to us; being committed to sit with what is and change the very way we understand and do our work individually and collectively; being able to sit in a space of not knowing as we cocreate solutions to our shared challenges. Radical self-care is just as much about the awareness that things must change as it is about the specific ways we can impact change. *Radical self-care invites,* *allows, and demands that we unapologetically advocate for ourselves and be unshakable in our belief that we are worthy of this care.*

Radical self-care is an antidote to the heaviness of our work. As strong as we are as helpers, healers, and changemakers, our work can wound us. There are also aspects of our work that we are not in control of, such as politics, social structures and systemic barriers we often have to push against. Radical self-care practices create foundational, sustainable, nurturing, and generative healing. Radical self-care holds space for the wounding in our work while encouraging holistic healing among our colleagues and throughout our communities. *Radical self-care encourages us to deeply honor the self while compassionately working for the collective.*

Radical self-care is a restorative practice and an emergent strategy. It is a holistic blueprint for well-being and self-actualization that gives us the capacity to show up in the world ready to make real change. This manifests as successfully managing the intersections of emotions and actions by practicing meditation, trauma-informed mindfulness, and self-compassion. We show up ready when we find and create healthy communities to engage in this collective healing work, when we are so resourced and nourished that we can face any opposition or pushback in our quest for total systems change. Showing up ready, we repair the harm done to us by the work we do in this world. *Radical self-care is how we move toward our individual and collective liberation with power and protection.*

It is in the spirit of and with deep respect for all the helpers, healers, and changemakers who have come before us that I offer this book as a contribution to the body of work on radical self-care. My intention is to expose the reality of our work and to share the deeply rooted, foundational practices (individual and collective) we can engage in daily to hold and protect ourselves (body, mind, and spirit) as we do the work this world needs.

This book is not THE answer; there is no single, magic answer. But I hope it is the start of some really compassionate and generative conversations in and between our helping, healing, and changemaking professions.

WHY RADICAL?

Becoming radical is giving ourselves permission to be more honest, more healed, more whole, more complete . . . to be radical is to constantly live in the territory yet undiscovered, the liberation yet unknown.

—Rev. angel Kyodo williams, *Radical Dharma*

When I started writing this book years ago, I knew the title would be *Radical Self-Care*. But as I began sharing the title with others, I was warned away from the word *radical*; it is overused, turns people off, or will be misunderstood. Some also suggested that I stay away from the term *self-care*, their concerns being the tired tropes of self-care as selfish, narcissistic, or "bougie." While I understand these concerns, I don't use any of these three words lightly.

Let's start with the word *radical*. For many people it suggests someone who professes utopian ideals, dissenting rhetoric, polarizing politics, or, at the very least, someone who is going to ruin your conservative family's Thanksgiving dinner. While the term is used in politics, radical is also used in the fields of mathematics, science, and medicine. The origin of the word *radical* means "forming the root" or "grasping the root."

I'm using this word to describe the socially embedded work we do as helpers, healers, and changemakers and to describe the deeply **rooted** care we need in order to continue this work in the world. The work we do touches the **root** of every sector of the global, social, and economic landscape in an effort to support the healthy function of our society and requires us to be innovative and unorthodox in our approaches. The work we do seeks to fundamentally (i.e., at the ***root***) change the lived experience of those we serve through advocating for political and social changes. The work we do challenges the status quo and demands complete systems change to meet the needs of our clients, students, patients, etc.

I ascribe to the philosophy of radical social work that believes another world is possible, and to see that reality, we must engage on both the individual/micro and the communal/macro levels. My role as a social worker is to see the individuals I serve within the greater context of their environment and social reality so that I may provide both individual interventions and social support that can move my students, their families, and their communities toward healing. Radical social work applies critical analysis to social problems as well as to the social work profession itself, ensuring that we are not used as tools of social control but rather we become advocates and agitators for change.

As a radical social worker, I also engage in antioppressive practices, believing it is my responsibility to challenge and change oppressive structures and practices (even inside the social work profession) by engaging in activism and advocacy beyond my day job to create equitable and justice-focused social change. My goal is to empower those I serve, not just so they no longer need my support but so they gain agency and create solidarity in their own communities. I do this radical work with humility, hope, courage, and a lot of radical self-care practices to keep me rooted in my wholeness. I engage in radical self-care practices that support my body, mind, and spirit to create a safe container from which I can engage those I serve without absorbing their traumas.

Our work is radical. Our work is vital and essential. Our work is deeply rooted in society. Our work challenges fractured social traditions and questions "the way it's always been." Our work disrupts and challenges entrenched systems. **It is imperative that our response to these realities be just as radical, because those of us who love our work and want to change systems *must survive long enough to make change.*** My goal with this book is to interrupt and disrupt the patterns of self-desertion, self-sacrifice, and self-surrender of helpers, healers, and changemakers so we can become more radically aligned with ourselves, each other, and the work we do in this world. Radical self-care is that disruption and the solution.

WHY SELF?

A strong practice of self-care is what allows me to continue to hold space. In some ways, for a space holder, this explains the connection between self and collective care. I cannot hold space without caring for myself and by caring for myself I am better able to care for the groups I am so lucky to hold space with and for.

—Michelle Cassandra Johnson, *We Heal Together*

Our inner work is connected to our outer work, so resistance requires great care for ourselves to feel connected and whole.

—Kaitlin B. Curtice, *Living Resistance*

There is a strong impulse among helpers, healers, and changemakers to avoid thinking about or speaking too much about ourselves. We see it as selfish in a culture where we feel we must sacrifice ourselves and subjugate our own needs to meet the needs of those we serve. We see other-care as more important than self-care, and we try to remove our "self" from the work to focus solely on those we serve. This passive sense of self keeps us in loops of hopelessness, burnout, and turnover in our professions. Radical self-care requires self-awareness, self-determination, self-regulation, self-evaluation, self-discovery, and self-recovery. Radical self-care disrupts those patterns of self-sacrificing, in which we become martyrs to our causes, and allows us to become abundantly resourced warriors who stand in solidarity with those we serve.

Jungian psychology sees the self as the coherent whole of our conscious and unconscious identity, the center of our total personality, including our character, attributes, and mentality, that distinguish us from others and make us who we are. Ultimately our self is our locus-of-control (the extent to which we believe we control our lives, the place from which action is initiated), and we must hold this position of self-sovereignty as we engage in practices that support our well-being and contribute to the communities within which we live and work.

In the Hindu body–energy chakra system, seven chakras represent a spinning vortex, an energy channel or flow of energy, that runs along the spine from the base of the spine to the crown of the head. In this system, the root chakra is identified with I AM. The root chakra sits at the base of the spine, and it is believed that all energy emanates *from the root.* When we get back to ourselves—our roots—and give ourselves the care we need, we shift the energy that emanates from us into all aspects of our lives and beyond, including in our work as helpers, healers, and changemakers. We must start at the root, *the self,* the I AM, before we can provide anything to anyone else. We have to go deeper into our "self," to the root of the suffering and the resilience, in order to find our own healing and to hold space for the many complexities in our work. We do this not by sacrificing our well-being but by insisting upon it. Ultimately, *knowing ourselves well protects us in the work of helping, healing, and change-making.*

We must be the ones who initiate, direct, and engage in our own care, but that does not mean we must do it individually or alone. Radical self-care focuses on humans in their environment, the individual *within a community.* The reality is that all social and collective change starts with the *purposeful action of individuals.* This is also true with radical self-care. We have a large community of helpers, healers, and changemakers who are dedicated to the work, and we can come together to support each other on this path.

WHY CARE?

Care is our individual and common ability to provide the political, social, material, and emotional conditions that allow the vast majority of people and living creatures on this planet to thrive—along with the planet itself.

—Care Collective, *Care Manifesto*

In the Care Collective's booklet, *The Care Manifesto*, care is defined as "a social capacity and activity involving the nurturing of all that is necessary for the welfare and flourishing of life" (Care Collective, 2020, p. 5). Care as a noun is defined as "the provision of what is necessary for the health, welfare, maintenance, and protection of someone or something; serious attention or consideration applied to doing something correctly or to avoid damage or risk." Care is also a verb, as many of us know very personally, that means "to feel concern or interest; attach importance to something; look after and provide for the needs of" (Oxford Languages, n.d.).

We often say "we need healing" without recognizing the immense amount of labor it takes to heal. We can only heal if we get to the root, and *the root work of healing is care.* Anyone who has been a caregiver for another being knows that *care takes work.* Care is hard. Care takes courage and requires action. Care requires patience and consistency. Care requires that we show up even when the person we're caring for is dysregulated. Care encompasses both love and compassion, both the joy and the suffering/suffering-with. Care also requires that we see ourselves as important and worthy of health, protection and attention to our well-being, fully understanding that we cannot care for others if we are not being cared for ourselves.

Care work has been devalued in our society, mostly because it is identified as "women's work." Care work is regularly underfunded, undercompensated, and often highlighted when challenges arise but ignored after the challenges pass. The labor of care can also be thankless work. I believe it's time to change the narrative around care. Our shared humanity requires that we be deliberate about care. We need to value care, to prioritize care, and to fund and resource care in our professions, agencies, organizations, and our communities. We need to value, prioritize, and support our own care with the practice of radical self-care.

THE NEED FOR RADICAL SELF-CARE

Self-care has many meanings, depending on the lens from which we seek to define it. After careful analysis of the many ways self-care is defined, researchers Nicole Martínez, Cynthia D. Connelly, Alexa Pérez, and Patricia Calero offered an integrated definition of self-care as "the ability to care for oneself through awareness, self-control, and self-reliance in order to achieve, maintain, or promote optimal health and well-being" (Martínez et al., 2021). This thorough definition encompasses three main attributes of self-control, awareness, and self-reliance and expands to include autonomy, responsibility, and self-direction. This integrated concept of self-care moves us beyond the basic and capitalistic self-care that we sometimes mistake as radical self-care.

Basic self-care is eating healthy food, drinking plenty of water, getting regular exercise or movement, having restful sleep, and connecting with others. Getting your regular medical check-ups and tests (mammograms, colonoscopies, etc.) are also part of our basic self-care. But just because they are "basic" doesn't mean they're easy to do nor that we all have the physical or mental capacity to do these activities for ourselves. We may need aides and support for our basic self-care, but sometimes we're just too busy to feed ourselves or go to the bathroom; sometimes we're too tired to get physical activity; sometimes we're too wired to get sleep. *When our basic self-care is off, that may be where we need to start.* But have you ever tried telling someone to drink more water or get more sleep? They tend to get defensive, don't they? Whenever someone pushes back against self-care, I ask them to try it first, and they usually find some relief. Once we find some relief by engaging in basic self-care, we can go deeper with our care.

Then there is **commercialized self-care**, where the goal is to feel good, to buy stuff, and to do it mostly independently of others. This kind of "self-care" is rooted in capitalism, consumerism, and an ego-based individualism that tells us we need more things to feel better. Commercialized self-care is additional, superficial, and external; it is something we add to our lives *when things get challenging.* Because we have so thoroughly internalized the capitalistic version of individualism that preaches self-over-others, carers tend to avoid anything connected to "self" to move away from this individualism, and thus we can easily be talked out of caring for ourselves in a meaningful way. This dismisses the reality that we are both the agent and object of action and change, which prevents us from moving into radical self-care to address our physical, emotional, psychological, and spiritual needs.

Radical self-care is foundational, fundamental, and internal; it is something that can be integrated into our lives consistently, *as a proactive measure.* Radical self-care is not an add-on but something already available to us and something we must initiate ourselves but don't have to do alone. Here's a breakdown of the differences, as I see them:

Commercialized Self-Care	Radical Self-Care
assumes burnout is inevitable	knows another way is possible
is reactive	is proactive
is an add-on	is an anchor
is superficial	is fundamental
is an escape	requires engagement
is a solo action	is a self-initiated, communal action
can make us feel good	can make us uncomfortable
is something we purchase	is already available to us
focuses on individual stress or trauma	focuses on communal healing and resilience

HOW TO USE THIS BOOK

We cannot achieve real, collective change without doing the personal work necessary to shift our induvial levels of thinking and feeling. Personal work allows us to become the people who can innovate new systems. Lasting change happens when we intentionally move the results of the personal out into the collective.

—Langston Kahn, *Deep Liberation*

This book is for anyone in the helping fields at any stage in the work and at all levels of our organizations. There are three levels of helpers, healers, and changemakers: those who are new to the game, those who are seasoned professionals, and those who are tapped out.

For those of you who are **new to the game**, just beginning your journey into the helping, healing, or change-making fields, I implore you to know yourself before you get too far in. Take some time to investigate *why you want to do this work*, what internal thread is pulling you, what your own traumas and triggers are, and what care you need so you can understand how the work will impact you. The first few years can be the most challenging, as your learning and understanding of theories and ideas meets the real world application of your work. **Use this book to seek out, try on, engage in, and build communities and practices of care that keep you rooted in your truth, in your heart, and in your body so you can be sustained in your education, licensure, or certification program and ultimately in this work.**

For those of you who are already knee-deep in these fields, my **seasoned pros**, I implore you to take time to remember who you are and reconnect with your true self, your true essence. Remember that you are whole, you are worthy, and you are connected to others. Remember who you are, why you came to this profession in the first place. This will help you *protect your passion from being exploited*. Doing so might cause you to leave the helping, healing, and change-making field, but that may be the radical self-care you need right now. You might also find meaning in becoming a mentor to newbies, sharing your wisdom and gleaning some of their new ideas, or being mentored yourself by someone who has been doing the work longer than you. **Use this book to help you unapologetically prioritize your well-being so you can continue to do the work you love or make decisions to shift your work in a way that honors and centers your care.**

For my friends who are **tapped out** and ready to leave the professions you love and have dedicated your lives to, *there is still some work to do to restore you to yourself.* This work may be separating yourself from all things "helping," or you may want to get more engaged by becoming a supervisor, a board member, a trainer, or even a foster parent. Your experiences and expertise can be used to mentor those entering the professions, your knowledge can be used to create new systems of care within your specific profession, and your awareness of structures can be used to dismantle and reimagine better systems. **Use this book to gain the courage, support, and healing you need to continue this work or to repair the heartbreaks you've sustained along the way.**

To all the helpers, healers, and changemakers at each level: *Thank you for your service.*

REFLECTIONS AND RADICAL TENDENCIES

At the end of each chapter, there will be a section called *Reflections.* The questions in these sections can be used independently, as you read through the book and reflect on your own journey, or they can be used for group discussions in educational or professional settings. I strongly suggest gathering a group of fellow helpers, healers, and changemakers for a book club/book study, community of practice, or just to build community. (You also have my permission to buy a nice new journal to keep your reflections in . . . because one can never have too many journals.) These questions are intended to help us think critically about the work we do and how we do it. Some may elicit discomfort, some may make you nod in agreement, and others may make you want to throw the book across the room. Notice what comes up around each reflection question and take note of that along with your responses to the questions.

Over the past decade, I have been piecing this book together, revelation by revelation, experience by experience, practice by practice. These practices are not new; many are cultural and ancestral practices that have existed for thousands of years, and many I found in community with other helpers, healers, and changemakers. I call these sustainable, healthy changes *radical tendencies* (radical ways of being) and will share them at the end of each chapter as a guide to creating your own radical self-care practice. Note or highlight the practices that resonate with you and explore them, then find what works for you, knowing that what works may change from season to season and from professional experience to professional experience.

START SMALL—JUST GET STARTED

Here are some simple truths about the practice of care to keep in mind as you go through the book:

Radical self-care does not require perfection. *You don't have to do all the things, all at once, all the time . . . but take a moment to be honest with yourself about where you can start.* This book can be used as a reference, as a "Choose Your Own Adventure" for getting the care you need. You can read it sequentially or hop between practices as needed. The recommendations for each radical tendency will include individual and community options for practices, where available. Choose something small and engaging, something you can incorporate immediately with the tools, time, and energy available to you in the moment. Then try another one. Then another. You don't have to be particularly "good" at any of them, so don't let fear of the unknown stop you. Oh, and you're absolutely allowed to have some fun!

Radical self-care isn't a crisis intervention, *per se*. The goal of radical self-care is to regularly, preventatively engage in these practices away from our work, allowing us to be vulnerable, drop into the practices, fully embody them. Then we are able to bring that embodiment, a memory of the felt sense, into the present moment when we are at work and facing a challenge. So, when you need to take a deep breath in a contentious staff meeting, it's not just an inhale and exhale . . . it's a full body memory of the calm space from which you practiced that breath. Now you're sitting in a staff meeting where tensions are rising but you're feeling a sense of grounded regulation, a kind of safe container, as you take a few deep breaths. Then you have the space to decide whether you get dragged into the chaos or respond from a place of calm control. *With radical self-care, you bring the felt sense from the practice into the present.*

Radical self-care is about consciously making small, sustainable, healthy changes that will allow us to shake the unconscious patterns that no longer serve us or our professions and to protect ourselves so we can stay sustained and can thrive in this work. The radical self-care practices shared in this book are not magic nor will you experience spontaneous healing the first time you engage them. (Well, you might, and if you do, good for you!) What makes them radical is their ability to be integrated into our daily lives as a foundation of support and nourishment as we do the work of helping, healing, and making change.

Radical self-care doesn't have to be practiced alone. Remember that "community" can be started with just one or two other people; but sometimes it can be helpful to start a practice solo then bring others in as you feel called to. Sometimes experiencing a practice in a large group—maybe a conference, public class, or retreat—might feel like a safer option so you know you're doing the practice correctly without risk of hurting yourself (e.g., yoga or another physical practice). Afterward, you can bring the practice into your daily schedule in ways that suit your care needs.

There's no wrong way to practice radical self-care. *Just get started.*

CHAPTER OVERVIEW

The answers to the challenges in our work start with a **reality check**, so we can be honest about the current state of the work we do. Then we **remember** why we chose this work and **reconnect** with the passion that brought us to this work by **regulating** our nervous systems and **rebalancing** our time, energy, and attention with strong boundaries. We do this by engaging in healing **rhythms and rituals** to sustain our spirits and provide us space to **rest and to restore** our energy. Once we do this, we can **reclaim** the power in our professions and find ways to move forward with a solid foundation of radical self-care.

Chapter 1: Reality Check attempts to paint a comprehensive picture of the true weight of our work. We cannot escape the reality of the work we have chosen as helpers, healers, and changemakers; daily, we are exposed to trauma and suffering that can cause very real changes in us that alter the way we think, feel, and see the world. It is hard to capture the depth, breadth, and radical nature of our work, so we must tell the truth about the heartbreak we experience from the vicarious trauma, moral injury, and burnout in our professions. This chapter also discusses the taboo topic of mental health breakdowns, death, and suicide in our work. *Please read this section with care and compassion for yourself and for our fellow helpers, healers, and changemakers who may currently be in this space.* Resources for immediate help are included.

Chapter 2: Remember and Reconnect encourages us to remember why we chose this challenging work. This chapter focuses on understanding why we come to this work and what may be triggered by the work, including the adverse *and* positive childhood experiences that subconsciously shape our *why*. We will investigate the role-switching, code-switching, and masking we do as methods of protection. We can become disconnected, dislocated, and dismembered by the wounding in our work, but remembering and reconnecting with our passion, people, and pleasure can bring us back to ourselves. We'll explore attachment, authenticity, agency, and authority in our work and how our radical self-care determines the expression of these in our work.

Practices in this chapter will help us remember and reconnect with ourselves, each other, and the work we love.

Chapter 3: Regulate and Rebalance speaks to the real ways our work impacts our emotions and our nervous systems, and how we can engage self-regulation and coregulate with our colleagues and those we serve. Understanding our window of tolerance, our stressors/triggers, and how our nervous system is wired is useful in our work; it can help us become aware of the transference and countertransference we may be experiencing. Understanding the empath/fawn/caregiver responses that may trigger overwhelm, overworking, and over-caregiving can help us prevent burnout. Boundaries help us rebalance the weight of the work we do, on the one hand, with our personal lives, on the other. We'll briefly discuss the vagus nerve and Polyvagal Theory, as well as their importance in emotional regulation. Practices in this chapter will offer support with emotional regulation and help us create safe and expansive containers to navigate the dysregulation in our work.

Chapter 4: Rituals and Rhythm are the containers for our radical self-care practices. In this chapter, we'll explore the many rhythms and rituals in our lives and in our work and their impact on us as well as ways we can engage with them to hold the weight of our work. Understanding resonance, entrainment, and the power of vibrations (not just good vibes) to heal will help us buffer and counteract the trauma we absorb doing our work. Some sacred rituals will be shared that help us release some of the pain our work can create. Practices in this chapter include ways to engage with vibration, sounds, and the elements to create rooted rituals for healing.

Chapter 5: Rest and Restore is a reminder that rest is a radical self-care practice to restore ourselves to wholeness. Our work as helpers, healers, and changemakers can be urgent and can demand all our energy, so rest is an appropriate counter to the hustle culture of overwork we often find ourselves in. The ways we restore our well-being—body, mind, and spirit—are vital and allow us to thrive as we hold space for the trauma and suffering of others. Practices in this chapter will remind us that sleep is vital, rest is available, and restoration, not productivity, is the end goal.

Chapter 6: Reclaim and Replenish is the culmination of our need for radical self-care, to move beyond our current ways of working toward a more caring, connected love ethic that can transform our professions. We must move toward our future with a full understanding of the current reality of our work as helpers, healers, and changemakers, but now with some tools for self-preservation and solid practices of radical self-care.

A WORD ABOUT CYNICS AND CRITICS

In every discussion of self-care or systemic challenges, there are always cynics and critics. Cynicism is easy to come by and requires no effort to change the status quo. In fact, it revels in the suffering and oppression of the status quo without feeling any responsibility to change the status quo they so readily critique. If we are cynical, we can easily fall into a space of refusing to see solutions because we are so stuck in our self-righteousness and being "right" about the problem. But this does not create an environment for change. Cynicism gets us nowhere and helps no one.

Cynicism and negativity can be deadly in our work as helpers, healers, and changemakers. Our cynicism might lead us to avoid an important meeting, ignore a needed intervention, or discount a complaint of pain from a patient. If we are jaded, helpless, and pessimistic, what chance do those we serve have? While I refuse to give in to the cynics of the world, I am open to critique. Critical awareness and critical dialogue move the conversation forward to a place where change is possible. Sometimes it's healthy to mistrust something or to not believe information at face value. That's where skepticism, instead of cynicism, can be helpful. Skepticism is a healthy form of discernment that causes us to get curious and investigate further so we can find the truth. Cynicism shuts down any attempts to find root causes or solutions.

If you are currently in this space (for very legitimate reasons), please give yourself lots of compassion as you move through these chapters. Being in a space of cynicism isn't easy; it's toxic to the person experiencing it and to those around that individual. You may find yourself reacting strongly to some of what I share, and I get it. I've been there. Just know that healing and growth can't happen from a place of cynicism. So, if you need to step back from your current profession or leave it altogether in order to shift out of cynicism (maybe into cautious optimism?), please know that *that is radical self-care too*, and may be the best place to start for you to be able to reset and reenter the work from a more grounded, compassionate, and resourced place.

RADICAL SELF-CARE FOR HELPERS, HEALERS, AND CHANGEMAKERS

1

REALITY CHECK

Being honest about the conditions of our work

> There's no liberation without actually leaning forward and looking at the things we habitually run away from, in order to see things as they really are, not as we have imagined them.
>
> —Lama Rod Owens, *Love and Rage*

> As healers, organizers, care workers, and those committed to change, our work is to hold horror and transformation in our own hands and in support of the people we are connected with.
>
> —Susan Raffo, *Liberated to the Bone*

For those of us who identify as helpers, healers, or changemakers, our nine-to-five job is to bear witness to wounding and to help the wounded in some capacity or another. We meet people on their worst day and see the worst things people do to each other, to animals, and to the planet. Whether it's child abuse, sexual assault, domestic violence, community violence, suicide, natural disasters, medical and mental health crises, unmet learning challenges, animal cruelty, climate change, or something else, we see it all and continue to show up and hold brave space for the wounded—and sometimes for the ones responsible for the wounding.

In yoga and meditation circles, you'll often hear a Rumi quote from the poem *Childhood Friends* paraphrased as, "The wound is where the light enters" (Barks, 2004, p. 142). It is read in yoga classes and comes up on my meditation apps often. This quote is used to comfort those who have been through hard times and to encourage those who feel their trauma may challenge their path to enlightenment or manifesting their dream life. While it's not necessarily meant to come across as dismissive of someone's pain, a form of spiritual bypassing, it is very telling that the part of the poem preceding these words is so often left out. It reads, "*Don't turn your head. Keep looking at the bandaged place.*"

This part of the poem reflects a reality that helpers, healers, and changemakers know well:

> *We are the ones who don't turn our heads, who keep looking at the bandaged place.*
> We're the ones trying to prevent the wound;
> We're the ones who get called when the wounding occurs;
> We're the ones who dress the wound so the healing can begin;
> We're the ones encouraging the wounded to look at their bandaged places to heal;
> We're the ones who seek justice for the wounded or hold the perpetrator accountable;
> We are the ones reminding the wounded that they are not broken, but that indeed, "the wound is where the light enters." (Barks, 2004, p. 142)

The work of helping, healing, and making change on behalf of individuals, families, communities, society, or organizations is messy but necessary. We work toward social justice, equity, and equality for those we serve, even when the systems we work within abhor change. We know we cannot do this work if we focus solely on the "light" and turn our heads away from the wounds. Sometimes our employers acknowledge the weight of the work, but often we're left to carry it on our own. When we try to deal with the heaviness of our work completely on our own, we have a difficult time finding our way to wholeness, well-being, or liberation. In fact, the heaviness of the work is often what causes us to leave the helping professions altogether.

But we don't have to do this challenging work alone. The very last sentence of Rumi's poem *Childhood Friends* speaks directly to the essence of radical self-care, and it reads:

> Do not look away. Don't turn your head.
> Keep looking at the bandaged place.
> And don't believe for a moment that you're healing yourself.
> (Barks, 2004, p. 142)

Regardless of the idealistic notions of our helping work, we must be able to share the challenges and be honest about the true cost of our care. Then we can demand change and seek the healing resources that can support us in our work. My intention with this chapter is to bring to light the reality of our work, to validate the many challenges we face as helpers, healers, and changemakers, and to highlight the need for radical self-care.

REALITY OF OUR WORK

> *Even from within large organizations and institutional structures, it is possible to work for social justice. It is possible to serve the interests of the poor and working class, people of color and women, lesbians, gays, and bisexuals and people with disabilities more effectively. But doing so is not without risk.*
>
> —Paul Kivel, *Social Service or Social Change?*

The COVID-19 pandemic and its impact on public education made the past few years the most challenging of my career as a school social worker. The challenge started on March 16, 2020, when we were sent home for what we were told would be an "extended two-week spring break." Famous last words.

As the McKinney-Vento Liaison for students experiencing homelessness, I saw high needs among those experiencing housing instability during the pandemic. I should mention here that I live and work in the San Francisco Bay Area where, in the right neighborhood, a tear-down house that is missing walls will still sell for a million dollars. Minimum wage is not a living wage for many working families in the Bay Area, so many folks must live "doubled-up," wherein multiple families share housing. This type of living arrangement is very common (along with families in hotels, shelters, cars, couch surfing, etc.) and qualifies students to receive extra services under the federal McKinney-Vento Homeless Assistance Act. Those extra services include immediate school enrollment, free lunch, and support with school supplies as well as partial credits for secondary students and school-of-origin rights to keep these students stable in school while their living situation is in flux.

In addition to the school-focused supports, I was able to provide food for families in need using COVID relief funds to purchase and distribute groceries or gift cards. I provided guidance on navigating the eviction moratorium and was able to refer families to various community agencies for 30–60 days of hotel support or up to four months of emergency rent relief. Even with all that support, I watched many families continue to struggle because their service industry jobs never came back.

At the very start of the pandemic, I served a family with four kids who had been living in a van, which we discovered when we tried to deliver an internet hotspot for the kids to engage in remote learning. With additional COVID-relief funds I was able to secure a 30-day hotel stay, but once that was up, the homeless shelter was their only option. The parents were a bit scared of the idea of taking their kids to a shelter, so I offered to do a "warm handoff" to be sure they got settled in safely. When I showed up to greet them, one of the kids asked me how my day was. This child was asking how my day was when he and his family were facing such a challenging situation. It took everything in me to calm the mix of sadness, helplessness, and rage I felt in that moment.

I took them to the shelter, got them checked in, and helped them get their sleeping space secured. The staff did their best to make the cold and unwelcoming converted warehouse "family-friendly," but the thought of children sleeping there made my heart sink. One of the youngest found a toy she liked, and her excitement helped the other kids settle in. I gave mom a big hug and told her I would check in on them the next day. I kept my composure as I walked to my car.

Then I cried the whole way home.

Crying myself home from work was not a new experience. Because being a social worker is heavy. I've cried myself home many late nights, especially when the help I can give does not provide a real solution to the suffering. Based on the conversations, podcasts, posts, and discussions I've had with my fellow helpers, healers, and changemakers during this time, I know I'm not alone in this. We did not create the COVID pandemic or the housing crisis, and it is not our responsibility to solve it all, even if that's how it often feels. *Knowing this reality doesn't remove the weight of this responsibility.*

In addition to the work we do on an individual basis, we are also living in a world where mass shootings are becoming a common occurrence, police violence is being captured on video and played ad nauseam, women's reproductive health and rights are being legislated away. Our LGBTQI+ siblings are under attack and our schools and teachers are being scapegoated for every social issue. We are seeing the direct impacts of unaffordable housing and lack of mental health care by the number of people experiencing homelessness on the streets of many communities. We are seeing the impacts of climate change in our weather patterns and natural disasters, further impacting the issues around health and housing. All of this is occurring in one of the wealthiest nations, as the number of billionaires climb, where inequality expands, and funding for social services continues to evaporate, yet we seem able to find billions of dollars to fund overseas wars.

The demands on helpers, healers, and changemakers to fix all these issues are ever increasing while the budget, the will, and the political support to do them is decreasing. Essential workers are exhausted, and what we're currently doing is no longer working. This is the reality of my work. The reality of *our* work.

I want to invite you to pause here and take a few deep breaths. It may be easy to sink into despair after reading these stories or considering the realities of your own helping profession. But I want to offer you a moment of present awareness, a sacred pause, a moment of stillness, to notice what this brings up for you before you continue reading. Feel free to pause and take a few breaths whenever you feel to, maybe even putting the book down to stretch or get yourself a glass or water or cup of tea. When you're ready, come back for more.

DOUBLE TROUBLE: CAPITALISM AND OPPRESSION

It is not possible . . . to engage in any serious conversation about inequality or equality without addressing capitalism.

—Angela Davis, *On Inequality: Angela Davis and Judith Butler* (SSEXBBOX, 2017, 27:15)

Caring for ourselves is an expression of our recognition of and value for humanity; it is a resistance to the plunder of neoliberalism.

—Tricia M. Kress and Jennifer Somma-Coughlin, "Mindfully Running the Course(s): Self-Care as Critical Praxis in Critical Pedagogy for Healing" (Kress, Emdin, & Lake, 2022)

Much of the work I do as a social worker is to relieve the impacts of capitalism and oppression on those I serve. While this book is not about these topics specifically, the work we do is to clean up the byproducts of oppressive systems and inequitable capitalism. It is important to define and explain these terms and to acknowledge their impact on us through our work.

In *Oppression and the Body: Roots, Resistance and Resolutions*, oppression is defined from a somatic perspective, as a form of trauma that "can be found at individual, interpersonal, social and institutional levels, and essentially works to dehumanize and undermine groups of people, manifesting in the form of racism, sexism, ableism, classism, heterosexism, and xenophobia, among others" (Caldwell & Bennett Leighton, 2018, p. 18). Oppression is a social force that holds one group back to the benefit of another group so that "there can be no oppressed group without a directly affected privileged group" (p. 19).

Oppression isn't the same for everyone, but it is real and we must address it in our work. Our identities are intersectional, so too are our oppressions. We must address *the intersections of oppressions*, and we must acknowledge when our work creates, upholds, or perpetuates oppression through policy, practice, rules, norms, or laws. To avoid adding to oppression, we need clarity when we are using our privileged identity as a helper, healer, or changemaker. We also need to maintain awareness of the ways these oppressions impact us outside of our work and through our work, even if we are not directly impacted. As a Black, biracial, cisgender, heterosexual, able-bodied woman, I'm aware that some of my identities are impacted by oppression while some provide me immense privilege. As a social worker, I recognize the privilege I hold in being the conduit between the families I serve and the resources they need and at the same time recognize that I am personally impacted by the housing crisis that I help others navigate.

The suffering we meet in our work is understood to be caused by oppression and inequalities in systems we now know are purposely designed to create these very conditions. In some cases, these inequalities are very lucrative and continue to create deeper class divides based on the hoarding of power and profit. This inequality has a root cause: capitalism. Capitalism uses "systems" as the delivery method of the inequality we seek to eliminate: the health care system, the education system, the child welfare system, the criminal justice system, etc. Capitalism creates competition that sees land, natural resources, and human labor (and sometimes human beings) sold to the highest bidder, for profit.

In the Bay Area, specifically Silicon Valley, where I live, we have both the highest rates of homelessness and the highest concentration of billionaires. You read that right. The average person needs a six-figure income to afford basic housing. Meanwhile, the wealthy have multiple homes that often stand empty until a specific holiday or event. Corporations and tech companies have office buildings that sit vacant and unused as the housing crisis gets larger and more intractable. The lack of affordable housing and increased homelessness in the wealthiest county, in the wealthiest state, in one of the wealthiest countries in the world is a direct result of capitalistic greed.

Capitalism creates false narratives of urgency and triggers feelings of scarcity and competition that cause us to fight over scraps and to gather limited resources we know aren't adequate for the work that is required. The challenge is the distribution of resources and wealth in a culture that prioritizes overwork, self-sacrifice, and profit over people. If you've been a helper, healer, or changemaker for a while, I have two familiar words for you: *unfunded mandates*. We know we could end homelessness, institute universal pre-kindergarten, provide free or affordable childcare, implement sensible gun control, invest in universal healthcare, care for our elderly, *and* address climate impacts if we had the political will.

But fixing systemic inequalities is not the concern of capitalism.

That's where we come in. While our jobs are not to dismantle capitalism directly, the work we do challenges these notions, or at least it should. Our work as helpers, healers, and changemakers is to ameliorate suffering for those who are oppressed by understanding the systemic inequalities while being skilled enough to navigate these systems to access justice and resources for those we serve. Our job is to provide resources toward individual healing while also noticing failures in the system and working collectively to change policies and practices within those systems. Getting involved in political activism at a local, county, state, or national level can also help buffer the impacts of capitalism on the people and communities we serve and give them the tools to be active participants in their own liberation, making ourselves obsolete.

This is the radical view of social service work that I ascribe to, as do many of you who do this work and picked up this book, and it is antithetical to the aims of capitalism where greed, scarcity, dependency, and competition rule. It is our job to make contradictions and oppressive practices in our work explicit, *to expose them and change them.* We should be skeptical of the ways our agencies or organizations may contribute to oppression via our efforts to help, heal, and make change through policies and practices like:

- required reporting of immigrants/refugees seeking care
- using corporate-funded assessments under the guise of public "accountability"
- offering book studies on equity, diversity, or inclusion without making any identifiable action toward actual equity, diversity, or inclusion.
- placing vulnerable, system-involved youth in for-profit residential or group homes

To escape the constraints of capitalism, many of us work for charities, public entities, nonprofits, or foundations with the intention of working toward the end of a particular kind of suffering. We fool ourselves into thinking we're not part of capitalism because we don't make much profit from the work we do. We are beholden to the charity of corporations or the kindness of politicians to champion our work and keep us funded. But if we're being radically honest, we must acknowledge that doing good isn't the same as doing what is right, and often our public or nonprofit work gets tied into capitalism in an unsustainable way.

> The tension at the heart of nonprofits remains that they are funded by the proceeds of an inherently unequal capitalist system, yet this system requires – indeed cannot exist without – humans who must be fed, housed, clothed, and cared for. In doing that caring work, nonprofits grease the wheels of that system; if they aim to stop its rolling, they may have to turn away from the work that allows the system to reproduce itself. This presents a difficult choice when that work is necessary for people to survive. (Jaffe, 2021, p. 155)

We are not here to perpetuate any system that upholds inequalities. We are not here to stand by, doing good, as systemic injustice occurs repeatedly. We do not want to see our students, clients, patients, or others we serve stuck in the same place year after year, even if that provides some level of job stability. When we do realize our true role and act on it, we will experience push back from those seeking to uphold the status quo, fund their special projects, or keep their institutions running. This is the resistance we may face in our work as helpers, healers, and changemakers that creates that sense of urgency in us that pushes us to our limits and keeps us in a state of hustle-hustle, go-go-go, the modern "work ethic."

This work ethic, also a product of capitalism, creates an unnecessary culture of overwork and overwhelm in endeavoring to fix privately created macro challenges with publicly funded micro solutions. We are made to feel that if we aren't working hard enough, the direct result is someone's suffering. If we aren't the one providing support for or being available to those we serve, we believe they won't get what they need. This is the lie we're told to keep us in this constant loop of overwhelm and overwork. The lie is perpetuated publicly when teachers, nurses, or social workers threaten to go on strike to advocate for better working conditions, and the narrative is, "they must not care about their students/patients/clients" rather than, "they care so much about the quality of their work with their students/patients/clients, they are willing to take this extreme step."

Helpers, healers, and changemakers are subject to the forces of capitalism, and those we serve are very much impacted by it. We often find ourselves buying into and extending this culture of overwork to deny ourselves the care we know we need. In her book *Emergent Strategy*, adrienne marie brown encapsulates this by reminding us that, "everything we are working on is actually urgent . . . setting aside time from our work can feel violently selfish" (brown, 2017, p. 199). This is the mentality that our higher education programs teach us; this is the mentality that the systems we work in want us to maintain; and this is the mentality that *many of us keep ourselves and each other stuck in*. It is toxic, and it is unsustainable.

DESTRUCTIVE BINARIES

Our healing cannot wait until the structures acquiesce, are dismantled, or come undone.

—Rev. angel Kyodo williams, *Radical Dharma*

We are beginning to fully understand the pervasive and long-lasting consequences of the trauma in our work, but for some reason, we haven't responded with the urgency the situation demands. Those of us who advocate for self-care are often met with folded arms and a jaded attitude. We are accused of ignoring all the environmental factors that add to our stress and of focusing too much on individual actions, or we face the dismissive suggestion that focusing on ourselves is selfish and that if we really cared about our work to change the world we should focus instead on changing systems. My favorite push back is that because we chose these professions, we just need to suck it up, keep it moving, and stop complaining.

I think the reason for this constant pushback is our attachment to destructive binaries that, ironically, keep the conversation about our well-being in the context of burnout and give us a way to condescendingly negate our own care. We use these binaries of self-care versus other-care to excuse ourselves and each other from having to take any personal responsibility for our health or well-being as helpers, healers, and changemakers. This keeps us fighting with each other instead of identifying and addressing the root cause of our challenges.

Nothing about radical self-care discounts the ways we are impacted by capitalism. In fact, if we truly are going up against the bastion of a "free market" economic system that benefits systems of power on a *global scale*, we have an even greater need for radical self-care. Radical self-care is responsive to and protects against the impacts of capitalism and oppression we find in our work. To engage this protective aspect, we must address the binaries that keep us stuck in overwork and keep us from caring for ourselves.

Radical Self-Care Versus Self-Sacrifice

We become accustomed to sacrificing ourselves for our work, for those we serve, and for our communities and families. But when we sacrifice ourselves for the good of others, we find ourselves in existential crises of our own making. It's an odd form of martyrdom, and it does little to progress our work or our own well-being. It also doesn't benefit those we serve, as we can begin to feel resentment when our sacrifice is not acknowledged or when the sacrifice we make has little positive impact on change. Self-sacrificing tendencies can make us believe we are the only ones who can do the work of helping, healing or change-making. This skewed view of our work (i.e., I am the *only one* who can do this. . .) keeps us in a posture of overwork, negating our own care, and makes burnout inevitable. Now more than ever, *we must come to our work in a way that allows us to show up for others without sacrificing ourselves.* Let's all agree to be done with this self-abandonment.

Radical Self-Care Versus Community-Care

Radical self-care acknowledges that while healing requires individual action, it also includes collective healing. The key to this is that we heal in *healthy* communities; communities made of individuals who are not well can create a toxic community. The most toxic communities are the ones where individual needs are subjugated for the collective (see above). The community can act as a silencing body rather than a healing body, especially when one person is harmed and is then silenced by the community for fear that their individual needs for validation and healing might disrupt the status quo of the group, like in religious communities, large institutions, or even families. However, when we do our individual self-care to be sure our contribution to our communities and collectives is that of well-being, we can notice when harm is happening in our communities and commit to creating cultures of care. *Investing in our radical self-care is, by default, investing in communal care.* We can act as a tonic to those in our lives rather than being a toxic influence in our families or communities. And when we truly practice radical self-care, we gain the clear-eyed perspective, the present moment awareness, and the deeply embodied courage we need to be in community with others.

Radical Self-Care Versus Systemic Change

We often talk about systemic change as a conflict, as the other side of the self-care coin, but we forget one small detail: systems are made up of individuals who perpetuate and hold up the structures of oppression because they, too, are being burned-out by doing the work. Some folks suggest that rather than investing in radical self-care, we should demand that the organizations or institutions we work for support our care, that we wait for our employer to give us the time and permission to take care of our well-being. These systems currently depend on us being dysregulated and disregarding our own care to serve their needs. However, similar to community care, we cannot neglect the care of the individuals who make up and work in these systems. This is why systemic change is so challenging and is not a small task. So why in the world would we think that we don't need a radical self-care practice to support us in this task? *There is a direct connection between our individual well-being and our ability to change the systems within which we work.*

Radical Self-Care Versus Professional Identity

For so many of us, our work becomes our identity. People know us by our profession because that's how we show up even if we're not still at work or on the clock. If we're honest, it feeds our ego a bit, but it also keeps us exhausted with no days off. When it comes to the topic of self-care, the reality is that we might fear what we will find if we step away from the work, take a moment to be still, and focus on our own well-being. We may find some unhealthy habits or unresolved traumas that need our attention, or we might find that the fire and passion that drew us to this work is no longer there. Worse still, we may have to admit that we are the ones (not our organizations, not our society, not our systems) keeping us from healing because we are so tightly bound to our professional identities and those powerful ego boosts. When we have a strong sense of ourselves and our ego is fed from more than just our work, our profession becomes *one aspect of our whole self* rather than the whole reflection of who we are, and our own care becomes nonnegotiable.

> Burnout is a charged topic that challenges our professional identity. Admitting burnout feels self-indulgent to a group of professionals who by nature strive to be selfless. Caring for patients is a tremendous privilege, and focusing on our own issues feels almost blasphemous. We see how ill and vulnerable many of our patients are, and by comparison, who are we to complain? Our education and training still idolize workaholism and martyrdom. And our promotion system still rewards it. (Joseph, 2018)

To suggest that we can ignore the very real health and community impacts of burnout in favor of systemic change or community care ignores the reality that we cannot provide care nor work for change if we are all sick, dying, or leaving our professions due to burnout. Safe, stable communities and organizations are not threatened by the individuals in them practicing radical self-care. We need to unapologetically reclaim our health and well-being and prioritize ourselves in the face of systemic inequalities.

CYCLE OF CARING

There are repetitive cycles in our work that can lead us toward burnout. Our work is a series of one-way relationships, and there are ways that we must professionally attach to those we serve and then separate from them to maintain that professionalism. Our awareness can protect us from the cycle of attachments and separations called the cycle of caring (Skovholt, 2005). Sometimes we are very aware of the phases of the cycle, and other times we are unaware of them (on autopilot?), but whether over a school year or a short crisis intervention, every helping profession engages this cycle in their care for others. This cycle is recreated over and over again in our work, and it can contribute to emotional burnout.

The four aspects of the cycle of caring are: empathic attachment, active involvement, felt separation, and re-creation. It is important to understand this cycle so we know how the basic nature of our work impacts us and so we can put some practices in place to help buffer their impacts.

Empathic Attachment

This is how we show up for the work. We have to be "on" and fully present with those we serve so we can attune to their needs and provide the right support. We become attached to them, taking in their narratives and histories, to learn where they are and to meet them there. This may happen quickly, in a matter of minutes, or we may gather this information over a period of days or weeks. We use our empathy and deep listening skills to assess their situation and then find the right interventions and resources for them. This requires a level of availability and vulnerability that we must be able to protect from exploitation.

Active Involvement

This is the area we spend the most time and energy, actively providing care for those we serve. We use our time, energy, attention, and skills to support others and provide tools for healing. This may be the case management aspect of our work, setting up sessions, office visits, home visits, connecting with additional support, and referrals. This is where our over-caring patterns can be triggered and exploited to overwork, which can lead to burnout if we get over-involved or we find that the care we are providing is not meeting the needs of those we serve.

Felt Separation

At this stage, our work is complete, and it's time to separate from those we have served because we have provided the skills, tools, resources, or interventions for them to support themselves moving forward. This can happen naturally, like when the end of a school year comes and your students graduate onto the next grade level or when a successful course of treatment allows a patient to be discharged from an institution. It can also happen suddenly, like when the youth you are serving gets released from your facility after a court hearing but before your sessions are up or the treatment goals have been reached—or when a patient, client, or student dies unexpectedly amid the course of treatment or engagement. Whether it is a natural separation or a sudden, unexpected one, this aspect can cause the most heartbreak for us, even if we're not fully aware of the impact.

Re-Creation

This is the part of the cycle where we step away from the work to reset and recharge. In the literature, this is where self-care comes in. Because each of the other aspects require a lot of energy and effort from us, this part of this cycle acknowledges the need to take a break before the next cycle of care begins. This break may be an hour before a new client comes in, a weekend between efforts, or a summer break between school years. Some of us may not get a break to step away, reset, or recharge, and this can cause irreparable harm to our health and well-being. If we do not take this step in a very purposeful way, our bodies may take the time in a very abrupt way, in the form of a physical or mental health crisis.

Rather than waiting until the end of the cycle to care for ourselves, we can engage in nourishing practices throughout this cycle to protect our hearts and to buffer the impact of all the trauma we might absorb. Within each stage, we can support ourselves (and each other) with check-ins and small practices in the moment, such as taking a deep breath, walking as we connect with our client, noticing the emotions that come up and knowing what is ours to hold or to release. We can also engage in rituals to close our time with others and prepare ourselves for the next cycle. Without this awareness and intentional support, the cycle of care can push us into burnout. *Having a radical self-care practice can help us hold the weight of this cycle of caring.*

BURNOUT AND TURN OVER

Burnout does not result from a genetic predisposition to grumpiness, a depressive personality, or general weakness. It is not caused by a failure of character or a lack of ambition. It is not a personality defect or a clinical syndrome. It is an occupational problem.

—Christina Maslach and Michael P. Leiter, *The Truth About Burnout*

According to the World Health Organization, burnout is a syndrome resulting from workplace stress and is characterized by three dimensions: feelings of energy depletion or exhaustion, increased mental distance from one's job or feelings of negativism or cynicism related to one's job, and reduced professional efficacy (World Health Organization, 2019). Burnout is now a full-blown epidemic, to the extent that the 11th revision of the International Classification of Diseases (ICD-11) recognizes it as an occupational phenomenon that impacts one's health. On October 1, 2023, burnout officially became a health diagnosis (ICD code Z73.0) eligible for reimbursement; however, burnout is *not* listed in the Diagnostic and Statistical Manual of Mental Disorders (DSM) as a *mental* health diagnosis (which is a good thing!).

Stated very simply, burnout is chronic stress from overwork that builds up over time. More specifically, it can be identified as work-related depression or anxiety that has a negative impact on one's health and well-being. Burnout's link to death and morbidity is finally being acknowledged, and it is being studied as a very serious threat to life on a global scale. Burnout is considered an *occupational* issue, not an individual issue. That said, the impacts of burnout are indeed felt by individuals.

Burnout is not a new phenomenon, by any means. Folks in the helping, healing, and change-making community have been ringing the alarm about burnout for decades. The term was first coined by psychologist Dr. Herbert Freudenberger in 1974 (Hillert et al., 2020) to describe the severe stress he witnessed among his colleagues working in an addiction clinic. The word *burnout* came from his observations of drug users he saw in the Upper East Side of New York City who, embroiled in their addiction, would sit and numbly let the end of their cigarettes burn all the way out. He used it to describe a phenomenon he observed in others in the helping professions after experiencing its debilitating symptoms himself. It seemed to impact people who had a passion for helping others and a drive to solve problems, specifically folks in health care, human services, and social services.

Building on Dr. Freudenberger's work, Dr. Christina Maslach spoke about burnout being an epidemic and a "soul erosion" in the book *The Truth About Burnout* (Maslach & Leiter, 1997). She created the Maslach Burnout Inventory, which offers 22 simple statements to help assess the levels of burnout. The three dimensions of burnout (exhaustion, depersonalization or mental distance, and professional efficacy) are inconvenient for any line of work, but the wounding in our work, specifically the immense amount of suffering we must hold for others, causes these three aspects to be felt a bit deeper for helpers, healers, and changemakers and to have a greater impact on those we serve, our organizations, and our communities. Let's explore these dimensions and the ways they show up for helpers, healers, and changemakers.

Exhaustion

This isn't just being tired but feeling it in your bones. The kind of tired that a nap can't fix. Like, I'm tired, all the women in me are tired, and *my ancestors are tired*. As shared by his daughter in an NPR interview (King, 2016), Dr. Freudenberger's experience with exhaustion from burnout found him literally unable to move his body to get out of bed. This is the kind of exhaustion we experience in the helping fields, and when we are exhausted, people can get hurt. We may miss something important in our work that could create harm for ourselves, our agencies, or those we serve, not to mention how our complete lack of any remaining energy after work will affect our spouse or our own children. Sometimes sleep deprivation or lack of rest may be a function of our job if we work night shifts or shifts that are longer than 10 hours. Sometimes insufficient rest or sleep is a function of the heaviness in our work, some call it a weariness of the soul. Whatever the cause, our experience of exhaustion, as it relates to burnout, is felt deeply, on every level, and takes more than a good night's sleep to fix. (More on sleep in Chapter 5.)

Mental Distance or Cynicism

Intense feelings of negativity or mental distancing from our work are how cynicism shows up. As I mentioned in the introduction of this book, cynicism is deadly among the helping, healing, and change-making professions. A toxic work environment can push us into cynicism, causing us to have a chip on our shoulder, become easily offended, or hold a defensive posture with supervisors and colleagues. It shifts our perspective of our work and those we serve, which can result in us being annoyed, disgusted, or showing bias toward our students, patients, clients, etc. It also impacts our families when we can't turn that negativity off. In an NPR interview with his daughter Lisa, it was revealed that Dr. Freudenberger was "not that pleasant to live with" (King, 2016) during his burnout. When we—gatekeepers of vital resources and support and providers of care to others—become cynical and negative, it can cause harm on many levels, including to ourselves.

Reduced Professional Efficacy

We're not making widgets on an assembly line, so when we feel like the work we're doing isn't making a difference, it can be heartbreaking. Usually we feel this not because our own skills aren't meeting the needs of those we serve but because we are thwarted by the bureaucracy of our work and are unable to be as efficient in our work as we know we could be. This can frustrate us to the point of burnout, especially when the limitations of our work are being imposed by people with no knowledge of the work we do (i.e., politicians making medical or educational decisions), and we are the ones left to witness and clean up the negative impacts of these limitations. We can also feel this reduced efficacy if we are passed over for promotions or if we feel stuck in our jobs because there are no promotions or areas of growth within our organizations. We may also feel stuck by our education or the degrees, certificates, and licenses we've accumulated (and the debt), especially if we find ourselves wanting to shift toward another profession or type of work.

Identifying the point when things start to get overwhelming is the key to avoiding burnout, which is the ultimate goal. These three dimensions of burnout are caused by six sources of work stress that can lead to burnout, and they are: workload, control, reward, community, fairness, and values. If you have experienced burnout, these will be very familiar to you, and if you are lucky enough to have not burned out yet, these will be areas to keep an eye on as you move through your career as a helper, healer, or changemaker.

1. *Workload:* This one may be the most obvious, but a high workload is the number one source of burnout. Having too much to do in the amount of time you have to do it, whether cases, students, projects, or deadlines. When we feel like we can't get to all the things we have to do, it feeds into being exhausted and feeling less than effective in our work—two of the three dimensions of burnout. Many of our professional guidelines have suggested ratios of workloads (caseloads, classroom sizes, patient load, etc.). When these are ignored, it can push us toward burnout.
2. *Control:* When you are doing work but have little control over the conditions of the work, the timing of the work, the resources required for the work, the outcomes of the work, etc., it can be easy to see how this lack of control contributes to burnout. This stress can be abated when we trust the people who make decisions; however, the larger the organization and the more moving parts, so to speak, the less control individual employees typically have in the decision-making process. Understandably, this increases the risk of burnout, especially for those in public education and in healthcare settings, where school boards or insurance boards create rules or conditions of work that educators, healthcare professionals, and social workers are left to contend with.

3. *Reward:* Lack of reward can push us to the brink of burning out. Very few of us come to the work of helping, healing, or change-making simply for the accolades, and many of us are hesitant to accept public praise, nevertheless, we all seek to be rewarded for the work we do. Rewards may come in the form of extrinsic/organizational rewards like PTO, additional benefits, or an increase in salary, or they may be intrinsic rewards, like praise from a supervisor, gratitude from a client, or respect from our peers. When these are lacking and we are continuing to do challenging work without any acknowledgment, it can cause the heaviness we face in our work to seem impossible to carry and can lead to cynicism or mental distance. Being given more challenging cases or the difficult patient or student is not a reward, but being acknowledged for managing the challenging cases can give us encouragement and support our resilience.
4. *Community:* We know how vital community is to our growth and happiness. The same is true for work communities; the healthy ones feed us, and the toxic ones drain us. Working in a toxic work environment or in a job that lacks any kind of collegial a healthy community contributes to burnout, especially with work as challenging as ours. The antidote to the heaviness of our work is a strong sense of comradery and colleagues who understand the work. If the larger work community is not healthy or supportive, we may need to create our own community at work. Having amazing colleagues who offer support, a shoulder to lean on, and sometimes just the space to vent when things get overwhelming keeps me from the edge of burnout. I call them my emotional support coworkers.
5. *Fairness:* Regularly facing unfair practices or unethical challenges in our work can burn us out. This may seem obvious, but sometimes fairness, or lack thereof, can stay under the radar for a long time before it bubbles up and can't be ignored. Whether it involves discrimination, impartial decisions, or a lack of good judgment (and whether it is

happening to us or those we serve), it can be challenging to stay hopeful and engaged in unfair conditions. Once there is a pattern of unfair behavior or decisions in addition to the real world consequences of the work we do as helpers, healers, and changemakers, we can see how easy it is to slide into burnout.

6. *Value conflict:* Values are the standards we live by, like loyalty, integrity, and honesty. In the same vein as fairness, facing conflicts of or a mismatch of values in the workplace makes our jobs very challenging. Working for a religious organization when you have different views might be one example. Working in a place where people who schmooze get advancements could be another. Value conflicts don't reach the depth of moral conflicts, but they can cause a disconnect between us and our work or may cause a kind of spiritual dilemma that creates distance between us and our work.

If we find ourselves facing most or all of these sources of work stress, we may want to reconsider where we are working and whether we feel aligned with the work we are doing. The impact we have diminishes as we approach burnout, and those we serve cannot afford to receive inadequate services. This isn't to suggest that we take personal responsibility for feeling this way, but rather that we notice and acknowledge when these aspects show up in an unbalanced way and that we take action before it's too late.

While burnout is not new, the challenge is that we still haven't adopted any real, fundamental changes in our professional training programs to act on or prevent the causes of burnout in our professions. And we are beginning to see the impacts. The United States is facing a major shortage of essential workers in the next few decades. While the populations who need our support (the elderly; the disabled; those experiencing homelessness, addiction, mental health crises, etc.) are increasing and becoming even more complex, there are forecasts of shortages among nurses, primary care physicians, teachers, social workers, childcare and elder care professionals, and first responders. Health pandemics (COVID, diabetes, cancer, etc.) and social epidemics (poverty, violence, suicide, etc.) seem intractable and exhaust those of us who work in these spaces.

Many of our institutions and organizations like schools, hospitals, and social services, will be directly and negatively impacted by these shortages. Those who depend on these social networks will have fewer and fewer supports if we don't shift this trajectory. We are burning out and turning over at alarming rates and we must do something to stem the tide. In order to do that, we need to address the root causes of burnout and to acknowledge that there is a cost to caring that goes beyond burnout for those of us who are helpers, healers, and changemakers.

THE COSTS OF CARING: BEYOND BURNOUT

These workers are expected . . . to give their lives over to the work because they believe in the cause; but it becomes harder and harder to believe in the cause when the cause is the thing mistreating you.

—Sarah Jaffe, *Work Won't Love You Back*

Those engaged in fighting for a more just, equitable, and joyous world have an urgent need to reckon with the pervasiveness of feelings of powerlessness, political inefficacy, apathy, and despair, and to explore how such sentiments influence struggles for social change.

—Deborah B. Gould, *Moving Politics: Emotion and ACT UP's Fight against AIDS*

When I started my work in rape crisis in 2003, some of my colleagues had 15–20 years of experience in that work. They knew the trajectory of policy change, they understood the many ways our work intersected with domestic violence and other social welfare disciplines, they were invested in their communities, had built relationships with local politicians and foundations, and they truly understood the need to be sustained in the work through self-care. Now, folks rarely stay in a position longer than three to five years, and in some organizations, the most senior worker may have only five years in that work. When we experience turnover in these professions, we are left with little to no institutional memory or historical context for the work, which necessitates recreating the wheel every three to five years when new workers come onboard. When people leave our agencies or organizations, their ideas, procedures, and programs often leave with them and we lose time, resources, and energy. Spending time recreating or rebranding old practices thwarts progress, which requires steady commitment and action over time.

We know that burnout is the main reason for this constant turnover, and while any occupation can experience burnout, I often say that helpers, healers, and changemakers experience a different flavor of burnout. What we experience is something beyond burnout because of the inevitable layers and intersections in our work. When our work exposes us to violence, oppression, or just plain negligence, we focus on the job at hand, but we often don't register that we are absorbing trauma. This can cause us to experience the symptoms of burnout but from a source that can be hard to name.

As described earlier, burnout is marked by exhaustion, depersonalization/cynicism, and lack of professional and personal efficacy. While these qualities can certainly be present for us, there are deeper causes/nuanced levels of work stress that some of us remain unaware of. Burnout "can definitely affect many helping professionals in addition to compassion fatigue and vicarious trauma, but burnout does not necessarily mean that our view of the world has been damaged or that we have lost the ability to feel compassion for others" (Mathieu, 2012, p. 10). Burnout is just one aspect of the impact of our work. Burnout does, however, make us more susceptible to the following "costs of caring" in our work, like compassion fatigue, moral injury, and primary, secondary, and vicarious trauma. Each of these can be experienced separately or in combination, so it is helpful to define them to better understand which aspect of our helping work is impacting us most, to allow for a more targeted application of our radical self-care practices.

COMPASSION FATIGUE

> *Professionals who listen to clients' stories of fear, pain, and suffering may feel similar fear, pain, and suffering because they care. Sometimes we feel we are losing our sense of self to the clients we serve. . . . Those who have enormous capacity for feeling and expressing empathy tend to be more at risk of compassion stress.*
>
> —Charles Figley, *Compassion Fatigue*

The first line in the book *Compassion Fatigue: Coping with Secondary Traumatic Stress Disorder in Those Who Treat the Traumatized* is, "There is a cost to caring" (Figley, 1995, p. 1). Charles Figley's foundational compassion fatigue research suggests that we will experience compassion fatigue if we are good at what we do. Some of us know this by other names, like injustice fatigue, lack-of-resources fatigue, or doing-three-jobs-on-one-salary fatigue. But seriously, compassion fatigue compromises the quality of the work we do and the quality of our personal lives. We may not have the energy for interactions with coworkers, family, or loved ones, which can impact those relationships. We may minimize the pain or suffering of others because we are in so much emotional pain ourselves. We may begin to close ourselves off from others in our personal lives and in our professional lives, shutting down our compassion to avoid further harm. We may also experience a traumatic-stress response similar to PTSD, sometimes referred to as "combat exhaustion." It can take us time to identify what is happening to us and to actively recenter ourselves and get grounded.

Described in the *Compassion Fatigue Workbook* as "the profound emotional and physical exhaustion that helping professionals and caregivers can develop over the course of their careers as helpers" (Mathieu, 2012, p. 8). Figley also suggests that "we know enough to realize that compassion fatigue is an occupational hazard of caring service providers" (Figley, 1995, p. 17). And while that may be true, calling this an occupational hazard or suggesting that those who are good at their work will inevitably experience this kind of pain gives power to oppressive systems. This is where our passion for the work and our heart as caregivers can be exploited even when we're suffering. *Our suffering is seen almost as a badge of honor, when it should be a sign for us to slow down.* Ultimately, while our compassion for those we serve can act as a buffer to stress in our work, compassion fatigue disconnects us from our empathy, our hope, and our compassion, which can deaden our passion for our work as helpers, healers, and changemakers. This may be a sign that we lack self-compassion, giving to others something that we ourselves may believe we do not deserve.

PRIMARY TRAUMA

> *Many social workers work in sites of structural violence, where oppressions intimately interlock in day-to-day interactions between those offering services and those receiving services.*
>
> —Chris Chapman and A. J. Withers, *A Violent History of Benevolence*

We are directly impacted by the trauma we are exposed to in our work, and I'm always amazed by how rarely our professions acknowledge this reality. The most obvious effect of the work is from direct exposure to trauma which can be working in physically dangerous settings, working with unsafe populations, or experiencing direct danger in our workplaces. First responders, members of the armed forces, social workers, medical professionals, and even some educators, may work in unsafe communities or workplaces that can cause primary trauma. Examples might be teachers who work in a prison or juvenile hall setting, social workers or probation officers who conduct home visits to known violent perpetrators, EMTs going to a scene to assist a victim while a shootout is in progress, or soldiers, photojournalists, or relief workers embedded in a war zone. When there is a risk to our personal safety, we may experience hopelessness, fear, anxiety, or we may begin to develop acute or chronic symptoms of posttraumatic stress.

It is admirable that we show up and keep doing the work even when it's hard, but our agencies and organizations must acknowledge these risks (not simply call them "hazards of the work") and prioritize safety as well as provide time and space to process traumatic incidents. Sometimes it can be helpful for those involved in a traumatic incident to have an opportunity to process their thoughts, feelings, and emotions immediately after an incident and to do so with others who also experienced the same incident. This strategy buffers our nervous systems from potential posttraumatic stress symptoms and provides us a space for collective healing in the aftermath of trauma.

Some law enforcement agencies require a mental health evaluation, a few sessions with a counselor, and/or a three to five day "deactivation" period after a traumatic incident before putting an officer back on duty. Some social work agencies do the same, but this isn't a systemwide practice, and it is very rare to find a school district willing to acknowledge these risks to teachers or to provide real security to their educators (beyond the poorly thought out ideas of arming teachers or bullet-proof white boards for classrooms). I've been in school districts and organizations where there is little consideration for the well-being of teachers or staff after a violent fight, a lockdown, or police action that may have been traumatizing to those involved. With this reality in mind, we need to develop individual practices that can hold us as we process the primary trauma in our work and that provide us a foundation of support from which to advocate for better care in our workplaces, to protect us from harm in the line of duty.

SECONDARY TRAUMATIC STRESS AND VICARIOUS TRAUMA

An initial step toward self-care for the helper is to have a framework for understanding the impact of doing trauma work. One important issue is to recognize that exposure to traumatized clients can affect the helper.

—Dena J. Rosenbloom, Anne C. Pratt, and Laurie Anne Pearlman, "Helpers' Responses to Trauma Work: Understanding and Intervening in an Organization in Secondary Traumatic Stress"

When I first heard about secondary trauma and vicarious trauma, the thought that my nervous system could react to a traumatic event that I hadn't personally experienced didn't make sense to me. When we are not the primary victim, it can be easy for us to reject the idea that we could be impacted simply by exposure to victimization. It wasn't until I experienced my first burnout while absorbing the stories of rape and sexual assault that I began to understand the insidious nature of the wounding in our work. As a Master of Social Work (MSW) intern, I spent hours combing through the files of convicted sex offenders to code their offenses and demographic information related to the offenders and their victims. It wasn't until my fellow intern quit unexpectedly (but also expectedly. . .) that I realized the heaviness of the work I was doing.

The terms *secondary stress* and *vicarious trauma* are sometimes used interchangeably and both fall under the umbrella of compassion fatigue. While they certainly overlap, I think it's important to understand the nuances of each. Ultimately, both are work-related trauma from exposure to traumatized clients or traumatic content, but secondary stress can happen in an instant, while vicarious trauma accumulates over time. In either case, because of our exposure to the realities of trauma in the world and in our workplaces, we are changed.

There are two categories of secondary trauma: the suffering of family members or close associates due to the trauma of a loved one, and the traumatic experience of being a direct witness to an incident and becoming overwhelmed by what is seen or heard even if you are not the primary victim (Rothschild & Rand, 2006). The traumatizing event often includes hearing, watching (via video, not in person), or reading about a traumatic event though you are not the victim. For example, being in a courtroom when graphic testimony of a traumatic event is given or watching surveillance footage of a crime occurring or reading through autopsy files or observing a forensic interview with a child abuse survivor. It could also happen while supporting a child or spouse through a terminal illness, directly experiencing the death of a loved one (without being harmed yourself), or witnessing an act of police brutality or some other mass casualty event that you are not personally impacted by.

Secondary traumatic stress can occur after one traumatic event, whereas vicarious trauma accumulates over a period of time and a series of traumatic events. As mentioned, secondary trauma can show up in a matter of days, whereas vicarious trauma may take months or even years to show up. Vicarious trauma is the "transformation in the therapist's (or other trauma worker's) inner experience resulting from the empathic engagement with clients' trauma material" (Figley, 1995, p. 151). It occurs when we are transformed by the stories, images, and details of trauma we didn't experience ourselves. "As a result of our exposure to the realities of trauma in the world, we are changed" (Pearlman & Saakvitne, 1995, p. 31).

Vicarious trauma is insidious and sneaks up on us. It is a cumulative process that happens over the course of our work. It shows up in our nervous system in subtle ways at first, but then creates a level of dysregulation that is hard to ignore. Vicarious trauma keeps us in a steady state of stress, accompanied by adrenaline rushes and cortisol spikes that cause inflammation in our bodies. This manifests as autoimmune disease or chronic pain with no specific medical marker, causing us to feel like we're going crazy or our body is working against us, when the root cause is the trauma we are exposed to in our work. In reality, those of us who have our own histories of trauma can be more vulnerable to the impacts of vicarious trauma (as I was with my rape crisis work), which we will explore further in the next chapter.

As helpers, healers, and changemakers, we must notice and address vicarious trauma, because the cost of not addressing it is too grave. "Unaddressed vicarious trauma, manifest in cynicism and despair, results in a loss to society of that hope and the positive actions it fuels. This loss can be experienced by our clients, as we at times join them in their despair; by our friends and families, as we no longer interject optimism, joy, and love into our shared pursuits; and in the larger systems in which we were once active as change agents, and which we may now leave, or withdraw from emotionally in a state of disillusionment and resignation" (Pearlman & Saakvitne, 1995, p. 33).

MORAL INJURY AND MORAL DISTRESS

Social work professionals have a political responsibility to act as agents for social transformation. Recognizing the systemic forces that impede anti-oppressive practice is a necessary first step in that social action. Moral distress is one concept that helps us to frame those structural barriers and social work's ethical responsibility to fight for societal change.

—Merlinda Weinberg, *Moral Distress: A Missing but Relevant Concept for Ethics in Social Work*

The term *moral injury* comes from the arena of war to explain combat-related psychological trauma. Moral injury is a betrayal of one's morals of "what is right," either by an individual or by a person in legitimate authority, in a high-stakes situation or environment (Shay, 2014). Moral injury violates a person's moral codes or deeply held moral beliefs, forcing us into actions that impinge upon welfare, justice, rights, and fairness. "Moral injury is emotional distress resulting from events or transgressive acts that create a dissonance within one's very being due to a disruption or violation of their existential orientation and values system" (Song et al., 2021).

Imagine a soldier in a war zone being given the order to kill a child who may be carrying a bomb. Because of the seriousness of the risk, the soldier must comply with the order whether that child has a bomb or not. Then that soldier is left to process the reality that they murdered a child as ordered by an authority. If this soldier then has to return home to their own child, possibly of the same age, the dissonance of those two realities can create deeper posttraumatic distress. You can see how the result may be a very deep moral injury. Especially if that soldier then returns from war to a lack of support from civilians or to anti-war protests that may feel like social stigma and that act to invalidate or even criminalize the very difficult actions that were demanded in moments of crisis.

As we do our work in a world that is increasingly violent and toxic, we are exposed to moral injury in our work as helpers, healers, and changemakers. For example, a child welfare social worker becomes aware of abuse in a foster home but is pressured to ignore it because that foster home is the only one that takes medically fragile children, and the agency doesn't want to lose the placement; the social worker is then left carrying the weight of knowing that a child is being harmed. Consider a nurse who is forced to discharge a sick, uninsured patient to make room for patients who can pay, when they know that person's illness will continue to fester without proper treatment. Or a judge who is forced to impose a mandatory minimum sentence on a defendant who would be better served by treatment or a more restorative approach. Any of these scenarios, all outside the arena of war, can also cause moral injury.

While the term *moral injury* originated from war, it is also referred to in research among nurses and other health professionals published since the COVID-19 pandemic. This research has found that the rates of moral injury among nonveteran populations is rising, in articles with titles like "Moral Injury Among Professionals in K–12 Education" (Sugrue, 2020), "Morally Injurious Experiences and Emotions of Health Care Professionals During the COVID-19 Pandemic Before Vaccine Availability" (Song et al., 2021), and "Prevalence of

Moral Injury, Burnout, Anxiety, and Depression in Healthcare Workers 2 Years in to the COVID-19 Pandemic" (Lennon et al., 2023).

A result of moral injury is moral distress, which "arises when one knows the right thing to do, but institutional constraints make it nearly impossible to pursue the right course of action" (Jameton, 1984). Moral distress creates disequilibrium in our bodies and nervous systems and can be compounded by multiple experiences of moral injury. Moral injury and moral distress are not the same as a moral dilemma. When dealing with a moral dilemma, we still have choices and some level of agency. Moral injury and moral distress occur when we do not have any choices and when our sense of agency is usurped by another authority, such as a supervisor, a leader, the institutions we work in, or the policies, laws, and legislation we are beholden to.

We must acknowledge the inevitability of being affected by the work—understanding the many ways our work transforms us and our worldview—so we can know exactly what radical self-care practices will help provide relief and healing. We also must understand the difference between being out of alignment with the work versus facing organizational challenges in the workplace, as they require different acts of radical self-care to navigate. To do this, we must acknowledge that our work is inherently traumatic (Stamm, 1999).

HEAVY CONTENT WARNING

If this topic makes you uneasy or triggers past trauma, please feel free to skip it, but come back to it when you can. If you or someone you know is having suicidal ideations or considering suicide, please call the National Suicide Prevention Lifeline at *988 or 800-273-8255 or reach out online at https://988lifeline.org/

Know that you are not alone, you are worthy of help, and **we need you.** Don't Clock Out is a website founded by health care workers for health care workers. Check out their resources at https://www.dontclockout.org/.

INDIVIDUAL/COMMUNAL PREVENTION

- Some ways we can individually and communally support each other are by being aware and noticing the signs of mental health distress in ourselves and our colleagues and accessing mental health treatment when needed or sharing those resources. Be watchful for the risk of suicide after a critical incident at work, a community trauma, or personal challenge. Remove access to lethal means or offer to help someone remove access (locking up weapons or medication, creating a safety plan for home and work). Support the healing process by allowing time and space for healing either in group sessions or individually.

ORGANIZATIONAL PREVENTION

- Some ways our organizations can support our safety are by training staff to recognize the signs and risks of suicide by learning basic mental health first aid. Be aware of the ways the work may create suicidal ideation and find ways to minimize them. Know what resources are available and make them available to employees while removing the stigma of seeking support by making it a protocol or policy. Provide spaces to process suicides (of colleagues or clients) when they do occur.

Seeking help when you are feeling distress is a sign of strength and courage. If this means pulling away from your work for a time to heal and find resources, please do so.

Staying alive is the ultimate act of radical self-care.

THE ULTIMATE COST OF CARING: DEATH AND SUICIDE

Some people work hard, day and night, in the field of helping others, but their strongest motivation is to stay busy so they can avoid feeling their own pain.

—Pema Chödrön, *Welcoming the Unwelcome*

Caregiver suicide is an ugly phenomenon. It devastates the care team, and even the whole system. It is one of the best-kept secrets in our industry, and we can no longer remain silent.

—Omar Reda, MD, *The Wounded Healer*

While compassion fatigue, secondary stress, vicarious trauma, and moral injury may be long-term consequences of our work, the immediate reality is that our work can expose us to death or increase the possibility of our own demise. Some of us work directly with death or with the possibility of death. Coroners and medical examiners obviously deal with death, but so do first responders, military members, rescue and pararescue personnel, medical professionals (human and animal), hospice workers, social workers, etc. The hope is that our training programs prepare us for the inevitable engagement with death or death-related content so we can process it and continue the work without being negatively impacted by it. But in addition to death being part of the work, many helpers, healers, and changemakers risk their lives to be of service when death is not an anticipated occupational hazard.

In fact, it was the death of a social worker that prompted me to become a social worker myself. When I was working for Court Appointed Special Advocates (CASA) in Columbus, Ohio, my job was to train volunteers to advocate for foster youth in the dependency system. I worked closely with judges, attorneys for children, as well as social workers with the local child welfare agency. On October 16,

2001, Nancy Fitzgivens, a social worker with the Franklin County Children Services (FCCS) was murdered at a home visit (Gillespie, 2001). She was visiting the home of a couple whose seven children had been removed due to drug use and reported sexual abuse. During the home visit, the father of the children stabbed Ms. Fitzgivens to death. Her death caused a wave of devastation and shock through the social work community. There was a scramble to implement safety measures for social workers in the field, and folks started checking in on one another. Her death came not long after 9/11, so the shock and trauma felt impenetrable, and the energy was heavy.

After Nancy Fitzgivens's death, I learned that she had had a long career as a teacher, and I was moved by her experiences with abused children. Even though I never had the privilege of meeting her, I felt an urgent need to carry on her work. Her dedication is remembered by the Nancy Fitzgivens Child Protection Award, given out each year by Franklin County Children Services in her honor, and the Nancy E. Fitzgivens Endowed Scholarship, established by the Annie E. Casey Foundation through The Ohio State University. It was her dedication that made me determined to become a social worker and prompted me to apply to graduate school for my MSW.

When we think of the risk of death in the line of duty, we often think of first responders or armed services members, but more and more helpers, healers, and changemakers are finding death or the risk of death a reality in their work. A few recent incidents shocked the social work community, surfacing continued concerns about physical safety.

- DCFS Worker Fatally Stabbed During Home Visit (Hundsdorfer, 2022)

  Dierdre Silas, a social worker in Illinois, was stabbed to death at a home visit, like Nancy more than twenty years prior.
- Police: Boyfriend at Texas Hospital for Baby's Birth Kills 2 (Bleiberg & Stengle, 2022)

  In Dallas, Texas, a man was granted bail to visit his newborn and went on to assault his girlfriend, who had just given birth, and in the process killed social worker Jacqueline Pokuaa and nurse Katie Annette Flowers.

- Homeless Woman Kills Shelter Coordinator With Ax in Front of Staff, Vermont Police Say (CBS News, 2023)
  Social worker Leah Rosin-Pritchard, who like Nancy became a social worker as her second career, was killed by a resident of the homeless shelter she ran.

Sadly, school shootings have become so common that if I referred to "the latest school shooting" as I write, I would not be referencing the same incident once this book is published. There is no end in sight, given our lack of change regarding gun control or intensive mental health supports. We have lost too many educators and school personnel to mass shootings. Education is a job that no one should have to risk their lives to do.

There is also the risk of protracted death based on being overworked, regardless of the content of the work. The Japanese have a word, *karoshi*, which literally means "overwork death." It was coined in the 1980s when Japan saw an alarming increase in middle-aged workers dying due to work stress. Heart failure, strokes, and suicides were the leading causes of the death—by overwork—and the alarm bells were sounded. Unfortunately, there was little movement globally to take this issue seriously or to make any reforms or corrective action to change how we work. By the time you're reading these words, there will have been more deaths of helpers, healers, and changemakers. We will learn some of their names, the ones that make it to the news, but others will go unnoticed, making this a silent epidemic among helpers, healers, and changemakers.

SUICIDE IN OUR WORK

Suicide is a public health epidemic and an occupational hazard of the helping professions that few want to discuss, but it is on the rise in the United States and globally, having increased 39% since 2020 (Sainato, 2022). Social workers, educators, medical professionals, first responders, and activists are at greater risk of negative physical and mental health outcomes, like addiction, disease, and even suicide. We must be aware that the distressing nature of our work can cause suicidal thoughts and reveal the truth about how common suicidal ideation and passive suicidality are in the work we do. We must not turn our heads from the unbearable pain some of our colleagues and allies have faced and the painful numbing some of us have experienced. There is a lot of fear and lack of understanding when it comes to suicide and suicidal behaviors, however, bringing this topic out of the shadows and into the light is the only way we can combat it and support those who may be bearing the ultimate toll of our work.

If we've been part of a critical incident that we can't shake, have experienced a moral injury that leaves us distraught, or if the vicarious trauma we have absorbed becomes just too much to hold, we may begin to have some suicidal thoughts or ideations. I know many helpers, healers, and changemakers, myself included, who have felt that the only way for us to get rest is to be injured or fatally wounded. If you've ever considered driving your car off a cliff or into a wall, if the idea of being laid up in a hospital bed sounds restful to you, or you've had other similar intrusive thoughts, you know exactly what I mean. Even then, we'd probably still feel the need to check emails. Maybe it's the general stress of the work or the way the public disregards the work we do that causes us to become passively suicidal. Some other reasons might be:

- heartbreak in the work, specifically with those we serve;
- futility or nihilism in the work when we work so hard but nothing changes;
- knowledge of the system; the more we know, the less we can deny its brokenness;
- distrust of a system, especially if we need help from similar services or colleagues;
- reluctance to seek help/fear of being stigmatized or punished for seeking help;
- denying the severity of the need for physical or mental health care;

- addiction or drug use/overdose; self-medicating the pain of burnout; and
- unethical or unprofessional behavior, leading to shame or professional ruin.

Working within systems that don't prioritize healing causes serious mental and psychological breakdown. I know several fellow educators, social workers, professors, and doctors who have had psychological breaks and have had to spend time in psychiatric facilities to recover. Some of them have expressed the fear of being shamed for seeking professional help, but this is another example of how we don't often extend compassion to ourselves in times of serious need. I applaud anyone—especially my fellow helpers, healers, and changemakers—for seeking the mental health care they need to address their own trauma wounds. *Seeking help is a very brave act of radical self-care and self-preservation.*

Among helpers, healers, and changemakers, educators and social workers have the lowest risk of suicide, but the research in this area is a bit sparse. Having a purpose-driven career and good professional training can act as buffers from self-harm, but still there are suicides among educators and social workers that are not reported as such. Unfortunately, first responders, physicians, nurses, and other health professionals are at very high risk of suicide, despite the passion they may have for their careers. It seems a well-known hazard of medical school that most classes will experience a suicide before they finish their residency. In fact, they are the only group of helpers, healers, and changemakers who have multiple books and articles written about the topic of suicide within their profession.

Cassie Alexander (2021) published a very raw take in her book *The Year of the Nurse*, written from her perspective as an ICU nurse in San Francisco who was brought to the verge of suicide by the COVID-19 pandemic. Using journal entries, responses to news articles, and her own direct work with dying COVID patients, she doesn't mince words.

> I just want to throw up and cry. . . . I try and I try and I do nothing but try and for what? What is even the point of all

> this trying? I'm breaking myself and for why or who or who the fuck cares? . . . I need someone to actually listen to me. All of this can't be for nothing. I can't take it anymore if it is. (Alexander, 2021 p. 201)

A recent study published in the *Journal of the American Medical Association* (*JAMA*) found that, "relative to nonhealth care workers, registered nurses, health technicians, and health care support workers in the United States were at increased risk of suicide" (Olfson et al., 2023). In his book *Why Physicians Die of Suicide*, Dr. Michael Myers, shares,

> There are also those who give too much to medicine, and they are the ones who are sitting ducks for burnout and its worst-case corollary, suicide. What makes their suicide even more tragic and ironic is that, in most cases, they have been killed by their work, lost their lives in the line of duty. (Myers, 2017, p. 31)

Tragically, the heaviness of the work and of the world has caught up with a few of our colleagues. Here are just a few examples:

- "My demons won today": Ohio activist's suicide spotlights depression among Black Lives Matter leaders (Lowery & Stankiewicz, 2016)
- New York City Police Officer Dies By Suicide—the 10th NYPD Suicide in 2019 (Law, 2019)
- "I Couldn't Do Anything": The Virus and an E.R. Doctor's Suicide (Knoll et al., 2020)
- Fourth officer who responded to US Capitol attack dies by suicide (Lowell, 2021)
- Searchers find body of missing Stanford nurse (Vainshtein, 2022)
- Sounding The Alarm: Firefighters Remain More Likely to Die By Suicide Than On Duty (Roberts, 2023)
- Four current and former L.A. Sheriff's Department employees died by suicide in a 24-hour span (Jany & Winton, 2023)

Ironically, the urgency of our work that can drive us to self-harm can also keep us from harming ourselves. An article titled "Why Do So Many Activists Commit Suicide?" shares the story of activists with suicidal ideations putting off their suicidal actions because there's important work to do, "You can't kill yourself today. . . . You've got this meeting, you've got to go protest at seven o'clock" (Raphael, 2016). Sadly, I have heard similar sentiments from other helpers, healers, and changemakers, that the only thing keeping them from suicide is the amount of work that still needs to be done.

This is a sad reflection on our helping professions and the lack of care we prioritize for those among us doing the most challenging work. It is painfully obvious that we need real change in the way we approach our work and maybe even the way our work is viewed by the public. It also means we must be engaging in our radical self-care practice, so we notice when we are sliding into suicidal ideation *ourselves* and we can seek the support needed before it gets too intense. A strong foundation of radical personal interventions are needed to hold one's heart and spirit when engaging in death- and suicide-inducing content.

When we engage our radical self-care we will also notice when a colleague needs some extra support and we can stand in solidarity with them as they get the mental health treatment they need. We must be the ones who accept when our colleagues might be suffering and reach out for help. Too often we are told to ask for help but are stigmatized when we do. In a letter to Dr. Wible, in her book *Physician Suicide Letters*, a physician named James wrote, "I suspect that you would be hard pressed to find one of us who isn't at least sometimes suicidal. We're just not allowed to admit it as it would end our careers" (Wible, 2016, p. 87).

Our work can contribute to our distress and suicidality. The heaviness of trauma and moral injury in our work requires a deeper understanding of the ways we must care for ourselves and each other. Radical self-care isn't just about doing things alone, and when it comes to the serious implications of death and suicide in our work, we must work together to be honest about this reality and take action to create better structures, policies, and practices in our organizations and within our professions to prevent these kinds of outcomes. We deserve the same compassion and care we give to others, especially around our mental health and well-being.

RADICAL TENDENCIES: BEYOND THE MASK AND THE CUP

The following concepts are a starting point for our radical self-care journey and will be a helpful foundational support as you move through the book and practice the radical tendencies shared in the following chapters. You're probably familiar with the oxygen mask analogy of self-care: If you're in a plane that is crashing, and the oxygen masks are needed for survival, it is vital that you put your own mask on before helping others with theirs. Makes sense. If you're busy helping others without your mask on, you will eventually pass out and be of no use to anyone. Even when there is oxygen available and being handed to you, if you refuse to use it because you're busy caring for others, you will most likely not survive that crash.

What if we looked a little deeper, beyond the mask, to acknowledge that *radical self-care is the breath.* In this analogy the mask and oxygen are provided (community care), but we still need to put the mask on *and take a breath* (radical self-care). Then, and only then, can we survive and be helpful to anyone around us. There are many proverbial "masks" and variations of "oxygen" available to us when we actively engage in our own well-being and prioritize our own care; thus it is our responsibility to take a deep breath, bring in the support we need, and act on our own behalf. Radical self-care requires that we initiate the action, that we take the first breath. The practices in this book are an offering of oxygen; *it's up to you to take a deep breath.*

In addition to the oxygen mask analogy, there is also a cup analogy we often use to address self-care. We say things like, "you can't pour from an empty cup" as a way of acknowledging the impact of our work. The goal is to ensure our cup is overflowing so that we keep what's in the cup for ourselves and give from our overflow. But what if we conceptualized this a bit differently?

In her book *Loving-Kindness: The Revolutionary Art of Happiness*, Sharon Salzberg shares a story about how the things in life that challenge us most are like salt. If we put a tablespoon of salt into a cup, it changes the quality of the water in that vessel, making it too salty to drink. But if we put that same tablespoon of salt into a lake . . . it does not change the quality of that water because the vessel is too large to be noticeably impacted.

> Even when the salt remains the same, the spaciousness of the vessel receiving it changes everything. . . . Our true work is to create a container so immense that any amount of salt, even a truckload, can come into it without affecting our capacity to receive it. (Salzberg, 1995, p. 43)

Like the oxygen mask analogy, if we are honest about our work and tell the truth about its impacts on us and those we serve, we must *get rid of the cup altogether and create a lake from which we can overflow.* I truly believe it is our job to expand our container. This is what allows us to show up for the work *without being changed by it* so that we can safely continue to effect change in our communities, organizations, and ultimately our world. The following chapters provide ways to expand our container and take the first breath by **remembering** why we chose this work and **reconnecting** with our passion, purpose, and true essence; by **regulating** our nervous system and **rebalancing** the energy we give to our work; by creating **rituals** and **rhythms** to help us stay aligned in our work; by providing space for us to **rest** and **restore** ourselves to wholeness; and by unapologetically **reclaiming** self-care and finding sources for **replenishing** in our work so we can move forward with radical change. Let's keep moving forward.

REFLECTIONS

This chapter was heavy but necessary. We often skim over or completely ignore the very real threats and traumatic impacts of our work as helpers, healers, and changemakers because we love the work we do and may see it as a calling. But being passionate about our work doesn't mean that we should ignore or deny the challenging aspects or that we should put up with the hurt and harm in our professions. My intention with this chapter was to get us thinking about the true cost of our work as helpers, healers, and changemakers so we understand the need for deep, courageous practices to hold our bodies, minds, and hearts as we continue to do the amazing work we have dedicated our lives to.

Here are some questions to reflect on before you move through the rest of the book:

- How do you tell the truth about the work you do?
  - What is the current state of your helping, healing, or change-making profession?
  - What happens to your mind/body/spirit when you are exposed to traumatic content in your work?
  - What are your thoughts about the burnout and turnover that is impacting your current profession?
- How can you do the work you love in a sustainable and generative way? What does that look like in your organization?
  - How do you work toward liberation for those you serve and for yourself simultaneously?
  - How do you do this challenging work while staying *grounded, regulated, aligned, present, embodied, and supported*?
- What would it look like (what would you need to see, hear, feel, know, and understand) if you were able to stand in your power, hold true to your values, and hold brave space in your work without harm to yourself or those you serve?
- What would it look like if a majority of helpers, healers, and changemakers unapologetically engaged in radical self-care that gave us the foundation from which to collaborate and support each other to really challenge the complex systems that no longer serve us?
- What if you were able to fearlessly challenge the status quo

and confidently move in the direction of true liberation for yourself and others without losing yourself or your identity?

- What would it look like (what would you need to see, hear, feel, know, and understand) if you could create radical change from a place of care, compassion, and joy?

2

REMEMBER AND RECONNECT

Why we do this work and how we do it whole

> Healing comes when the individual remembers his or her identity—the purpose chosen in the world of ancestral wisdom—and reconnects with that world of Spirit.
>
> —Patrice Somé, *The Healing Wisdom of Africa*

> Radical collective memory is a major threat to the status quo.
>
> —Aurora Levins Morales, *Medicine Stories*

When I present on radical self-care, I know there will be some folks in the space who are just not feeling it. There's always someone in the back of the room with folded arms, their head cocked sideways, delivering a steady stream of eye rolls and exasperated sighs. They tend to be the people who are most burned-out or very close to it—the people I most want to reach. So when I was presenting at a child abuse prevention conference many years ago, I noticed a few of those folks in the room.

After the presentation, several attendees came up to me to share their stories as helpers, healers, and changemakers. As they were talking, I noticed one of the women who had her arms folded throughout my presentation waiting behind the crowd. As I made my way through the crowd to talk to her, I braced myself and prepared to defend my work. What she said shocked me but also let me know I was on the right track regarding radical self-care.

The woman started by asking if she could give me a hug. She held on for a while and when we separated, she had tears in her eyes. She pulled away and said, "I wasn't going to come to this conference today, but my boss made me. Sitting here listening to you made me realize that I've been dealing with the impacts of vicarious trauma in my career for decades without having a name for it." She shared that her passion to care for children led her to a lifelong career as a pediatric ICU nurse. The heaviness of that work, even though she loved it, wore her out, impacted her health, and fractured her relationships. She said she fell into alcohol addiction to cope with the weight of her work and that led to multiple divorces and losing touch with her own children. All while providing life-saving care for other people's children.

She shared that as she listened to me talk, the anger projected toward me slowly turned to sadness when she realized that if she had been fully aware of the wounding in her work and about radical self-care, she might be in a very different place. But because there wasn't a culture of care in her workplace, she was left to believe that the dysregulation she was feeling was a personal short-coming and that she wasn't as strong as her colleagues, who seemed to be able to do the work without being negatively impacted by it. I emphasized that others *seemed* to be able to do the work without being impacted, but everyone is impacted by trauma-facing work whether they show it or not; it's that insidious.

As we parted, she said the most important thing for her to do at that moment was to remember why she got into nursing, to reconnect with that passion and to reconnect with her loved ones. We shared another hug and she encouraged me to keep up this work and maybe even write a book about "all this radical stuff you're talking about." I've had similar interactions at most of my presentations or workshops, and it's the spark from these conversations that pushed me to write this book.

DISMEMBERED AND DISCONNECTED

The professional work centered on the relief of the emotional suffering of clients automatically includes absorbing information that is about suffering. Often it includes absorbing that suffering itself as well.

—Charles Figley, *Compassion Fatigue*

The challenging work of helpers, healers, and changemakers can cause a rift between our professional and personal selves. The stress and trauma we absorb causes a disconnect within ourselves which can cause us to become fractured, compartmentalized, and dissociated. These are all forms of self-protection and, in some ways, attempts to create a buffer between the work we do and our personal lives, but this disconnection can cause us to be "dismembered" and disconnected from ourselves and the rest of our lives, creating fragmentation that eventually can lead to burnout and beyond.

Disconnecting from our work from time to time is a good thing, however, we need to be able to safely toggle between our roles at work and our roles at home. This provides a clear delineation and protects both spaces. In their book *Healing the Traumatized Self*, the authors acknowledge that "such strategies are entirely healthy, normative ways of managing and tolerating everyday distress, so long as one does not step back too far, too often" (Frewen & Lanius, 2015, p. 16). The authors suggest that becoming a detached observer is a healthy way to navigate distress, but when we disconnect without intention or conscious awareness and this happens over and over again, it can exacerbate our stress and push us over the edge. We become unable to control the overwhelm we feel, and we find ourselves out of alignment, fragmented, and disconnected in places and with people with whom we want connection. This is what makes us more vulnerable to the impacts of compassion fatigue, vicarious trauma, and even burnout.

There are many aspects of our work that can cause disconnection. First are our attempts at professional objectivity in our work that may see us necessarily creating separation and healthy disconnection. To avoid bias or misunderstandings, sometimes we have to set aside our personal beliefs and ideas so we can objectively see who or what is in front of us without influencing the process. For instance, I may reach out to the parents of a youth I am working with, and they share a questionable parenting technique that I disagree with. Assuming it's not abuse or neglect that needs to be reported, it is not my place to give parenting advice, so I do my best to be objective, to listen, and to provide the support the youth needs.

Depending on our specific work, each client, patient, or student may also require us to show up in a certain way for them that may be different for others, and maybe even different from how we show up in our personal lives. How I show up for a student who had just assaulted another student will be different from how I show up for a student who experienced a death in the family. How I show up to check in on an elementary school student is different than how I show up when I facilitate professional development with adults. They all get my compassion and professional care, but my affect with each of them may be slightly different based on their emotional regulation needs at the moment. How I show up after work for dinner with friends may also be different. You can see how this can be a kind of healthy fragmenting but can lead to a more disconnected existence.

Second are our attempts to protect those we love from our work or to prevent our work from encroaching on our time with those we love. We attempt to keep work at work and home at home so we don't "cross-contaminate" between the two and so we can enjoy time with family and friends. An EMT must focus all their attention on the patient strapped to the gurney rather than worrying about their child's grades or an upcoming school event. A soldier or journalist in an active war zone must focus all their attention on what's happening on the ground rather than thinking about their family members back home. A surgeon must focus all their attention on the patient at the end of the scalpel rather than being preoccupied with a conversation they had earlier with a coworker or spouse.

In the Netflix documentary *Lenox Hill* (Shatz & Barash, 2020), which follows doctors at the storied New York City hospital, the doctors share the challenges of disconnection in their work. In Episode 2, Dr. David Langer, the chief of neurosurgery, speaks to this challenge as he is about to head into the operating room to remove a brain tumor for a patient after taking a phone call with his son. "I used to get so stressed because I wanted to be a good dad. There's just so much emotional energy that goes into doing this well and having a piece of yourself that you can share with your wife and kids." This can create a separation that works and might even allow us to be more productive in our work, but it still is a disruption in our connection to ourselves and others that, over time, can have ill effects.

Lastly, disconnection occurs when our idealized version of our work clashes with reality. We optimistically assume that our agency, institution, or organization has the best intentions for our work; that healthcare agencies heal; that child protection agencies protect children; that the justice system seeks real justice; that our social services agencies serve the public, etc. But when we realize that sometimes our agency doesn't have our clients', students', or patients' best interests at the core of their work or, worse, that our agencies or organizations might actually be perpetuating the problems we are working so hard to change, we begin to feel disconnected from the passion that brought us to the work. If we are not conscious of it, overtime we can find ourselves disconnected from our core selves, unsure of who we are outside of our professional roles. There is a danger to our well-being when our whole identity is solely about our work as helpers, healers, and changemakers.

Sometimes we disconnect from colleagues because we don't feel they are as dedicated to the work as we are or because the overwhelm prompts us to isolate (because, like my nurse friend, we assume we're the only one who "can't handle it"). Sometimes we disconnect from our passion because it becomes exploited by agencies or organizations, and we may become disillusioned. Sometimes we disconnect from our families as a way of protecting them from the pain of our work (or we use our work to gain distance from our family). Sometimes we disconnect from our community due to misunderstandings, disagreements, or the challenging nature of our work. Sometimes we disconnect from ourselves and the world due to the constant triggering of trauma, vicarious trauma, and moral injury in our work. We disconnect from our passion, our purpose, and our people. Let's discuss the specific ways helpers, healers, and changemakers disconnect as well as the risks and benefits of the different forms of disconnection.

Compartmentalization

In her article in the *Huffington Post* titled, "I had my dream job as a death investigator. Then it morphed into a nightmare," M. Bridgette Golden shared how she was able to compartmentalize her work and disconnect herself while at work until that became too challenging and, "suddenly the trauma of it all started to leak out of the carefully labeled boxes in my brain where I had packed it away" (Golden, 2023). She began to see death in everyday activities, like cooking tofu or seeing plastic bags on the side of the road, and she found herself crying herself home. Sound familiar?

When it comes to our work, compartmentalizing is a helpful stress-management skill that allows us to separate personal and professional events and to suppress our thoughts and emotions so we can adapt to situations that may be overwhelming. Done safely and in the short-term, it's a great defense mechanism. It allows us to keep our work in perspective and to keep the emotions we might experience in our work from leaking out into nonwork situations. Sometimes it is impossible to keep the emotions contained, and if we're not conscious of the emotions we carry and aren't releasing them in some healthy way, we may harm ourselves or those we love. We may show up to family functions, still stressed about a situation at work, and while we are physically present, we may be emotionally unavailable. You're there, but you're *not really there.* A healthy level of compartmentalization requires some way to release what is being held.

Dissociation

When we daydream, we are dissociating in the simplest sense of the word. We are physically in one place but mentally in another. We disconnect from reality momentarily to find respite. Dissociation is a way our brains separate emotions, thoughts, meaning (derealization), and even separate our sense of self (depersonalization), especially when we experience chronic stress or trauma. If we are in control of our dissociation, like in the case of daydreaming or meditating, and can safely return to ourselves, it can be an amazing protective practice. "Go to your happy place" is a common prompt that may feel a bit silly but offers a container for dissociating safely.*

As self-protection, we may dissociate during a traumatic event to survive, and that adaptive trauma survival response can become something our minds do automatically as a way of protecting ourselves in later stressful situations. Dr. Bruce Perry simplifies this by sharing, "if dissociation is your preferred mode of stress adaptation for long periods of time when you're young, you end up with a sensitized dissociative response to any challenge" (Perry & Winfrey, 2021, p. 172). It can be triggered by something in our current environment, usually connected to our senses (something we see, smell, touch, taste, hear), and it causes us to numb-out or feel detached from ourselves and our work.

The challenge with dissociation in our work is that it is often out of our control, and that lack of control causes more stress. Pathological dissociation—when we "leave" without conscious awareness—can negatively impact our sense of agency and control. Interactions with our bosses, colleagues, collaborators, or even those we serve can cause dissociation, and it's important to be able to identify when it happens (what is the trigger?) and have some tools, like the ones at the end of this chapter, to bring you back to the present moment. Being able to choose when we "leave" and when we return to the present moment is a radical self-care skill that can act as a supportive structure of self-protection in our work.

**Safety is relative and depends on many factors, including your past experiences of trauma and your current environment. Please do not attempt to "go to your happy place" while driving or operating heavy machinery. Also, please seek additional support if you find yourself dissociating often, without the ability to bring yourself back, as it may be an early warning sign of distress and is important to pay attention to; you may need some additional support.*

Role-Swapping

Many of us hold several different roles in our lives. I am a social worker, a daughter, a sister, a wife, a foster parent, an auntie, a friend, a neighbor, a board member, a colleague, etc. While all these identities make up the whole of me, there are times when I have to lean more heavily into one of those roles, depending on the situation. In some roles, I feel very competent, and in others, I'm still learning. Switching between these roles is normal and natural, but sometimes we can get stuck in one role . . . often our professional caregiving role. This can impact our personal relationships when we try to maintain some of our power, control, or authority with family members who may need us to just be a parent or partner. We can also be impacted when we are in a personal situation, but our relatives, friends or neighbors ask for legal advice, mental health support, or social work insight. This makes it harder for us to separate or swap roles.

Being the one with the solutions or the one who handles the hard cases can be difficult to switch off when we get into a different space and need to be more reciprocal or to ask for help from others. When we're in a caregiving role in our work for the majority of our days, it can be challenging to shift to being a parent or a spouse/partner, especially shifting into a mode of romance or sex. Pleasure isn't often the focus when we're at work (in fact our work can kill our libido), so we may just need some time to decompress between work and home so we can shift out of caregiving mode and become available for the other roles we wish to inhabit.

Juggling too many roles at the same time can lead to burnout. This is especially true for women who often inhabit the roles of caregiver at work and at home. "Since most women burnouts pride themselves on their endurance and ability to volley and cope with their many roles, they rarely own up to inner exhaustion until they become physically ill" (Freudenberger & North, 1985, p. 18). Intentional role-swapping may involve some work around boundaries to allow us the space to soften and inhabit our personal roles more fully in the face of the challenges of our work as helpers, healers, and changemakers.

Code-Switching

Code-switching is "a complex dance of reconciling one's own inner awareness with the outside pressures associated with expressing racial, ethnic, and cultural identities" (Caldwell & Bennett Leighton, 2018, p. 186). The formal definition of code-switching refers to toggling between languages, like English and Spanish or standard English to African American Vernacular English (AAVE), to assimilate to the dominant culture. Many helpers, healers, and changemakers do this literally as part of their work, translating or interpreting between languages, cultures, or systems. But code-switching can also be used to describe behavior, like changing who we are or how we show up at work.

Sometimes our work requires us to wear a uniform and "dress down," meaning no makeup, no tattoos, and sporting a simple or conservative hair style, but on our own time, we can switch it up and express ourselves with clothes, makeup, body modifications, and hair styles. This can be a protective measure in our work, depending on our specific profession, like working with youth or working in a carceral setting. It can also be a protective measure for us personally, like tying long hair up into a bun so it can't be pulled by a human or get caught in a machine. There are times, however, that changes demanded of our dress and hairstyles have nothing to do with professionalism or personal safety, but rather a possible racial or gender bias. This is when code-switching becomes a protective measure to buffer oneself against the challenges of our personal identity not being accepted in our workplaces.

When I worked in rape crisis, I attended a conference for the Violence Against Women Act (VAWA) grant recipients and went with a male colleague of mine. We met at the airport, where I showed up in comfortable blue jeans, a sweatshirt, little make-up, and a backpack. My coworker, a black man, showed up in a full suit with his briefcase. I was shocked by the formal attire he had on, so I asked him if he always traveled in a suit, and his response broke my heart. He said, "I don't like wearing a suit when I fly but I've found that if I'm wearing anything less professional than a full suit, I tend to get 'randomly selected' for TSA searches. Happens every time, so now I dress as professionally as I can." He was forced to code-switch for his own safety, and we can only imagine the lack of control he felt having to make that switch as a protective measure rather than because he just liked wearing a suit.

Code-switching is often tied to a core identity we feel we must protect or switch out of as a way of safely assimilating to our work environment. Examples might include an LGBTQIA+ teacher who can't share their marriage to their same sex partner, a Black physician's assistant who is told box braids or locs aren't professional in a medical setting, or a journalist who is reprimanded for speaking their native language while at work. I remember feeling that I had to straighten my curly hair to be seen as professional, so I did it for years, most likely impacting my health with chemical straighteners. I've also heard plenty of helpers, healers, and changemakers of color talk about using their "White voice" at work to be perceived as more professional. Not being able to show up in our work with our whole selves puts us in a constant state of vigilance, causing a disconnect that may seem minor but that can accumulate to the point that we lose connection with ourselves.

When we control the switch, it can empower us, but if we are forced to code-switch when we work in a space that doesn't honor all parts of us, it can do harm. In his book *Black Magic*, Chad Sanders shares his code-switching challenges as the only Black man in the tech firms where he worked: "it took me a very long time to come to grips with exercising duality in a healthy way versus fighting and being willing to murder myself internally or externally to avoid it" (Sanders, 2021 p. 56).

Masking

Masking often refers to the behaviors people on the autism spectrum use to engage in our neurotypical society. When we have to hide who we are or how we function and behave in the same way as everyone else to gain social acceptance, we are masking. In a way, it is similar to code-switching, in that we are suppressing one way of being to adopt another, more acceptable way of being. We may hide aspects of ourselves that might be threatening or unusual to others; we may change our outward expression to stay safe or be included; or we may use masking as a way of showing positivity when we're in distress. Smiling when someone else smiles, even if we're not particularly happy; making small talk with a colleague to join in office culture, even if we would prefer to be left alone; responding "fine" when we're asked how we're doing, rather than sharing that we're having a really hard day at work, are all examples of masking in relation to our work.

Masking is a coping mechanism that allows us to navigate challenges in our work and to protect ourselves, but it involves shutting down our emotions, and that can cause long-term harm. Ultimately, masking forces us to hold all our emotions by ourselves or to suppress them for the greater good, and that is never healthy. Masking also suppresses who we are in favor of who we think we need to be, and that causes us to lose connection with ourselves.

Disengagement and depersonalization speak to the different flavors of fragmentation, dismembering, and disconnection that pull us further from ourselves and from one another. The disconnection feels so uncomfortable that we numb out, isolate, pull away, or just shut down. Many of us pull further into the work, picking up extra shifts or challenging cases to keep us in a productive state of disconnection, allowing us to do what feels like good work, while ignoring the nagging feeling that something is off.

In their book *Women's Burnout*, Dr. Freudenberger and Gail North explain twelve stages of the burnout cycle that help illuminate the ways disconnection, dismissal, and denial show up on the path to burnout (Freudenberger & North, 1985):

1. ***The compulsion to prove/Ambition:*** "I must prove myself. I can do this."
2. ***Intensity/Working harder:*** "I must do more."
3. ***Subtle deprivations/Neglecting needs:*** "I don't have time for this/myself."
4. ***Dismissal of conflict and needs/Avoiding conflict:*** "Nothing is wrong. it's fine."

5. *Distortion of values/Revising values:* "This is more important."
6. *Heightened denial:* "The problem isn't me, it's work, others, etc."
7. *Disengagement/Withdrawal:* "I need to be alone."
8. *Observable changes/Concerning others:* "I'm fine, don't worry about me."
9. *Depersonalization:* "I just need to make it through the day/week/year."
10. *Sense of emptiness:* "I don't feel anything anymore."
11. *Depression:* "Nothing matters anymore."
12. *Total burnout exhaustion:* "I can't keep going."

It is vital that we notice when our work is causing any kind of dissociation or unnecessary role- or code- switching. Catching our burnout as soon as possible and giving ourselves permission to engage our radical self-care practices helps us stay present to what we are feeling rather than dissociate or fall into patterns of compulsive caregiving.

WHY *THIS* WORK?

If our work dismembers and disconnects us, why do any of us do it? That's a question I always get from folks in other professions when I express the challenges of being in a helping profession. It's a valid question, given how our work impacts us. The helpers, healers, and changemakers I know are talented and intelligent and could do well in any other profession, but as we've already discussed, our passions, purpose, and people are the reason we do this work, so the more important questions are: *what brought us to this work?* and *what keeps us in it?*

Our draw to this work of helping, healing, and change-making often originates from our lived experience, whether because of it or despite it. This may be an obvious statement, but if we're not cognizant of why we came to the work, the wounding we experience can leave us confused or can catch us off guard. It's important to consider that our choice of work, the very reason we become caregivers, is often a direct response to our trauma patterns from childhood. Gabor Maté says we choose work in the helping professions for conscious reasons (*I want to help*) and unconscious reasons (*I have to justify my existence*). Among my fellow helpers, healers, and changemakers, I have observed that we come to this work for two main reasons:

1. Some of us experienced a wonderful childhood with support and love, and we want every human to experience what we did.
2. Some of us experienced a difficult or traumatic childhood, and we want to ensure no one ever experiences what we did.

This is one of the things I love most about my fellow helpers, healers, and changemakers: that we take our past experiences and take action to change the things we know didn't work for us or our loved ones. I know folks who became firefighters or peace officers after being saved from a house fire or an abusive home. I know folks who became social workers after experiencing the challenges of living in group homes or foster homes. I know folks who became nurses or doctors because they witnessed a parent or sibling go through a terminal illness. I know folks who became teachers after having one teacher believe in them and encourage their learning. I know folks who became peace corps or Red Cross volunteers because they survived war themselves or grew up in refugee camps. And I know folks who became activists after experiencing the horrors of war and wanting peace for others. These are the reasons I love us and want us to be consciously aware of why we do this work, *so the extra layer of our personal experiences can be a strength in our work rather than a liability.*

No matter what our experience, we may come to our healing work with deep wounds; some we may be very aware of, and some make their way to the surface when triggered by the work. Many of us had both wonderful and traumatic experiences and have some insight on how those experiences shaped us. We also come to this work with deep reserves of resilience and knowledge gained from our experiences. Even those of us who have had wonderful childhoods may have experienced trauma or we may have had to behave a certain way to appease the adults in our lives, whether they were violent, absent, or just overwhelmed. We are human, so there is no way to fully separate our adult selves from the traumas we survived in childhood, however, remembering who we are and where we come from is a good place to start.

REMEMBERING WHO WE ARE

If some people forget their past as a way to survive, other people remember it for the same reasons.

—Malidoma Patrice Somé, *Of Water and the Spirit*

I believe there exists in humans a fundamental, primal drive toward wholeness and health. This includes access to a part of ourselves that has always been within, that lives beyond any trauma, and is eternally whole and undamaged.

—Peter A. Levine, *An Autobiography of Trauma*

What we "do" in the world by way of occupation is not all that we are or all that we have to contribute to society, but it can be easy to let the work become our excuse for running away from ourselves. Remembering who we are at the core of our being (i.e., our true essence, fundamental consciousness, core self) helps us gain an understanding of why we are drawn to the work of helping, healing, and making change and can buffer us from exploitation. Theorists and researchers debate if there is one true essence, an authentic self, or if we actually hold a multiplicity of selves depending on the environments and situations we navigate, but what I mean here is simply the unique aspects that make you who you are and that differentiate you from others.

When I say, "remembering who we are," I'm not talking about self-help or self-obsession, but rather self-awareness that allows us to truly get down to the root: who are you when no one is watching, when you're not posting to social media, when you don't have to perform your professional identity, when you don't have to mask or code-switch, when you can *just be you*? In his book *The Wounded Healer*, Dr. Omar Reda reminds us, "we caregivers bear witness to the stories of our clients, but we should not neglect our own" (Reda, 2022, p. 2). Remembering who we are starts by recalling our own stories, the major formative experiences of our childhoods. I'll share a few of mine to help you begin to remember a few of your own.

I grew up in the '80s and '90s in the land of Kristens, otherwise known as Ohio. As a biracial middle child of three girls raised by a White mother and a Black father, I had a wonderful childhood filled with love, compassion, protection, and support. My parents were both veterans who enlisted after high school (Army and Navy) who completed their college degrees later in life and taught me the power of a work ethic, selfless service, and honorable morals. My mother was a stay-at-home mom who was declared "the best at momming" by my sister's best friend (you guessed it, Kristen), and when tasked to explain what my dad did, I jokingly say my dad was the Black Homer Simpson. He was a nuclear reactor operator at the Perry Nuclear Power Plant (think of the opening credits of *The Simpsons* that show Homer at work). Take Your Daughter to Work days were very interesting. We got to tour the control room and the cooling towers and, yes, we got donuts and glow sticks.

My dad sometimes worked night shifts at the power plant, so when we were home during the day and my dad needed quiet to sleep, my mother would get us out of the house and into the community. We spent time checking out books at the Mentor Public Library and the Cleveland Public Library, we rode escalators and watched airplanes take off at the Cleveland Airport, and we played on our local playgrounds and Ohio's Metro Parks. My mom signed us up for swimming lessons at the local civic center along with soccer, softball, and summer Junior Olympics, where we got to run relays and win medals. We took typing classes at the local community college (which we hated as teens, but appreciate as adults) and got to explore natural history museums, art museums, and botanical gardens. My mom did a lot of work to make sure my dad could sleep uninterrupted and to make sure we were engaged in local community learning events, hence "the best at momming."

We visited often with relatives in Pennsylvania, and I had wonderful connections with my aunts, uncles, and cousins. Every summer for most of my childhood, my extended family spent a week at Cedar Point, the largest amusement park in Ohio. Holidays and birthdays were made special by my amazing maternal grandma Nancy, who always reminded me that I was loved and that I could be anything and do anything if I worked hard and applied myself. From the time I was very young, I've had a desire to help, which was enabled by my Christian faith, as women did most of the caretaking in the church. Like many helpers, healers, and changemakers, I was an overachiever perfectionist who went out of my way to excel. My parents raised us on a cul de sac in a suburb of Cleveland with the best schools, and I had amazing K–12 teachers who saw my hunger for knowledge and encouraged me along the way. I had a diverse group of friends, I excelled at academics and athletics, and I was elected by my peers to be the class representative from 1st through 12th grade. My overachieving tendencies led me to seek more leadership positions, and I became senior class president and captain of the track team my senior year. I graduated with honors, a year's worth of college credits under my belt, and earned a leadership scholarship to college.

Overall, **I had a wonderful childhood. *And* I experienced trauma.***

**Note: I'm going to share some of my own childhood trauma. This may stir up something in you, whether your stories are similar or you're just experiencing empathy. Please take care of yourself as you read the next few paragraphs.*

Growing up in a White community, I often felt the intense need to be better and do more to prove I was worthy of existing as a Black/biracial person. Being mediocre wasn't an option, as my actions often reflected on *all* Black folks rather than being just my own, and I felt that pressure. All the time. Much of this was due to microaggressions that I absorbed as internal oppressions. I was told very directly, "You're not like other Black people . . . you're better/different" or "You're so good/smart/pretty . . . for a Black girl," and it didn't take much for me to feel the weight of wanting to be a good representation of Blackness. When I got the highest score on a test or won a scholarship, if I wasn't accused of cheating, I was accused of only achieving success because of affirmative action rather than on my own merits. At the same time, I was often reminded by folks in the Black community that I wasn't Black enough. As you can imagine, this caused plenty of heartbreak, but also cemented my quest for perfection.

I was a hypersensitive, highly intuitive, painfully empathic child, who picked up on energies and injustices very quickly even though I didn't always have the words to share what I was experiencing. I could sense issues between adults and feel when there was tension in the air. I was the kid who had simply to hear that my parents were disappointed in me to feel immediate shame and change my behavior. As a typical middle child, I adjusted myself so as not to take up too much space or cause too much burden. I often had stomachaches and strep throat, which came on when my parents argued or when things were "off" at home or school. Once, I heard my parents arguing about the cost of co-pays for doctor's visits, with my father asking if all the visits were necessary. This is a totally normal adult conversation, but hearing their raised voices made me think something was wrong and it was my fault. I decided the solution was to simply not tell my mom when I was sick or in pain so she wouldn't take me to the doctor and my dad wouldn't be mad about the co-pay. Weeks later, I got a sore throat and rather than tell my mom, I just put up with the pain . . . until it turned into scarlet fever, and I had to be rushed to urgent care after becoming so lethargic I couldn't get off the couch. While this incident was not due to neglect by my parents but rather to my adolescent brain interpreting their fighting as my fault and to my juvenile "solution" to the problem, my somatic issues were most likely the result of other traumas in my childhood.

When I was five years old, I was molested by a relative at a family function on my paternal grandmother's side. Thankfully, I was able to tell my mom as soon as I was safe at home, she believed me and protected me from that relative. Therapy wasn't as common or available back then, but in the years following, my mom and grandma would often ask me if I needed to talk about it or if there was anything more I needed to share. It was years into being a rape crisis counselor as an adult before I could use the words *sexual assault* and acknowledge the impact of that one act on the trajectory of my life. I had certainly felt the impacts of that traumatic experience, becoming even more hyperaware of my environment and those around me as a means of threat detection and self-protection. I also became hypervigilant to the injustice and victim-blaming that occurs often in the media, society, and even in churches. Whenever someone made a disparaging comment about a news report of a rape, suggesting that the victim was at fault, or I overheard someone at church suggest, "that's what you get when you do worldly things," I would second guess whether I was at fault for my own sexual assault. Following rules and being a "good girl" became the only way I could convince myself that the assault wasn't my fault, because the societal messages about who could be seen as a victim had seeped deep into my subconscious.

My first experience of community trauma was the January 28, 1986 Space Shuttle Challenger disaster. I was in first grade, and because Christa McAuliffe was going to be the first teacher in space, it was a big deal in schools. Our teachers held lessons about space and astronauts, we got to eat freeze dried astronaut ice cream, and there was a lot of fanfare leading up to the launch. My school, Fairfax Elementary, gathered us all in the gym to watch the launch, only for it to explode 73 seconds after takeoff. It was a shocking event for the nation, but particularly painful for educators. I could see the anguish in the faces of my teachers, but I don't recall how they managed to continue the school day nor how they explained the tragedy to us. I recall a sense of sadness and helplessness but also the feeling that this was a bigger loss for our teachers than we students could possibly understand. It was a national tragedy that had greatly impacted many across the United States.

In October of 1989, when I was in fifth grade, the kidnapping of Amy Mihaljevic from a shopping center in Bay Village, Ohio, captured the attention of the nation. When I saw her picture on the news and on missing persons posters, with her side ponytail and horse silhouette earrings, the image was burned into my memory. I felt an immediate connection to her. We were the same age, both born in December of 1978, and I saw myself in her. She was lured to a shopping center, after answering a call from a man who claimed to know her mom, under the guise of getting her mom a gift. Her kidnapping and subsequent murder (her decomposed body was found months later) set off a decade of stranger-danger frenzy and families creating code words in case they had to have another adult pick up their child from school. It deeply affected the way I saw the world and my safety in it.

That same year, later in fifth grade, I had a racially biased teacher who targeted me. As an overachiever, I did very well on tests and often had the top score in the class. This was the era of grading curves, where the highest score often "broke the curve," but anytime I got a 100% on a test or assignment, this teacher would accuse me of cheating or plagiarizing. She would sometimes stop me in the middle of a test and make me submit it, marking the questions I didn't complete against me. Then there was the time we had to make a billboard for our favorite book and I did mine on *The Island of the Blue Dolphins*. I was so proud of the dolphin that I painstakingly drew, but just a few days before we were to present our billboards, she called me to her desk to tell me that my paper was smaller than the other students' and that wasn't fair to them since they had more space to fill. Even though she was the one who cut the paper and gave it to us, she threw mine away and made me start over. I remember being so devastated and crying in the bathroom. She eventually felt comfortable enough to tell my White mother that she didn't think Black children learned the same way as other kids and that I should be tested for special education, since I seemed to cheat a lot and she wasn't sure of my actual academic aptitude. To call her bluff, my mom agreed to have me tested and . . . I tested into the gifted program. But that experience broke my little heart and only added to the sense of needing to achieve more than others to prove my worth.

My first personal experience of death was in fourth grade when my

Pap died. My great-grandfather was elderly, so while it was sad, it made sense to me in the order of life. However, when I was in sixth grade and my best friend's mom died suddenly, I had a harder time processing it. (Yes, my best friend was also a Kristen.) Her mom had been playing basketball in the driveway one summer afternoon. My sisters and I had to leave to go run errands and when we returned, there was an ambulance and fire truck on our street. It was hard to wrap my brain around the idea that someone I just saw was now deceased, but I mostly couldn't understand how a parent could just die . . . before their kids were even grown. This was also my first time acting as a caregiver, sitting in the back of the funeral home with my friend who didn't want to go near her mother's casket, and holding space for her grief.

Then in the summer of 1995, when I was 16, my friend John Stout died in a car accident. My mom got a call from one of my friend's moms, then she sat me down at the kitchen table and told me about his passing. I was no stranger to death by then, but the reality that someone my age could be here one day and gone the next left me numb. Teenagers are supposed to be invincible, or at least we thought so. John was one of the nicest people, especially for a teenage boy in the '90s. He would walk me from class to class and would often carry my books. He also stood up for me once and almost got into a fight when another student said something racist about me. John was such a sweet soul. I couldn't cry until his funeral, but after the burial, on the way to the car, I sobbed in my mother's arms. My sense of teenage invincibility was gone.

All these traumatic experiences, some primary and personal, others secondary and communal, impacted my childhood and shaped who I am now. They also stirred in me the passion and purpose of protecting children, no doubt leading me toward the helping professions. It is possible that our traumas brought us to helping, healing, and changemaking professions as a matter of need: the need to relive aspects of our traumas in safe-ish environments. To reconstruct a comprehensive narrative that connects us to our true selves and to understand why we chose this work as helpers, healers, and changemakers, we must certainly acknowledge our Adverse Childhood Experiences (ACEs). But to come into radical clarity, we must also acknowledge and celebrate our Positive Childhood Experiences (PCEs). Let's explore these positive and adverse experiences, sometimes referred to together as PACEs.

POSITIVE AND ADVERSE CHILDHOOD EXPERIENCES (PACES)

> *In some people, adversity can foster perseverance, deepen empathy, strengthen the resolve to protect, and spark mini-superpowers, but in all people, it gets under our skin and into our DNS, and it becomes an important part of who we are.*
>
> —Dr. Nadine Burke Harris, *The Deepest Well*

Just so it can be said, we don't have to have experienced trauma to be helpers, healers, or changemakers, nor do we always enter these professions from a place of victimhood, focusing only on the negative experiences we survived. Those of us who *do* bring our wounds to the work, as Wounded Healers, also come to this work with deep reserves of resilience, and we can tap into these stores when the work gets heavy. Our lives are complicated, and many of us have experienced our fair share of both adverse *and* positive situations that drive the decisions we make and the roles we take on. To understand why we do the work we do, it's helpful for us to know and acknowledge the diversity of our experiences.

The original work on ACEs (Felitti et al., 1998) captures the case reviews of nearly 17,000 adult Kaiser patients, connecting their longer term, negative health outcomes with a survey of ten adverse experiences (listed on pp. 68–69). Their work has been instrumental in validating the fact that trauma, especially that experienced during vital childhood developmental stages, has very tangible health implications that affect us long after the trauma is experienced. Their research found that almost 70% of participants had at least one adverse experience, while 48% experienced one to three ACES, and 21.5% had experienced more than four ACEs. This was the first major study of its kind to document the widespread reality of trauma and to link it directly to specific health outcomes later in life.

Experiencing trauma as a child can increase the risk of future victimization and substance abuse, educational challenges, delayed brain or body development, and it can cause toxic stress that directly impacts brain development and the regulation of the nervous system. ACEs do not necessarily directly cause these negative outcomes, but left unprocessed and unresolved, are highly correlated with toxic stress and trauma that cause chronic inflammation in the brain and body. This inflammation can result in memory problems, stress disorders, learning disabilities, and health issues, such as heart disease, diabetes, Alzheimer's disease, dementia, cancer, and autoimmune diseases like fibromyalgia and arthritis.

While the original ACEs study captured the negative outcomes of adversity among mostly White, middle-aged participants who were able to afford private insurance (Kaiser), in true scientific inquiry, there was a desire to see if the same outcomes could be found among a more socially and racially diverse group of adults. To capture the full diversity of experiences of childhood trauma and adversity on a larger scale, the Philadelphia ACE Project (Cronholm et al., 2015) researched the prevalence of adverse experiences among 1,784 Philadelphia residents. Of the 1,784 residents surveyed, more than 83% experienced at least one ACE, compared to 70% in the original study. The study also added five additional categories to the original ACEs, called the Expanded ACEs or Urban ACEs, that describe community-level adversity, experienced outside of the home, and that capture more fully the kinds of negative impacts of trauma that we come across in our work as helpers, healers, and changemakers.

Abuse and Neglect	Household Dysfunction
Physical abuse Sexual abuse Emotional abuse Physical neglect Emotional neglect	Separation/divorce Mental illness Addiction to drugs or alcohol Incarceration Witnessing domestic violence

Extended/Urban ACEs
Bullying
Community violence
Neighborhood safety
Racism
Living in foster care

There is no trauma competition; trauma is trauma. Each of us will respond differently to experiences that may be similar. An example might be if a group of people experienced a natural disaster, but some folks pick up the pieces and move on with their lives while the shock and impact of that traumatic event may cause others to fall apart. It is also not uncommon that someone may experience one ACE that impacts their lives in unimaginable ways, while someone with a higher ACE score may be able to minimize the impacts. It is important to remember this so we don't discount our own traumatic experiences by comparing it to the trauma we see among those we serve.

This was something I unintentionally did as a rape crisis counselor, minimizing my own sexual abuse trauma after working with victims and survivors of violent assaults. The youth I served had to endure multiple assaults, sometimes by parents or caregivers, they didn't have anyone they could tell, or if they did, they weren't believed or kept safe; so in comparison, I didn't think I deserved to feel victimized or to acknowledge the harm that resulted from my one adverse experience. My traumatic experience happened once, by someone who was not a parent or caregiver, and I was able to tell an adult who believed me and kept me safe, so I discounted the chronic stress my body was trying to address through somatic illnesses. Minimizing my own trauma and its impacts on my life by focusing on the trauma of those I served allowed me to ignore my need for healing. Comparing my trauma to the trauma of those I served kept me from practicing radical self-care, which ultimately led to my burnout during that time.

Childhood adversity is very important to understand because it helps us make sense of our lives in a fuller way. Everyone I know who has read the ACEs study or assessed their own ACE score (a simple tally of the experiences) felt that understanding how those experiences had shaped their adolescence and have impacted their adult lives was a form of validation. Validation that there were consequences to the trauma(s) they experienced and validation that some of the challenges they face as adults are not necessarily all in their heads *nor are they their fault.* The revelations and clarity that come from being able to link the challenges in adulthood directly to childhood traumas allow us a level of self-compassion to see that we are not broken by our trauma.

Understanding our ACE score can also explain why we've chosen our current professions as helpers, healers, and changemakers. Something else that stopped me from fully identifying my own ACE was the fact that I didn't want to let one trauma, something that was done to me without my consent, define me or limit the story of my childhood. As I shared earlier, I had an amazing childhood despite the traumas I experienced, and I didn't feel like a victim because there was so much love and support in my life. Focusing only on the adversity in childhood felt like something was missing. I wasn't just a victim, I was a survivor, and I felt like the ACEs weren't enough to tell the full story of who I am or why I became a social worker.

Luckily, there has been more research to show that the impact of adversity in childhood can be countered—and sometimes even prevented—by the following seven Positive Childhood Experiences (PCEs) (Bethell et al., 2019), which are:

- we were able to talk to family about feelings;
- had family that stood by us during difficult times;
- enjoyed participating in community traditions;
- felt a sense of belonging in high school (not including those who did not attend school or were homeschooled);
- felt supported by friends;
- had at least two nonparent adults who took genuine interest in us; and
- felt safe and protected by an adult in our home.

These experiences can sometimes be more impactful than those that create trauma, even though they may seem fairly simple or obvious. For example, my ACE of child sexual abuse was undoubtedly buffered by my ability to talk to my family about my feelings and to feel supported and protected by them when things got difficult. I had very supportive friends and felt a sense of belonging that helped buffer the racism I experienced in high school, and my teachers and coaches were safe nonparent adults who cared about my success and invested time in me.

I want to be clear that this is in no way suggesting toxic positivity, nor do these positive experiences negate the traumas we may have survived. Rather, it is to affirm that positive experiences in childhood can act as a buffer to the negative experiences and lessen their impact on us. Peter Levine speaks to this in his book, *An Autobiography of Trauma* (2024), sharing a few cherished childhood memories before recalling a violent assault he endured as a teenager. "Holding these 'body memories' of being cared for helped make it possible for me to encounter many times of great distress, without being completely overwhelmed and annihilated" (Levine, 2024, p. 3).

We come to our work as helpers, healers, and changemakers with all these experiences and have opportunities to show up either with a victim mindset or show up standing in our power as survivors. It is important to acknowledge the childhood experiences that create trauma in our lives but also the ones that create strength and resilience. I experienced one ACE but seven PCEs, which tells a fuller story of my life and my reasons for choosing to work in a helping profession. So, when we are asked "*Why this work?*", we can be confident that *it is not just from our traumas but from our strength and resilience that we choose to become helpers, healers, and changemakers.*

Our childhood experiences are linked to the ways we show up in our work and they can contribute to our risk of burnout if we're not paying attention. We may engage in self-soothing or self-harming behaviors, or engage in risk-taking behavior we otherwise might not engage in because we can't see the hurt in our work or its repercussions in our lives. Our ability to numb out and get the job done can keep us stuck. If there are childhood wounds we still need to heal, it is imperative that we invest our time and energy into healing, so we have clarity about what is *our* trauma material and what we are absorbing from those we serve. This is key to avoiding burnout and to building resilience for the work that is still to come.

CAREGIVING AND PEOPLE PLEASING

> *If we are not made to feel important for just who we are, we may seek significance by becoming compulsive helpers.*
>
> —Gabor Maté, *The Myth of Normal*

Some of the ways my own childhood experiences showed up was through excessive caregiving and a tendency toward people pleasing at the expense of my health. These characteristics are very common among those who choose helping professions. I shared earlier how I was a hypersensitive, empathic child who took on the stress I felt around me, even when that wasn't the intention of the adults in my life. There are several reasons we move toward over-caring and people-pleasing, and while some include a level of stress, not all of them involve a kind of purposeful abuse or neglect.

Some childhood situations that might lead to excessive caregiving/people pleasing include:

- being the child of immigrants or a parent with a disability and being exposed to adult issues by translating for parents in medical situations or other sensitive situations;
- surviving chronic illness or disability as a child and feeling the need to protect your parents or others from your pain and suffering;
- being an older child in a large family and being expected to take care of younger siblings, or noticing your parent's overwhelm and helping often;

- being raised by relatives (grandparents, aunts, uncles, etc.) and feeling that you needed to be good or "perfect" to ease their burden;
- being raised in foster care or being adopted and feeling the need to be grateful to your guardians or be "good" so you didn't jeopardize your placement;
- surviving the death of a parent or sibling and feeling the need to relieve the grief or to ease the burden on the surviving parent/sibling(s);
- growing up in a house where domestic violence occurred and trying to protect siblings or distract the abuser by placating them (by being funny, getting good grades, being a star athlete, etc.);
- hearing stories from elders about their traumas (war, immigration, poverty, etc.) and feeling like any challenges you faced paled in comparison; or
- being the child of a helper, healer, or changemaker who dedicated their lives to their work and dismissed their child's emotions or minimized them in comparison to the people they served.

All these are examples of ways we may have been impacted, even if our parents or caregivers had the best intentions. We turn to compulsive caregiving and people pleasing in an effort to gain back some level of control in our lives, however, as Gabor Maté lays out in his book *When The Body Says No* (2011), this can make us more susceptible to disease and chronic illness. If we can mediate our tendency to care for others more than we care for ourselves, we can turn these experiences into the fuel we need to do good work as helpers, healers, and changemakers without sacrificing our own well-being.

ATTACHMENT AND AUTHENTICITY

The imperative to survive overrides everything, and that survival depends on the maintenance of attachment, at whatever cost to authenticity.

—Gabor Maté, *The Myth of Normal*

Attachment is formed in childhood, in relation to our caregiver's responsiveness to our needs, and can have an interesting impact on our ability to be authentic. Having our needs met by our caregivers is a vital aspect of basic survival, a core need. Our authenticity is also a core need, and is directly impacted by a secure attachment to safe, loving caregivers, but if that attachment is disorganized or dysfunctional, we will sacrifice our authenticity for attachment. Those of us who are sensitive to the needs of others around us may have had to moderate our authentic selves to accommodate the needs of others during childhood. This is often an unconscious adaptation that can have long lasting implications for our well-being.

John Bowlby, a pioneer of attachment theory, proposed that there are four different attachment styles that impact our lives: secure, anxious, avoidant, or disorganized. The quality of our attachment style has consequences for our well-being throughout our lives and dictates how we behave in relationships. Our attachment styles can show up in our work lives as well, especially in our relationships with our supervisors, colleagues, and those we serve. Each of the distinct attachment styles manifests differently:

Secure attachment: Our caregivers met our physical and emotional needs. We are able to build strong relationships with colleagues; we have a sense of agency and autonomy in our work; and we are open to feedback and collaboration. We will seek and provide support, perform well under pressure, and can be flexible in our work plans.

Anxious/Ambivalent attachment: Our caregivers were inconsistent with meeting our physical and emotional needs. We are loyal and dedicated but may constantly seek approval and validation from colleagues. We seek connection but may have difficulty with criticism and can be sensitive to the slightest rejection. We may micromanage or become overly controlling in an effort to control our environment, feeling overwhelmed when things don't go as planned.

Avoidant attachment: Our caregivers didn't sufficiently meet our emotional needs. We are self-sufficient and independent but may become isolated or become emotionally distant with coworkers. We are comfortable working alone and can be self-directed but can come off as cold or aloof. We thrive in competitive environments and are results-focused but may lack empathy when others don't meet our expectations.

Disorganized attachment: Our caregivers were erratic or violent and unable to meet our needs. We thrive in fast paced, chaotic environments and can be resourceful and adaptable but can also be inconsistent and unreliable. We may lack clear vision or direction and may struggle with motivation. We may seek approval from others but can be prone to conflict and drama, which can make it challenging to form close bonds with colleagues.

Similar to understanding our adverse childhood experiences, it can be important to understand our attachment style. It simply gives us more information about ourselves and about how we show up in our work as helpers, healers, and changemakers. I have worked with supervisors and colleagues who were not aware that they were constantly creating drama or pushing others away or micromanaging, and I wonder how our workplace interactions would have changed if those coworkers had been aware of their attachment styles and had some tools to mediate their feelings of anxiety or avoidance. With this awareness, we are better able to take control of the overwhelm we may feel at work that results from our behaviors connected to these styles, which can be a radical self-care practice in and of itself.

Authenticity is being true to who we are as individuals, being who we say we are. "To be authentic is to be true to a sense of self arising from one's own unique and genuine essence, to be plugged into this inner GPS and to navigate from it" (Maté, 2022, p. 106). While our authenticity can be impacted by our attachment to a caregiver in our early years, we may also find this dynamic showing up as adults, compromising our authenticity to stay attached to a job that meets our needs for survival. Getting a paycheck to keep a roof over our head, food in our fridge, and the lights on is so important that we may feel we have no option but to sacrifice our authentic selves to stay connected to a job that demands our time and energy. We may put up with a toxic workplace, toxic coworkers, or unfair policies because we fear not having our needs met by collecting a salary.

If we are unable to be ourselves in the workplace, especially with our high-intensity work as helpers, healers, and changemakers, we may compromise our values, suppress our true selves, trade our integrity to keep quiet about injustices, or begin to isolate ourselves from others. We might also compromise our principles to engage in behavior like gossiping, taking credit for other people's work, or spreading rumors to feel part of the work culture. This can cause us to give up our personal boundaries, become emotionally exhausted, or develop negative coping mechanisms, so we can bear the work. Certainly, losing a sense of authenticity will impact our work with those we serve and can add a level of stress and a risk of unintended harm. If we start to question our decisions, disconnect from the work, or lose connection with ourselves, we are just stockpiling tinder for burnout.

Awareness of how others view us, as well as of whether our behavior is consistent with our internal values, is foundational to building relationships. We are obliged to act from a place of integrity and care.

—Joanne Zannoni, *Drowning in Hats!*

In a recent conversation with a retired social worker, I asked how retirement was treating her, and her response was enlightening. She said that with each new employer she worked for, she had to take on aspects of personality to fit the mold of the job and be successful in that work. She had worked for several decades and realized that some of the behaviors and beliefs she had adopted weren't really "her," so she had been spending the first few years of her retirement peeling away the layers of habits, language, and even postures that she had adopted over those years of work. She said it took her years to be able to drop some of the ways she had disconnected and dissociated from her authentic self and others to hold the weight of her work. As she spoke about removing these layers of self that she had taken on, her body and face softened. We don't have to wait until retirement to shed these layers and become our authentic selves. We can engage self-awareness to understand the ways we may compromise ourselves and can then make conscious choices in how we show up in an authentic way.

HEROES, SAVIORS, AND WARRIORS

> *Being heroized was lonely. Once you're the hero, no one helps you. By definition, heroes have their shit together. They have everything under control. It was a trap. . . . People died in that narrative.*
>
> —Jennifer Murphy, *First Responder*

> *The problem is, warring takes a toll on the warrior, and our western society is not good about taking care of these brave and noble individuals.*
>
> —Kim Colegrove, *Mindfulness for Warriors*

One of the most insidious aspects of the pandemic was the very public labeling of essential workers as heroes and saviors. Many of us showed up to serve for others while also managing the impact of the pandemic on our own families and our own health. The brutal human toll of the pandemic was carried heavily by helpers, healers, and changemakers. Once the pandemic was declared "over", society went right back to devaluing the work of helpers, healers, and changemakers they once lauded as "essential" and "heroes." Those of us who were helping others get through the pandemic felt like we were being ignored, gaslit, and scapegoated. What felt like true recognition of the work we did as helpers, healers, and changemakers was used to keep us overworked and forced to endure unsafe working environments.

It can certainly be an ego boost to be called a hero, and it feels good be seen as a savior or a warrior, but this positions us in a questionable hierarchy in relation to those we serve. Heroes are able to find solutions to every problem, saviors "fundamentally believe they are better than the people they are rescuing" (Flaherty, 2016, p. 18), and warriors are seen as stronger than others. We begin to believe everyone we encounter needs saving and every challenge we face is a battle that requires a fight, keeping us in patterns of confrontation or overreaching to save others when that may not be what they need from us. It also keeps us in a state of denying our own needs as we carry the unbearable weight, the invisible wounds, and the negative impacts to our worldview and our well-being that may result from our work.

These labels of hero, savior, and warrior, can become identities that we cling to for validation and to help make meaning of the work when it gets hard. But being put in these roles (or positioning ourselves in these roles) may compromise how effective we feel in our work, should something go awry or an intervention fail. In a way, we are set up to feel a sense of impotence or helplessness when we can't meet the moment with the skills our profession requires, even if much of the situation is out of our control. Of course, this puts us on a direct path to burnout because these impossible expectations demand perfection when circumstances may not allow us to engage in the ways we would like.

The reality is heroes don't get help, no one saves the saviors and warriors don't get rest. When heroes need help, it can be challenging to ask for it, and just as hard to receive it. This is identified as the "John Wayne Syndrome," especially in male-dominated helping professions, but it can cause us to suffer with stress and overwhelm because "crisis workers perceive role conflict when they themselves must seek help" (Mitchell, 1985, as cited in Figley, 1995, p. 75). Sometimes it can make others uncomfortable when the more stable person in their lives becomes untethered. If a hero or warrior needs rescuing, then what hope do "regular" folks have? This can keep us from acknowledging the need for care and can create an undercurrent of subjugating our needs to perpetuate a facade that creates an environment where trauma and chronic stress are ignored and can fester.

By contrast, certain indigenous cultures view warriors as protectors of the community who stand in the path of harm and safeguard the most vulnerable among them. The Wabanake word for warrior means helper and shield, "to stand in the path of harm, using just enough force to prevent the harm from occurring, without causing any harm in return" (Mitchell, 2018, p. 152). The goal of the warrior was not fighting for the sake of violence, but rather as service to the community. The Lakota culture views warriors in a more holistic light:

> The warrior, for us, is one who sacrifices himself for the good of others. His task is to take care of the elderly, the defenseless, those who cannot provide for themselves, and above all, the children, the future of humanity. (Mitchell, 2018, p. 152)

Coincidentally, indigenous cultures also *honor and take care of their warriors*. If we take on these intentions and humble actions as our warrior mentality, we may be less impacted by oppression in our work as helpers, healers, and changemakers and can move toward the radical change we need in our communities and our systems.

AGENCY AND AUTHORITY

It is not easy to be a professional, to lay claim to professional authority and esteem and side with ordinary folks, especially poor folks. It is not easy to be a bureaucrat intent on rising within the bureaucracy and side with the clients and victims of that bureaucracy.

—Roy Bailey and Mike Brake, *Radical Social Work*

In order to prevent ourselves from falling into the traps of being a hero or a savior, we have to be aware of the privilege and the power we hold in our work as helpers, healers, and changemakers.

Agency is the sense of control we have over our lives and our work. A sense of agency gives us the ability to create our own thoughts and behaviors based on our own desires without limitations put on us by others and to be able to control the outcomes of our actions. Having a strong sense of personal agency gives us the motivation to set achievable goals, gives us a sense of empowerment in social situations, and increases our ability to be resilient. Stress and trauma can interfere with our sense of agency, causing us to feel helpless and less able to make decisions that can move our lives forward in a positive direction. Without agency, we are more vulnerable to victimization, but a strong sense of agency reminds us that we are worthy and enough. It also helps us understand our power, allowing us to use our strengths to build solidarity in our work while keeping us from doing harm. With a strong sense of agency, we can also increase our capacity to be in connection with others in ways that enhance our own resilience.

In our work, agency allows us to advocate for ourselves, stand in the space of advocacy for those we serve, and to speak up and push back when we see things that are not right within our workplace or in the larger profession. In the same way radical self-care can empower us with a sense of agency, my goal as a radical social worker is to empower my students and clients with a sense of agency in their own lives. As an advocate for students experiencing homelessness, I use my personal agency and lack of fear of retaliation to strongly speak out on their behalf. Almost any email I send could be my last, as it sometimes takes pushing back against authority to get the resources my students need and deserve. We can also build a sense of collective agency through unions and professional associations that represent groups of likeminded people who push for important changes that make our work easier to navigate. Our sense of agency impacts how we show up in the position of authority often bestowed upon us as helpers, healers, and changemakers.

Authority in our work can be a tool for change and creation or a tool for domination and oppression. We need to recognize the positions of authority we assume in our work via our level of education, title, or position and use that power in a positive way. How we wield our authority is important and needs to be done in a mindful way for the benefit of those we serve, not just the systems or institutions we work for. When combined with a strong sense of agency, we can use our authority to uplift important issues and work across organizations and professions to move toward real systemic change.

In the book *A Violent History of Benevolence*, the authors warn that "social workers have to be incredibly careful about how they navigate very real power & [*sic*] authority in people's lives" (Chapman & Withers, 2019, p. 347). When we have the authority to detain someone, provide or withhold lifesaving treatment for someone, or remove someone's child, it is so important that we use that power wisely. In my role as a school social worker, I am sensitive to fact that certain parents or students perceive me as someone who may punish them or make their life more challenging instead of helping them. I try to always be aware that they may perceive my job title alone as a threat, and I often provide a bit of a disclaimer that my job is to keep them safe and remove barriers to their child's education. I never want a student or parent to fear asking for help or working with me simply because others in similar roles may have abused their power.

Unfortunately, some folks in the helping professions abuse their authority by threatening or harassing coworkers, discriminating against clients, or violating the trust of those they serve. Much of the violent behavior we see among some police officers, teachers, medical professionals, and others is a direct result of abuse of authority to gain power over others more vulnerable. We have to be especially careful when our work demands that we make decisions for our clients or against their wishes. In his book *Power in the Helping Professions*, Dr. Adolf Guggenbühl-Craig (a social worker who became a medical psychiatrist) warns that we are all susceptible to the "power shadow" that shows up in our work, "a social worker prompted by power motives may nevertheless make decisions [that are] helpful to his client. But there is a great danger that the more the case worker pretends to himself that he is operating only from selfless motives, the more influential his power shadow will become until it finally betrays him into making some very questionable decisions" (Guggenbühl-Craig, 2021, p. 24).

Our abuse of authority, our "power shadow," causes more damage than we realize, eroding confidence in our professions and organizations and thwarting the change work we need moving forward. Abuse of our authority is not an issue if we put our work in its proper place within the larger scope of our lives and if we don't use our professions as our entire identity. We can take notice when there is an abuse of authority by a supervisor or colleague and take action to hold them accountable and push back against the oppressive nature that may show up in the systems we inhabit as helpers, healers, and changemakers.

ABUSE OF AUTHORITY: PREDATORS IN OUR PROFESSIONS

Many of us navigate roles as agents of places and forces we would like to fundamentally transform or abolish. Alongside work towards such fundamental change, we also need people who work in these places to locally cultivate dignity, agency, freedom, and more equitable distributions.

—Chris Chapman and A. J. Withers,
A Violent History of Benevolence

The flip side of some folks identifying as a hero or savior is that there are predators in our professions. Given the urgency of change we need and the systems in which we need the most change, this section may be more radically honest than some are ready for, so let me cut to the chase: Not everyone in helping professions is there to help. Some people become helpers to gain access and to harm. Some people become healers to exploit. Some people become changemakers to grift.

Police, priests, and politicians are among the professions whose members are at higher risk of abusing their power to exploit the vulnerable. There are White supremacists and misogynists who go into policing so they can use the cover of the badge to target and kill minorities or harm women with impunity. There are pedophiles and predators who go into the priesthood so they can use the cover of religion to gain the trust of parents and attain unquestioned access to molest children. There are narcissists and fraudsters who go into politics so they can use the cover of their position in government to create policies that intentionally harm groups of people they don't like or to maintain oppressive policies for their personal financial/material gain.

Millions of people have been traumatized by predators in these male-dominated professions with histories rooted in racism, patriarchy, and abuse of power. Report after report and video after video reveal these heinous acts and expose the ways these systems create environments for predators to hide. Police have a monopoly on the use of force, priests (and pastors, deacons, rabbis, gurus, etc.) have a monopoly on faith, while politicians have a monopoly on government control. They use secrecy to hide their abuses and abusers, moving predators from precinct to precinct or church to church with little accountability or concern for the safety of those they "serve." They exploit the authority of their positions, and their manipulation of power is real. In their current iterations, they create violence and toxicity in our society, leaving other helpers, healers, and changemakers to clean up the damage.

As a social worker, I have served survivors of violence from all three of these professions. I have attended many protests and marches and helped pass legislation demanding change in these specific professions. While it is necessary to call these professions out for their bad behavior, if we want the change we say we do, *we must call these professions in and hold them accountable.* This is hard to do in a politicized space of hostility and high emotions, as valid as these emotions are after an incident of police brutality, another disclosure of sexual abuse by a priest, or the latest political move that disenfranchises millions of people. I am not suggesting that the violence or sordid histories in these professions should be ignored, accepted, or go unpunished.

On the contrary, these issues are very real and must be addressed head on. But we must acknowledge that the divisions among our professions are being purposely created to keep us in a state of fear and disdain for each other and to further push us into our separate professional silos that keep us from making real change. The radical truth is that some of us must be brave enough to bridge that gap and make connections between and among our professions. The only way for these systems to be dismantled and reimagined is for courageous folks inside these systems to do that work in collaboration with those on the outside. We need people who speak the language, know the culture, and understand the history and hierarchy within these institutions. We need folks outside of these professions to be open to working toward change rather than isolating these professions or seeing them as filled only with predators. We must support the folks inside doing good work *and* we have to hold their institutions accountable at the highest levels.

In his book *My Grandmother's Hands*, Resmaa Menakem presents two chapters on what he calls "the Police Body" (Menakem, 2017). In Chapter 8, "White-Body Supremacy and the Police Body," he reminds us that "the chaos and confusion that make up contemporary police culture are wreaking havoc on police bodies and psyches. . . . Police bodies are visibly suffering from their own form of trauma and, in turn, inflicting unnecessary harm on the less powerful, including some of the people they have pledged to protect" (p. 117). Later, in Chapter 17, "Mending the Police Heart and Body," Resmaa, whose brother is a police officer, implores law enforcement to engage in "strong and consistent self-care," adding, "caring for your body may save your life. It may also keep you from unnecessarily taking the life of a stranger" (Menakem, 2017, p. 216). The same can be said of priests and politicians. We need police, priests, and politicians who are committed to their own radical self-care, so they have the internal resources to push against the systems they work within, and they have the courage to root out the predators among them.

> *Whether working inside or outside of these institutions, our communities have relied upon radical practitioners willing to provide care that is rooted in abolition and liberation.*
>
> —Cara Page and Erica Woodland, *Healing Justice Lineages*

Predators are not only found among police, priests, and politicians. Those of us in education, social work, healthcare, and other helping professions also need to be aware of the questionable roots of our own professions (assimilating kids for industrial work, controlling the poor under the guise of benevolent welfare, and the eugenics movement that experimented on Black bodies without anesthesia, respectively) and the exploitation of positions of power to harm others. Some recent headlines that demonstrate this include:

- New York doctor is charged with drugging and assaulting patients (Mascarenhas, 2023)
- Nurse pleads guilty to replacing fentanyl with saline (Associated Press, 2023b)
- Social worker arrested for helping child sex trafficker (Margolfo, 2022)
- California "Teacher of the Year" accused of child sex abuse (Associated Press, 2023a)
- Court Clerk and Defense Lawyer Are Charged in a Cash-for-Clients Scheme (Meko, 2023)
- Former Children's Court judge sentenced to 9 years for child porn (Vielmetti, 2021)

It infuriates me when someone who claims to be a helper, healer, or changemaker uses the authority of their position as power over others. I have served survivors of abuse by teachers, coaches, doctors, and even other social workers, and I often wonder how these folks are able to hide among us. The reality is that many of us are so overwhelmed in our work, using all our energy to stay in survival mode, that we miss the yellow flags that turn into red flags, and then we're blindsided when we hear about abuse, mistreatment, or misconduct by a colleague or within our profession.

This responsibility falls on those of us who are true helpers and healers to protect those we serve, weed these predators out and clean up our professions, especially the helping, healing, and changemaking professions that serve vulnerable folks. We must be unafraid. Radical self-care allows us the clarity and control to see and identify these predators among us. Radical self-care gives us the courage to call them out. Ultimately, radical self-care gives us the solid foundation from which we can disrupt what isn't working, repair the harm done to our people and our professions, and reimagine what is possible.

We keep saying we have to do this work in community. It's time to expand our community to include those from professions we know are harmful, hold them accountable, and change the narrative. We can reclaim our professions from the infiltration of predators at all levels. Vulnerable people should be able to access help and healing without being preyed upon, exploited, or harmed. Period. We can no longer turn a blind eye to this reality. Not today. Not ever. Not on our watch.

RECONNECTING WITH OUR PASSION, PURPOSE, AND PEOPLE

And if we believe that we are all connected, then we must all recognize that our well-being influences the well-being of our families, our communities, and the larger world that we are tied to. Therefore, self-care isn't a self-indulgent luxury, it is an absolute necessity.

—Sherri Mitchell, *Sacred Instructions*

> *Once we come home to our whole selves, then we can hold space for the fullness of others—for we all contain within us the seeds for mindful as well as harmful actions.*
>
> —Amy Wright Glenn, *Holding Space*

We wouldn't do this challenging work if there wasn't a compelling reason. Those of us who choose helping, healing, and change-making work do so because it is our passion, our purpose, or we are serving those we see as our people.

Our passion is a powerful or intense emotion that compels us to action. It gives us the deep devotion to our work or to an ideology we feel "called" to work on behalf of, like making sure every child has a safe home or ensuring clean water in our communities. **Our purpose** is the reason we feel we must do the work, and provides the focus we need to pursue our professions. An example might be organizing indigenous communities against the threat of oil drilling on sacred land, despite the threats we may face for doing so. **Our people** are the constituents, clients, students, patients, etc. who are the focus of our energy and our advocacy. Children, the elderly, folks with chronic illnesses, or those experiencing war, homelessness etc. may be the focus of our concern and our work. Our people are also our colleagues and fellow helpers, healers, and changemakers across the globe, those with whom we seek solidarity through professional organizations, conferences, or communities of practice.

Every year I attend the annual conference of the National Association for the Education of Homeless Children and Youth (NAEHCY*) and get to spend a few days learning and connecting with thousands of my fellow McKinney-Vento/Homeless Youth liaisons throughout the country. (Full disclosure: As of this publication date [2025], I am the president of the board of directors for NAEHCY.) Since many of us are solo practitioners in our school districts, it is the one time we all get to come together and share expertise that can make the work we do easier. The conference is a breath of fresh air for me, and I can often feel the stress of my day-to-day work being lifted simply by being in the same space as my fellow liaisons. It is a gathering I look forward to every year that truly helps prevent burnout from that August through October slog at the beginning of each new school year.

Our passion, purpose, and people are the drivers in our work and may be the reason we show up excited to engage and care for others, but they can also be the reason we put up with the negative aspects of our work. We are the ones who stay in challenging situations or stick it out in toxic work environments so we don't feel we're abandoning our colleagues or clients, or failing our students. Our loyalty to those we serve can be exploited when our agencies and organizations use our dedication against us, reminding us of our passion when we demand fair wages or suggesting that if this work was truly our purpose, we shouldn't go on strike to demand better patient care or better funding for education. Once we remember who we are and why we do this work, we begin to understand how our passion is used (or abused) to keep us overworked, overwhelmed, and underpaid. Then we're able to use the power of remembering our passion, purpose, and people so that we can reignite that fire to keep us sustained in this amazing work we love. This is very important because "the difference between how a person navigates their part in a dehumanizing system can make an enormous impact on those subjected to the system" (Chapman & Withers, 2019, p. 348).

Shifting how we see our work will help us navigate these systems and can buffer us from burnout. Many cultures have a phrase or a way of describing their passion and purpose that ties them to something beyond our titles and education. In Costa Rica, *plan de vida*, or soul's purpose, is our reason for getting up each morning and taking care of the things that need to be taken care of. While getting up and going to work may not always feel like our soul's purpose, it is an opportunity to reconnect with our own *plan de vida* and go about our work in a humble and dedicated way. The Japanese have a similar theory, *ikigai*, or our reason for being. *Ikigai* is a way of understanding what we love, what we're good at, what the world needs, and what we can get paid to do. This theory also speaks to the joy we can have as we pursue our passion and purpose in our profession that gives meaning to our lives. It's a good reminder that we are allowed to enjoy our work and even find pleasure in aspects of our work as helpers, healers, and changemakers.

RECONNECTING WITH PLEASURE AND PLAY

The reward, the real grace, of conscious service, then, is the opportunity not only to help relieve the suffering but to grow in wisdom, experience greater unity and have a good time while doing it.

—Ram Das and Paul Gorman, *How Can I Help?*

The topic of pleasure makes folks uncomfortable. I think it's because we often associate pleasure with sexual intimacy, and that is already a taboo topic, let alone in connection with our work. Professional ethics, you know? But reconnecting with pleasure in our work is vital for our well-being and impacts the effectiveness of our work. Pleasure can be defined simply as finding joy, happiness, and satisfaction; and when we can find joy, happiness, and satisfaction amid the many challenges of our work as helpers, healers, and changemakers, we can tap into a strong source of resilience.

Some of us may have started our work with a sense of joy, happiness, or satisfaction but quickly fell into unhappiness and stress. We may even feel like any level of enjoyment in our work is an affront to the challenges of oppression and suffering we confront in our work. Maybe it's the intensity of the harm we see in our work that pulls us back from engaging in fun but risky activities or allowing others to, like those working in substance treatment who swear off drugs or alcohol even in social settings, those working in child welfare who refuse to allow their children to attend sleepovers, or those who work in the medical field refusing to partake in any activities they know could cause harm or death, like jumping on a trampoline or eating hard candy. In an effort to protect from or prevent the harm we see daily, we may inadvertently become buzzkills or killjoys to ourselves or to those around us.

We need constant reminders that we do not have to suffer to be good at our jobs. We are not martyrs. We are allowed to come to our jobs with a sense of joy and playfulness that counteracts and helps contain the suffering of those we serve. In her book *Pleasure Activism* (2019), adrienne marie brown suggests that joy and pleasure is resistance. One of the first ways we can bring pleasure back into our work is to remember what we used to enjoy about our work and notice what has changed. We can identify the specific aspects of our work that became draining or stressful (sometimes it's *all of the aspects*), and we can consider what systemic or organizational changes may have contributed to our dissatisfaction. Maybe a systemic shift is causing our discontent, but it could also be that we underestimated some aspects of our work or that we have been assigned more than we can manage, and that has stolen our joy.

> *Pleasure—embodied, connected pleasure—is one of the ways we know when we are free. That we are always free. That we always have the power to co-create the world. Pleasure helps us move through the times that are unfair, through grief and loneliness, through the terror of genocide, or days when the demands are just overwhelming. Pleasure heals the places where our hearts and spirit get wounded.*
>
> —Adrienne Marie Brown, *Pleasure Activism*

Remembering the purpose and meaning of our work, remembering why we came to this work in the first place, and reconnecting with the intrinsic motivation that drives us in our work can help us regain our joy. One of the small things I do is keep a folder of any thank you notes or printed emails from those I serve to ground myself back to the joy of my work when things get particularly challenging. Tapping into a sense of gratitude helps shift me out of a stressful state and into a more pleasurable one. I also try to celebrate even the smallest successes of my students; maybe a habitually truant student comes to school but skips class. The win is that they came to school at all . . . and then we can work on getting them to class. If we only measure success by the end result, we will be miserable and constantly feel like we are failing in our work as helpers, healers, and changemakers. So celebrating the small wins can bring a sense of accomplishment, satisfaction, and pleasure back into our work.

> *When we play together, we feel physically attuned and experience a sense of connection and joy.*
>
> —Bessel van der Kolk, MD, *The Body Keeps the Score*

Bringing play into our work might be a bit more challenging. Here again, the urgency and seriousness of the work we do might make play seem inappropriate or silly. How can we play when we work with suffering? At the 2024 Child Abuse Symposium hosted by the Santa Clara County Child Abuse Prevention Council (of which I am a former Chair), Dr. Thomas D. Lyon, PhD, director of the USC Child Interviewing Lab at the University of Southern California Gould School of Law, shared his protocol for forensic interviews with child survivors of abuse and violence. He shared clips from interviews with child victim/survivors responding to disturbing but necessary questions like, "What did he do with his hands?" His presentation brought a sobering energy to the room full of veteran helpers, healers, and changemakers.

During the question-and-answer session, I asked Dr. Lyon how he supports the well-being of his graduate students and colleagues who conduct these interviews, and how he protects them from vicarious trauma, given the intensity of the work they do. His response was, "play." He said he takes time with his students and staff to deliberately find times to engage in play, take retreats, and engage a sense of humor to buffer the heaviness of the important work they do. He shared that by incorporating play, they build camaraderie among the staff that they can depend on when an interview gets too intense, or the reality of their work gets too heavy.

When we cut off pleasure and play as a protective measure, we naturally cut ourselves off from the full human experience and a natural way to support ourselves in times of stress and overwhelm. We must find ways to deliberately incorporate pleasure and play into our work. If you are a supervisor, professor, principal, superintendent, manager, chief, or anyone else in a position of authority in the helping fields, I urge you to find ways to incorporate pleasure and play for your staff. It will help them manage the heaviness of their work and provide cohesion (and possibly retention) among your staff and make your workplace a healthy one.

RADICAL TENDENCIES: REMEMBERING AND RECONNECTING

Radical self-care is not about getting caught up in the distraction of consumerism, the commodification of care, or the false cures we seek to feel good. Radical self-care requires that we, rather than numbing out, dissociating, or distracting ourselves, sit with discomfort long enough to find the root cause of it, and then find a practice that can truly alleviate the discomfort at the root. This allows us to move toward healing and liberation as we protect ourselves from dismemberment and disconnection.

The practices in this chapter are intended to counter or prevent some of the ways our work dismembers and disconnects us. We protect and care only for the things and people we feel connected to, and connection is one of our superpowers as human beings—one that can help us heal the stress and trauma we absorb in our work. To care for ourselves, we have to reconnect with ourselves and with each other. As you engage each of these practices, do so with compassion and care and notice what comes up for you. Your body might surprise you! We begin to unravel the root causes of our stress and overwhelm when we take time in the space of remembering.

REMEMBERING OUR DEEPLY ROOTED "WHY"

"We do it for the outcome, not the income" is a common quote I hear in the social work world. I loathe it. Often, we feel we are tasked with bearing the heaviness of the work because it is the work we've chosen; it is our "why" in the world. This is where our passion becomes a "calling" and can be dangerously used against us. Here I hear Nietzsche's famous quote as a warning, "He who has a why to live for can bear almost any how." so I want to be clear: *I'm not asking you to remember your why so you can forget you're underpaid, overworked, unsafe, or being exploited in your workplace.* In fact, I'm not asking you to remember your why for any other reason than to decide if this is still the space where you feel fulfilled. It's a good opportunity to check in with yourself and reflect. But I suggest we go a little deeper. **Five Whys** is a practice I like to do whenever I have a big decision to make, but it's also helpful for uncovering the deeper reasons we come to the work of helping, healing, and change-making. Here's how to practice the Five Whys:

- Get out a piece of paper or a journal. Write the word *WHY* on a line, then allow a few spaces and add another *WHY* until you have five of them on your page.
- Take a deep breath and consider, very simply, why you became a [fill in the blank]. Using Gabor Maté's example from page 59, it could be as simple as "I want to help."
- Then move to the next *WHY* and consider why you want to help. This might be something a bit more serious like, "I want to help because no one helped me when I was (a child, sick, new to the country, etc.)."
- Continue teasing out the whys until you feel you've distilled it down as far as you can. Maybe you don't need all five spaces to get to the root of your why. This conscious practice will help identify our purpose in the work of helping, healing, or making change and can be an anchor when things feel overwhelming or we're second guessing our profession.

THERAPY

When I know who I am, I am you, when I don't know who I am, I serve you.

—Ram Dass and Paul Gorman, *How Can I Help?*

It is best practice in many of our helping, healing, and change-making professions to be receiving some level of therapy or counseling. Quite frankly, it should be standard practice in *all* helping professions, especially since therapy is more available, more affordable, more accessible, and (slowly) becoming more diverse than it's ever been. Having a therapist as we do this work helps us stay grounded and connected to ourselves as we work with others. It is also a helpful counterbalance to our work and can be a strong resource if we find ourselves facing burnout.

Many of us are so passionate about our work that we are willing to bear the negative conditions of the work. But if we go into the work with our eyes wide open and are doing our own healing work, we will find that radical self-care is necessary. The challenge comes when we are oblivious to this connection or we try to use our work for our own trauma healing. This isn't to say we should wait until we're fully healed (whatever that means) before we join a helping profession, but *it does* mean that *we need to actively seek our own trauma therapy and professional support for healing alongside our work.*

Solo

As you start your helping, healing, and change-making work (or find yourself in the midst of it) consider finding a therapist to help you process things as you move through your career. There are so many ways to access licensed therapists who understand our work, practice their own radical self-care, and can be part of our support system. Also, find out whether your employer offers an Employee Assistance Program ("EAP") as part of its employee benefits. EAPs vary, but many offer free, confidential short-term psychological counseling for people who are dealing with mental health issues, as well as referrals.

Collective

We can also benefit from group therapy with other helpers, healers, and changemakers as a reminder that we are not alone in this work or in our struggle to hold all aspects of the wounding in our work. I encourage those of you with experience in the helping fields to consider becoming a licensed therapist yourself. We always need folks who fully understand the work to help support those of us in the eye of the storm, and what better way than doing this with our fellow helpers.

MINDFUL AWARENESS

> *Mindfulness not only makes it possible to survey our internal landscape with compassion and curiosity but can also actively steer us in the right direction for self-care.*
>
> —Bessel van der Kolk, *The Body Keeps the Score*

To fully know the reality of our work and to be able to see what needs to be changed, it is helpful to first get still. We don't trust stillness or ease because they feel too vulnerable. Our bodies have become used to the hurry, hustle, and even the chaos in our work. But stillness is where the magic happens, giving our brains and bodies a bit of space to process all that we carry. One way to find some stillness is through mindfulness. Mindfulness is a way of being in the present moment by purposely focusing our attention without judgment. Mindfulness is a way of showing up for ourselves and those we serve. There are a few different ways to access mindfulness and they can be done solo as personal practices or collectively as work strategies. Here are a few:

Deep Listening

Our work requires attunement to those we serve so we can meet their needs. Attuning to the needs of others requires deep listening so they feel seen, heard, and respected. Deep listening is a technique of being fully present and holding space for someone in a way that leads to empathy and compassion. When we are in the space of deep listening, we are not trying to solve anything or find solutions, rather, we are just sitting with and bearing witness.

- As you listen, see if you can relax your body, starting with your face and shoulders and slowly moving down your body. (A body scan is included in these practices [see p. 98]; you can use that as a guide.) This will help you be more present and focused on the speaker.
- If thoughts, solutions, or the urge to interject come up, notice them, and release them.
- Observe the nonverbal communication, like posture, gestures, and facial expressions. See if you can subtly mirror the speaker's body language to create a sense of trust.
- You can ask for clarity from the speaker as a way of engagement, but keep an open mind and stay curious and nonjudgmental in your clarification questions.
- Afterward, reflect on the conversation and jot down a few notes about key points. You can run these by the speaker to be sure your observations are accurate. This can help validate their feelings and will let them know you were listening.

Guided Meditation With Imagery

Meditation is a controlled form of mindful dissociation, and when done in a conscious manner, we can create a container to make it a safer experience. Guided imagery has many benefits and is used to treat trauma among veterans of war, to speed healing among cancer patients, and as a tool for success among professional athletes. This guided practice is one I do often when I feel I have reached the limits of my support for a student and don't want to be left with the feeling of failure, especially when I can't protect them from the suffering they might encounter. When I'm dealing with compassion fatigue or moral injury, I pull into this practice to relieve myself of the anger and rage I may feel about the injustices I see in my work and in the world.

This particular guided meditation is my **purple bubble meditation** for calling in safety for someone you know who may be in harm's way. This bubble will be a space of love, light, and protection—surrounding them with positive energy and strength—and can help us put down the worry we have for this person even when we aren't able to help in a more tangible way. It goes a little something like this:

- Find a comfortable position where you can sit or lie down undisturbed. Close your eyes or soften your gaze downward if it feels comfortable. Take a few slow, deep breaths, feeling your body relax with each inhale and exhale.
- Imagine a beautiful purple light swirling around you. This light is warm, calming, and filled with love. Feel it envelope you completely, creating a safe and protected space.
- See this purple light extending outward, forming a large bubble around you. This bubble is strong and impenetrable, shielding you from any negativity or harm. *Hold this feeling of self-protection for a few moments.*
- Think of the person you care about who may be in harm's way. Visualize them clearly in your mind's eye. See their face, their body, their surroundings. Hear their voice or maybe a phrase they are known to say.
- Imagine the purple bubble gently expanding, encompassing them within its protective embrace. Feel your love and compassion flowing into the bubble, surrounding them with positive energy, support, and safety.
- See the purple light filling them with peace, strength, and courage. Envision them safe and protected from any harm. Imagine the best outcome for them, no matter how challenging that may be in real life. Visualize them graduating, visiting

a family member, or having a day full of joy. This can become a form of manifesting goodness on their behalf.

- Spend a few moments holding this image in your mind. Feel the connection you have with this person, and know that your love and positive energy are with them always. *Trust that they will get the love and support they need, even if you are not the one who can give it to them in this moment.*
- As you slowly come back to the present moment, carry the feeling of love and peace within your body. Remember, even if you are physically apart, your love and purposeful connection can create a powerful force of protection for those you care about.
- When you feel ready, gently wiggle your fingers and toes, and take a few deep breaths. Slowly open your eyes, return, and orient yourself to your surroundings.
- Carry the positive energy of this meditation with you throughout your day. Remember that you can always create a purple bubble of safety for yourself and those you serve.

Body Scan

There is no right or wrong way to do a body scan. Just tune into the sensations you feel as you move your attention through your body. The benefits of regularly reconnecting with your body are not small. It can help reduce stress and anxiety, manage pain and discomfort, and promote relaxation and sleep. Before we start, there is a warning and a few variations you can consider:

- WARNINGS: Safety considerations before you start.
  - If you are anxious, start your scan with the feet and move to the top of the body; you may wish to start with the feet, scan to the top, and scan back down to the feet, maintaining a sense of being grounded. If you feel a sense of panic at all during this practice, STOP.
  - DO NOT DO A BODY SCAN WHILE DRIVING. Once you have mastered or personalized your body scan practice,

you might find it helpful to engage when you're driving or doing other activities, but if this is a new practice, please do it somewhere safe, preferably in a place that isn't moving.

- VARIATIONS: Some ways you can personalize your practice.
  - You can shorten or lengthen the practice by what body parts you focus on. If you're short on time, you can focus on the larger body parts (head, chest, hips, and legs); and if you have a bit more time, you can focus on all the small parts, including the space between the toes.
  - You can include music or ambient sounds to accompany your body scan if you'd like. Bonus points if you have the option to do a body scan in the woods or near a body of water.
  - You can add visualization to your scan by imagining your breath sweeping over each part of your body as you scan and name them. This can help relieve tension or give you something to focus on as you scan.

Now let's get into the body scan: Find a comfortable position, standing, sitting, or laying down, and feel free to use blankets and pillows to make yourself more comfortable. Close your eyes, if that feels good for you, or soften your gaze downward, or toward the floor to minimize distractions. Take a few slow, deep breaths to ease your body into relaxation.

- Bring your attention to your toes. Notice any sensations you experience there, such as warmth, tingling, pressure, or stillness. Notice if they are cold or warm, simply observing and acknowledging these sensations without judgment.
- Gradually move your attention up your feet, noticing any sensations in your soles, arches, and ankles. Take your time and explore each area with gentle curiosity. Roll the ankles if that feels good.
- Continue moving your attention up your legs, noticing any sensations in your calves, shins, knees, thighs, and hips. Allow yourself to feel the weight of your limbs resting on the ground.
- Move your attention to your torso, noticing any sensations in your abdomen, chest, back, and ribs. Observe the subtle rise

and fall of your breath as it enters and leaves your body. Bring gentle awareness to any tension you feel in the chest, and see if you can release it on an exhale.

- Explore the sensations in your arms and hands, beginning with your fingertips and moving up your forearms, elbows, upper arms, and shoulders. Notice any tension or tightness in these areas and allow it to soften. If it feels okay for you, ball your hand into a fist and release it. Do this a few times.
- Move your attention to your neck and head, noticing any sensations in your jaw, scalp, face, and ears. Observe any thoughts or emotions that arise without judgment and let them go with each exhale. Bring awareness to your forehead and the space between your eyebrows, allowing it to soften.
- Now, take a moment to rest your attention on your entire body. Notice any overall sensations, such as a sense of warmth, tingling, or energy flow. Simply observe and acknowledge these sensations without judgment.
- When you're ready, gently wiggle your fingers and toes and take a few deep breaths. Slowly open your eyes, or keep them closed if that feels more comfortable.
- Take a moment to appreciate the sensations in your body and the space you occupy.
- Carry this sense of awareness and presence throughout your day and come back to this body scan as many times as you need.

RECONNECTING WITH OURSELVES, EACH OTHER, AND NATURE

Fundamental consciousness is self-knowing. . . . To know ourselves as the subtle ground of our being is a distinct shift from fragmentation to wholeness, but it is who we actually are.

—Judith Blackstone, PhD, *Trauma and the Unbound Body*

When our work threatens to disconnect us, it is a radical act of self-care to remember that we are one with others, one with nature, and that we can reconnect with ourselves. Disconnection can happen unintentionally and even unconsciously, but we have the power, and even the obligation, to reconnect with our true nature in a very intentional way. By consciously engaging in practices that keep us present and fully engaged, we can prevent or alleviate the stress and trauma we absorb in our work. When we remember that we are all one, it can keep us from taking everything on ourselves and it keeps us from taking ourselves too seriously.

Shedding Layers and Roles

As shared earlier in this chapter, we may find ourselves moving between roles and social codes to assimilate to the cultures in our workplaces. This can cause us to take on identities that don't align with our fundamental consciousness, leading us toward burnout. One of the practices we can engage in to uncover our true selves is to shed layers of our professional identity and get to our true beliefs, thoughts, and opinions. We can do this by finding activities that bring joy, pleasure, and satisfaction.

Solo: Pursue creative passions by finding small pockets of time or take a full day off and commit to doing something creative that brings you back to a sense of enjoyment. Maybe it's painting, sewing, gardening, vision boarding, pulling tarot cards, dancing, or rock climbing. You don't have to be good at it, and it never has to be shared with anyone (or on social media), so allow yourself to be fully in it, and don't worry about who might see it or whether it will be critiqued.

Collective: Find like-minded people to pursue these passions with. Join a recreation league or a local book club; find an online community with similar interests; attend a local workshop or event in your community; and be open to meeting people. If you are open to new experiences and are compassionate with yourself in your learning, this kind of engagement can be a buffer from burnout.

Sound Healing to Remember and Reconnect

The goal of healing . . . is to create harmony out of disharmony. But healing can also be a means of connecting with our innermost essence, so that we expand our identity beyond a limited, ego-based definition of self.

—Dr. Mitchell L. Gaynor, *The Healing Power of Sound*

Stress can put us out of sync with ourselves and each other. Music, in the form of sounds and vibrations, can help us remember and reconnect in a way that connects us to ourselves and the world around us. I will share more about the healing power of vibrations on our regulation (Chapter 3) and the power of rhythm in our work (Chapter 4), but we can start here with simple sound healing practices that can bring us back into the present moment, bring more joy into our work, and help us move toward connection.

Solo: Create a playlist of music that evokes different moods and emotions: anger, sadness, joy, etc. Jam out in your shower or car. Find a song that reminds you of your childhood (preferably good memories), or a song that evokes a strong emotion and allow yourself to feel it. You might also purchase a crystal sound bowl or a Tibetan singing bowl to create your own sound healing.

Collective: Go to a concert with friends or family. This can also be a call back to childhood by attending a concert of a musician or group from your youth. Lauryn Hill and Earth, Wind, & Fire concerts are two throwback events that evoke positive memories for me. Attending a drum circle or sound healing session at a local yoga studio can also be a way to collectively engage in the healing power of sound.

Yin Yoga to Reconnect the Body

> *Yoga offers self-care strategies that help individuals recognize the value of self-awareness and self-regulation as foundational for overall health and well-being.*
>
> —Gail Parker, PhD, *Transforming Ethnic and Race-Based Traumatic Stress with Yoga*

The ancient practice of yoga is an eight-limbed system of well-being, a way to practice discipline toward a state of enlightenment, a spiritual path. The eight limbs include yamas (principles on how to treat others and engage with the world around us; niyamas (standards of self-discipline); asana (the physical postures, or what we know in the West as "yoga"); pranayama (breath control); dharana (concentration and the ability to focus the mind); dhyana (meditation); and samadhi (a state of enlightenment). Often when we hear people say they practice yoga, they mean the asana postures. That is the focus of this section on yin yoga, but I would be remiss without mentioning all eight limbs of the full yoga system.

As a practice of physical postures matched with our breath, yoga asana and pranayama has many healing abilities. More specifically, yoga unifies the body and the breath, creating an amazing full-body connection we can experience when we practice. Yoga can be practiced solo, at home on our yoga mats, or collectively in a class or studio. Yin yoga, specifically, in which poses are held for longer periods of time, allows the body to slow down, get still, and settle into a state of calm ease. The challenge of yin yoga is the stillness; however, it is in this stillness that we can begin to see what care we need to heal the stress we are experiencing. *Staying with the stillness is the practice.* There are many yin yoga guides and videos available if you want to start a yin yoga practice, or you can find a local studio and try a class with others. Yin yoga is a radical self-care practice that reconnects us with our bodies and brings us back into a state of well-being. (Tai chi, Qigong, and other similar practices can have the same benefits as yoga asana, as they also unify the breath with physical movement.)

Nature and Green Spaces

> *We know we feel relaxed when we look at green trees. A shady green view even improves our health . . . the color green calms our minds and promotes healing.*
>
> —PETER WOHLLEBEN, *The Heartbeat of Trees*

> *A thoughtfully engaged relationship with a natural environment enables you to recover with ease, without imposition, your personal capacity for self-control and action, as well as cognitive decision-making abilities. It gives us the space to reconnect with ourselves.*
>
> —MARCO MENCAGLI AND MARCO NIERI, *The Secret Therapy of Trees*

Nature creates a safe container to help us protect our energy and buffer our bodies from absorbing too much stress. Studies have shown the immense value of reconnecting with nature, from camping to forest bathing. Our bodies crave being in tune with nature, and this attunement can counteract the stressful fast pace of our work environments. Some things to consider when it comes to bringing nature into our radical self-care practices:

- **Nature reset:** Camping in nature for three nights or more can shift the vibrations in our bodies and put us back in sync with nature. Connecting with nature can reconnect us to ourselves. If you can't camp or be out in the woods for days at a time, a walk in nature or near a body of water can have a similar effect.

- **Nature-viewing:** Simply looking at pictures of nature has a calming effect on our bodies and helps us reconnect with the environment. Watching a video of nature has a similar effect. Some teachers show their students nature videos during times of group work or studying for an exam to keep students engaged and connected. You can employ this practice by having a nature screen saver, hanging a photo of nature, or taking a break to look out your window during the day. You can also engage in "walk and talks," where you take your meetings outside and incorporate movement. I do this often with my students if they want to talk with me about a difficult topic. It seems to help them articulate what is bothering them without sitting in the discomfort of it. This may seem overly simple, but it can help release stress from our bodies.

CREATING A SPACE FOR PLEASURE AND PLAY

As we do our work, we can purposely surround ourselves with beauty as a way of creating space for joy and satisfaction in our work. We can consciously and compassionately bring playfulness into our workplaces to enhance learning, impact emotional regulation, and encourage problem-solving. Consider these options for creating a space for pleasure and play:

- Bring plants and aromatherapy into your space. I have an office full of plants, and everyone who comes into my space smiles and tells me how calm and happy it makes them feel.
- Keep windows open (if this is an option), bring some mirrors into the space to open it up, or consider furnishing your desk with a soft light so you can keep harsh overhead lights off or dimmed.
- Create a calm space (even just a section of your desk) that can be kept visually clear or can hold some items that bring you

comfort, like a picture, crystal, or any personal visual representation of joy.

- If you're able, bring in candles, tea, or coffee for those times when you just need a break.
- Create "play breaks" or create a space in the workplace where play is encouraged. Maybe it's an outside green space, a basketball hoop in the parking lot, or a game room.
- Encourage play outside of work by offering discounted gym memberships or organizing "field trips" to a local climbing gym, a community pool, or an ice skating rink.
- Cultivate times for retreats, whether facilitated for the whole staff, or allowing folks to take a day for themselves.
- Engage restorative practices as a way to bring constructed play. Get folks in a circle and use a game as an energizer. It's a great lead in for group conversations and restorative conferences.
- Hang positive affirmations and quotes in your space or wear clothing with funny sayings that relate to your profession. This can bring a sense of levity to you, your colleagues and those you serve. My students particularly like my "Your Favorite Social Worker" T-shirt.

SELF-COMPASSION: LOVING KINDNESS (METTA MEDITATION)

No matter how well we do our work, we can't end all the suffering or heal all the trauma. In those moments when we have done all we can, to ease our hearts we can do a metta meditation of loving kindness to hold space for them and ourselves. Metta meditation assumes that all beings deserve happiness and freedom from suffering. This is a way to strengthen the connections between ourselves and others by receiving loving kindness and sending it out to others.

- Sit comfortably. Close your eyes if that is comfortable, or soften your gaze toward the floor (to avoid distraction).
- Bring your awareness to your breath, and begin to slow the exhales.
- When you're ready, repeat these words as an offering of loving kindness to yourself: May I be happy. May I be healthy. May I be safe. May I be free from suffering.
- Repeat the sequence as many times as you like, then move on to someone you love and care about. Bring them to mind and offer them the same loving kindness: May they be happy. May they be healthy. May they be safe. May they be free from suffering.
- Consider if there are others you would like to offer this loving kindness:
  - someone you are acquainted with but maybe not very close with;
  - someone with whom you may have a difficult relationship, like coworkers, clients, the person who cut you off in traffic, or family members.

REFLECTIONS

- As you read this chapter, what came up for you?
- What brought you to your current work of helping others, and is there a quote, a saying or an event that got you interested in this profession?
- What keeps you in this work? Why *this* work? *Go deeper.*
- Can you identify your passion, purpose, and people, and have any of those changed since you started this work? In what ways?
- How do you feel about incorporating pleasure and play into your work?
- Were you able to identify your ACEs and PCEs?
  - ACEs Score: /10
  - PCEs Score: /7

- How do you think your PACEs (adverse and positive childhood experiences) contributed to your becoming a helper, healer, or changemaker, if at all?
- Can you identify your own attachment style? If so, what is it, and how do you think it impacts your work?
- Have you ever abused your authority in your role as a helper? Have you witnessed others abusing their authority? How did you reconcile these incidents?
- Are you currently in therapy? If so, how has it helped you in your work as a helper, healer, or changemaker?

3

REGULATE AND REBALANCE

Regulating our nervous system: breath, balance, and boundaries

> As you care for people with your heart wide open, you often don't realize how much of what you are exposed to is being taken in and held in your body. It isn't until later that your body starts to let you know.
>
> —Laura van Dernoot Lipsky with Connie Burk, *Trauma Stewardship*

Once we become aware of the ways we carry the weight of our work, we begin to notice that the disconnection in our work is caused by dysregulation and lack of balance. We become dysregulated because the work we do as helpers, healers, and changemakers is intense and challenging. *We are the intervention*, and as we put ourselves directly in the work we do, especially when working in spaces of suffering, oppression, or injustice, we will necessarily be dysregulated by it.

When we are overwhelmed with work stress, we may have trouble finding our balance and find it difficult to choose which to focus on: the day-to-day alleviation of suffering or identifying and addressing the larger systemic inequalities that cause the suffering. We become unbalanced when we attempt to juggle the micro and macro aspects of our work without considering our own care as we do it. Intently focused on others, we often neglect the signs we see in ourselves, so it's important that we learn how to identify imbalances and dysregulation early, engage radical self-care practices, and prevent burnout altogether. Understanding the dysregulation we experience and how to regulate gives us an opportunity to rebalance ourselves and each other in the helping professions.

SURVIVAL MODE

> *If an organism is stuck in survival mode, its energies are focused on fighting off unseen enemies, which leaves no room for nurture, care, and love. For us humans, it means that as long as the mind is defending against invisible assaults, our closest bonds are threatened, along with our ability to imagine, plan, play, and pay attention to other people's needs.*
>
> —Bessel van der Kolk, *The Body Keeps the Score*

We are energized to do the work we love but become deeply exhausted by the conditions in which we do the work. In speaking with fellow educators and social workers while writing this book, many of them expressed similar sentiments of exhaustion and despair because of the dysregulation and the lack of balance they feel while doing their work well. We know the only way to do this work is to balance both the micro and macro aspects of being a helper, healer, and changemaker. This means working one-on-one with individuals or in small groups while also organizing communities, working to change policies, and creating workable systems. This means engaging in change work with administrators, executive directors, and boards of directors and engaging in legislation and political advocacy.

This challenge of where to focus our energy is expressed in the commonly shared upstream/river parable. You've likely heard this one (paraphrased):

> *As you're walking along a riverbank, you notice a person struggling to swim, near drowning. You jump in, pull them to safety,*

> *provide CPR and heroically save them. Then a few moments later, another person is struggling in the water, and you jump in again to save them. This happens over and over again: you see a person struggling, pull them out, and provide life-saving support until the next one floats by. And while you're busy jumping in and pulling bodies out of the water to safety, you have no time to walk upstream to find out why these people are falling into the river in the first place, let alone to put in a preventative measure to stop the flow of bodies.*

This parable, initially used to explain the importance of prevention efforts in public health, speaks to the overwhelm of our work. It also speaks to the work we do to alleviate immediate suffering for individuals and how it can keep us from seeking the root causes of these conditions, such as advocating for broader political, societal, and economic change that might prevent some of the intractable suffering we tend to see in our work over time: a micro-focus versus a macro-focus. Many of us may not have the option of choosing one level of focus.

This keeps us in perpetual loops of stress and crisis in which we can't breathe and focusing on our own well-being seems impossible. So, we let our own needs sit by the wayside while we save others and use up all our energy, time, and attention on our work, then when work gets overwhelming, we feel stuck or at a loss for what to do next. The ability to be creative and to imagine possibilities are key to liberation and making real change, but it can be impossible to imagine "what could be" when all our energy is being focused on what currently exists and on what is failing. The reality of our work is that while we are too exhausted from the nonstop work of pulling bodies from the proverbial rivers to ease the suffering of some, those at the river head keep sending bodies downstream, and we often find ourselves stuck in survival mode. In order to get out of these loops of stress and crisis, we must understand how we get there and have some radical self-care tools to help us get unstuck from survival mode.

We know what survival mode looks like in those we serve: It is the undocumented student who drops out of school to work so their family doesn't get evicted. It's the survivor of domestic violence who has left a violent relationship but finds their way into the arms of the next abuser. It's the youth who recants their disclosure of abuse because they don't want to risk leaving their younger siblings. It's the student who acts out in the classroom , using their behavior as a cry for help.

We know what survival mode looks like for others, but we must be able to recognize when we are in survival mode, too. It's the social worker who barely sees their own children because they're working overtime caring for others' children. It's the first responder who avoids going home at the end of the day because it's too painful to see their family and hold the grief of their workday simultaneously. It's the educator who teaches all day and can't find time to eat lunch or even use the restroom during the school day. It's the journalist or activist who survives on energy drinks and fast food so they can respond to the never-ending breaking news cycle of injustices.

Survival mode is being in a constant state of self-preservation where our brain and body are on high alert for potential threats in our environment. This is a prolonged stress state that can cause us to experience fatigue, memory loss, irritability, lack of focus, along with a host of physical symptoms. We may notice we are in survival mode when everything seems urgent and it is hard to prioritize (see Upstream Parable); we may find ourselves canceling or missing meetings; we may find ourselves unable to say NO or take on extra work without considering the impact to our own well-being; we may feel a lack of joy or are unable to enjoy the things we once found pleasure in; and we may feel ourselves in defense mode, reacting to things in our environment rather than being proactive or preventative.

Some of us have been in survival mode for months, years, possibly even our whole lives. The challenge is, we may have difficulty identifying this in ourselves because our ability to sense our own needs is impaired by years, or even decades, of working within systems that deny our individual humanity while helping others with their survival. For many of us, caregiving is an adaptive survival response we carry from childhood, and it can make us oblivious to this inherent trauma we carry. This is why, I believe, so many of us find ourselves parked long-term in survival mode; it is a state that we have become accustomed to. Helpers, healers, and changemakers are masters at anesthetizing ourselves to the pain and suffering in our work and to the conditions surrounding our work so that we can do what needs to be done. Sometimes the only way to hold the stress is to numb out. In his book *The Wild Edge of Sorrow*, Francis Weller suggests that Western civilization is guilty of two sins, "amnesia and anesthesia—we forget and we go numb" (2015, p. xx).

Survival mode causes us to forget about our own needs until they become too obvious to ignore. When we've been in survival mode for too long, we start to see the impacts. We hold the stress and trauma of those we serve in our bodies. One of the first signs that we may be in survival mode is a lack of physical balance. We feel more clumsy than usual, bumping into people or immovable objects. We may notice bruises on our body and aren't sure how they got there or that we seem to "fall over" when we were just standing still. We may get a little dizzy every time we stand up, but we brush it off and keep moving with our day. We may even begin forgetting small things, like losing our cell phones or misplacing our keys. Assuming we don't have a chronic condition and are sober, these can all be early signs of our physical bodies going into survival mode. These things may have been happening for a long time so it's easy to dismiss them and continue with our work.

By the time we notice the physical imbalances, we may already have experienced lack of balance and dysregulation in other areas of our lives. We may have missed medical appointments, left bills unpaid, or otherwise ignored our own personal needs to focus on the work. Overwork and chronic caregiving can become our survival adaptation, or we can shift into complete shutdown to escape the weight of our work. When we are stuck in survival mode, we become exhausted just from maintaining the hypervigilance that it requires. That loss of energy keeps us from caring for ourselves, as van der Kolk (2014) suggests in the quote at the start of this section, but it also keeps us from imagining, playing, and learning, which are how we create change in our professions. To get out of this unrelenting cycle and move back to a space of care, we have to understand how our individual nervous system is wired and how it reacts to threats, traumas, and triggers in our environment.

STRESS, TRAUMA, AND TRIGGERS

> *Trauma pervades our culture, from personal functioning through social relationships, parenting, education, popular culture, economics, and politics. In fact, someone without the marks of trauma would be an outlier in our society.*
>
> —Gabor Maté, *The Myth of Normal*

> *Not only can trauma be healed, but with appropriate guidance and support, it can be transformative. Trauma has the potential to be one of the most significant forces for psychological, social, and spiritual awakening and evolution.*
>
> —Peter Levine, *Waking the Tiger*

In 2007, after years of working in rape crisis and surviving a major burnout, my husband finished his PhD in sociology and we moved to California from Connecticut. I was looking for work in the same field I'd been working in, and when I shared that I had an interview for a position at a rape crisis coalition, my husband very lovingly pleaded with me to do *anything other than* rape crisis work. He had watched me struggle during my experience of burnout and saw how bad the health issues and triggering became. He also saw how most of my symptoms of stress abated immediately after I left my job for our cross-country move. I agreed with him and figured I'd shift from the world of rape crisis into education because "there's probably not a lot of trauma in schools." (Insert laughing/crying emoji here.) This is the constant reminder that trauma "pervades our culture" and is especially inherent in the work we do, no matter the specific profession or location.

In our work as helpers, healers, and changemakers it can be

challenging to differentiate if we are dealing with stress or experiencing trauma. Stress is the body's response to any challenge or demand which "consists of the internal alterations—visible or not—that occur when the organism perceives a threat to its existence or well-being" (Maté, 2011, p. 28). Trauma is not the event, but rather what happens within our brains and bodies as a result of the traumatic event, "a psychic injury, lodged in our nervous system, mind, and body, lasting long past the original incident(s), triggerable at any time (Maté, 2022, p. 20). In her book *Trauma and Recovery*, Judith Herman shares, "Traumatic events overwhelm the ordinary systems of care that give people a sense of control, connection, and meaning" (Herman, 1997, p. 33). Trauma overwhelms us, impacts our normal development, and changes the trajectory of our lives, causing disconnection and confusion, throwing us off our life's path. Like a crimp in a hose that stops water from flowing freely, experiencing trauma slows or stops the flow of care for ourselves in the moment.

Trauma can be experienced in the following ways:

Acute Trauma: A one-time traumatic event, regardless of the duration.

Chronic Trauma: Ongoing, repeated or prolonged trauma with no respite or recovery.

Complex Trauma: Multiple, different traumatic events over time.

Systemic Trauma: Exposure to traumatic systems (educational, medical, carceral, etc.)

Generational Trauma: Trauma passed down through generations through behavior.

Epigenetic Trauma: DNA and gene expression activated by extreme stress in our environment and passed to future generations.

There is no trauma competition, but it is important to acknowledge the nuances of trauma and the different ways it impacts us. Similarly to our varied experiences of ACEs, we all may experience an overwhelmingly stressful event at the same time but based on our previous personal experiences and available resources, some of us may experience it as a trauma that impacts us for a long time, and others may experience it as a trauma that has minimal impacts, and some may not register it as a traumatic event at all. The intensity and duration of the experience and our relationship to whatever or whoever is causing the threat can dictate how we experience trauma and how healing happens afterward. Our age and other basic demographics (e.g., education level, class, race, mobility, physical ability) can also determine our access to safety, healing, and recourse after an event which can contribute to whether the event is cemented as more or less traumatic.

When we experience a traumatic event, we experience it through our senses, allowing our brains to catalog what we see, hear, smell, taste, or feel during the event. We can then use that information to detect and avoid similar experiences in the future. However, there may be times when this information recall impacts us negatively. We may recall the tone of a voice that reminds us of an abusive parent, the smell of perfume that reminds us of a strict teacher, or a cold chill that reminds us of living in a home without heat. Each of these sensory memories will, in turn, create an unpleasant body sensation that can take us back to the full memory of the traumatic event, even if it occurred years prior. While these memories can be stimulated through the senses, they can also evoke emotions or cognitive distortions that pull us into dysregulation. This is what we call *triggering.*

Triggering can come in the form of flashbacks, intrusive thoughts, nightmares, uncontrollable flooding of strong emotions, hyperarousal, dissociation, or even physical symptoms, like headaches, stomachaches, and nausea. I want to be clear that triggering is a very real experience for trauma survivors and is not the same as simply being made uncomfortable, nor is it an excuse for avoiding accountability. If we are unaware of our own traumatic responses and our specific triggers, we can wind up with the double whammy of our own primary trauma combined with vicarious trauma we are exposed to in our work. Our coworkers and colleagues can also trigger us. Let me share a story to illustrate this point.

One day, I was sitting in a school district-level staff meeting feeling particularly off, but I couldn't tell exactly what was bothering me. My work was stressful, but there was something else I had been feeling for a while and couldn't name. All I could do was engage the feeling and practice my radical self-care. I made sure I was hydrated; I moved my body; I meditated; I talked to my therapist; but I still couldn't shake this feeling. So I started paying more attention at work, to see where my discomfort was coming from and get to the root of what was bothering me. For context, this staff meeting was slightly contentious, as there were some interpersonal issues among folks, but the administrator facilitating the meeting claimed it was a "safe space for courageous conversations." I was asked to share about a challenge I was having with another colleague, and right after I shared, the administrator said, "Thanks for sharing. But you know, there's always two sides to every story."

As soon as she said the words, my blood ran cold, I felt heavy in my seat, unable to move, and I saw a few other people in the room shift in their seats. It was at that moment I realized that the phrase "there's two sides to every story" triggered a full body reaction that I'm not sure I can put into words. Processing it later, I connected the phrase to a feeling of not being believed as a survivor of an adverse childhood experience. While my mother believed me and protected me from further harm, there were others who listened to my story of sexual abuse and responded by saying something like "well, there are two sides to every story. . ." and what they clearly meant was *they didn't believe me.* My fellow survivors know how crazy making not being believed can be. While that is not exactly what the administrator meant at that moment, *my nervous system didn't know the difference.*

This is how triggering works. Something happens to us in the present moment that puts us back into a past experience where we had little control. Our whole body feels the intense resurfacing of strong emotions from the past in the present moment. Triggers, in the context of regulation, are important for us to be aware of, because it is the emotional material we bring to the work: it can make us more vulnerable to dysregulation, or we can harness the power of our nervous system to fuel our resilience as helpers, healers, and changemakers. My own trauma was triggered at work by a colleague, and it took me some time to figure out what was causing my dysregulation. The moment I was able to connect the intense feelings of arousal I felt in those meetings to a tangible memory recall from my past, it made sense and deescalated the intensity of those feelings immediately.

The challenge with triggers is that we don't know what they are until they're activated, and if we're not aware that the sensations we're experiencing are from the past, we may project them onto people and situations in the present. Bringing in a sense of control and meaning by noticing when I was being triggered and engaging my radical self-care practices to hold space for myself as I did the work of uncovering the root of the trigger, I no longer felt out of balance at work and avoided burnout. Because our jobs are people-centered and often support folks through challenging experiences, we will inevitably come up against their triggers and trauma responses. Knowing our own traumas and triggers can help us navigate the trauma responses of those we serve and create compassion for our own responses.

ALL THE Fs: FLOCK, FIGHT, FLIGHT, FREEZE, AND FAWN

Intolerable experience can also happen when we become so habituated to narrowly focusing on work or so unused to active rest that a real juicy experience is threatening simply by contrast. The intolerable experience stimulates a fight-or-flight reaction, making the body tense, agitated, and eager to do something to relieve the situation.

—Christine Caldwell, *Getting Our Bodies Back*

Trauma isn't simply what happened to us but how we (our nervous system) respond to the traumatic event. Our nervous system responds to threats, *real or perceived,* that we pick up on through our senses. What we see, hear, smell, feel, and taste can give us clues about our general safety, and our bodies react before we have time to think about a response. This is called neuroception, the unconscious detection of safety or threat. When our brains sense a threat (stress and trauma are threats), chemical reactions occur in our bodies to ready us for survival. To help my students to understand their stress responses, to help them learn to trust their nervous system responses, and to know that their body and brain are always working to protect them in amazing ways, I use this example: Imagine you're at work and you suddenly smell something burning. It may be a familiar smell, but the smell of something burning sends a warning signal to your brain that says, "Something is wrong, we're not safe," and it quickly jumps into action, releasing stress hormones to help us physically move our bodies to get to safety. We begin to orient ourselves to the room, seeking the source of the smell.

If we find that someone is standing outside our door smoking a cigarette, and that this smoke is wafting in on the air and that is what we smelled, we may realize there is no threat, and our nervous system will cease producing stress hormones so we can go on about our day. However, if we notice that there is a fire in the corner of the room we're in, we obviously need a much different response. Using adrenaline, our bodies leap into action, moving us through the room, out the door, away from the threat, and toward safety. Cortisol is also released and acts as an inflammatory agent or pain suppressant so we can get to safety without stopping if we get hurt. Once we get to safety or the threat is neutralized, our nervous system halts adrenaline and cortisol production in our body so that we can return to the prethreat state we were in, a state we call homeostasis, or our baseline regulation. If there was a true threat and we had to mobilize to stay safe, we may need some time to process all the adrenaline and cortisol that accumulated. This release might take the form of shaking, talking about the incident (using voice to regulate ourselves), taking a few deep breaths, or another kind of physical release.

Our brains take action to keep us safe by activating a stress response or trauma response to help us survive a threat in the moment. While these reactions are instantaneous and automatic, we can attune to our nervous system responses, understand them, and gain some level of control over the situations and environments that activate them. That's not to say we can prevent ourselves from having these responses (nor would we want to), but knowing our responses gives us some wisdom and space to manage how we respond. Let's explore all the Fs.

Flock: Seeking connection to others and comfort in numbers.
Fight: Physically defending ourselves from the threat.
Flight: Removing ourselves from the threat or running away from it.
Freeze: Becoming immobile until the threat has passed.
Fawn: Accommodating, or appeasing to deflect the threat.

We may have one strong default response, or we may exercise different responses based on the threat. When we initially sense a threat, we may seek safety in numbers and become hypervigilant to our environment (flock). That hypervigilance allows us to gauge the reactions of those around us to better assess the threat and determine what needs to happen next. If we can act, we can run away from the threat (flight) or address it head on (fight). If we can't run away or fight, it may be in our best interest to pacify the threat by being still (freeze) or by being agreeable or self-depreciating (fawn). Our brains and bodies work together to determine the best response to each threat, even if we have trouble understanding why we had a certain response. For example, when we freeze in response to a threat, we may ask ourselves why we didn't fight back, why we didn't run away, or why we didn't call out for help. This can compound the trauma we experience by adding a layer of guilt or shame rather than a rooted awareness that our trauma response kept us alive. *We are survivors, regardless of—or because of—the automatic response we had in the moment.*

We may also see these responses as residual reactions in our work. For example, a **flock response reaction** might show up as a constant seeking to be part of a group or a level of codependency with colleagues or those we serve. A **fight response reaction** may look like defensiveness with colleagues, micromanaging others, or feeling like you're being targeted when that may not be the case. A **flight response reaction** might manifest as not staying at a job longer than one to three years or going relationship to relationship, moving on when either work or a relationship start getting too intense. A **freeze response reaction** may turn up as procrastinating on that deadline, putting off that phone call you need to make, or isolating yourself from colleagues or family members. And a **fawn response reaction** may take the form of weak boundaries and workaholism due to an inability to say no for fear of reprisal or being seen as rude or unpleasant.

Fight, flight, and freeze are opposites of the "tend and befriend" responses of flock and fawn, but any one of these responses can be engaged depending on the threat and the environment we are in. If we are alone and could flee, maybe flight would be our first response, but if we have a child, client, or coworker with us, we might fight or flock instead. Flock seemed to be a universal response to stress and trauma during the COVID-19 pandemic, as the herd mentality took over many of our decisions while we were all figuring out how to respond to the global threat of the illness. I noticed the residues of each response type early in my own professional life, moving jobs frequently, overworking, feeling the need to defend myself often, and procrastinating when difficult situations arose.

By identifying those responses and acknowledging that they were no longer needed to keep me safe, I was able to release the stress (and stress hormones) of constantly feeling like I was under threat, and was better able to stay engaged and regulated in my work. Knowing how our nervous system regulates itself is important, so we can know when we are dysregulated and can have some tools to bring us back to a baseline of calm regulation with a helping dose of compassion for the ways our bodies keep us safe and alive. While it's not as important to know the anatomical specifics of our brains, it can be helpful to get a basic map of the parts of our nervous system that are engaged when we are regulated so we can better identify when we are not.

EMOTIONAL AND NERVOUS SYSTEM REGULATION: BODY–MIND CONNECTION

Part of the grace of the nervous system is that it is constantly self-regulating. What you can't process today will be available to be processed some other time when you are stronger, more resourceful, and better able to do it.

—Peter Levine, *Waking the Tiger: Healing Trauma*

Over the past decade, society has gained awareness of how our bodies and minds work together. We are learning more about how the brain and body impact each other and how our environment impacts our nervous system, which in turn dictates our behavior, our emotions, our immune system, and our overall health and well-being. Emotional regulation plays a large part in how we handle the content of our work with others. Emotions are just energy and when we are aware of our emotions, we have the power to stay regulated. The chemical action of an emotion only lasts for 90 seconds, but as humans we can extend our emotional reactions well beyond that, holding grudges or emotional material in our minds for months, years, and even decades. Sometimes strong emotions like fear, shame, or anger might freak us out, especially if the emotions center around the folks we serve or work with, and that may cause us to shut down or become dysregulated. In her book, *Little Book of Big Emotions* (2004), Erika M. Hunter shares, "We can't escape from our feelings—not without consequences. But by learning to listen to and work with our feelings, we can be more in control of our lives, rather than feeling compelled, impelled, propelled, expelled, or repelled by our emotions" (p. 11). We can gain emotional intelligence by being more aware of how our emotions are triggered in our work.

We are affected not only by the people we serve and the work we do but also by the environment in which we do it. Our physiology cannot be separated from our environment, which is why it is so vital that we become aware of how our chosen professions impact our health. All helpers, healers, and changemakers should have a basic understanding of the nervous system and regulation because they impact how we show up in our work and are foundational aspects of our radical self-care. How we show up is important. We are the intervention, so our tone of voice, our posture, the words we use, and how we position ourselves matter, and this requires us to show up present and grounded in our body and mind. We require a certain level of nervous system regulation to stay present with our students, clients, patients, etc.

While it is important to understand the nervous system, it is outside of my scope of expertise, so I will offer a simplified explanation to help us start to make the connections with how our work impacts us on a deep, internal level. In order to gain more insight into nervous system regulation, I highly recommend reading the works of Peter Levine, Gabor Maté, Nadine Burke Harris, Babette Rothschild, Stephen Porges, Bessel van der Kolk, and other medical and psychology professionals.

As I understand it, our nervous system has many interconnected parts that work seamlessly together to keep us alive and well. The brain and body communicate with each other via the nervous system, a complex network of chemicals and nerves drive all the actions that make us human. From respiration to reproduction, digestion to dementia, heartbeat to headaches, it is our nervous system that controls our thoughts, feelings, and movements. The **central nervous system**, made up of our brain and spinal cord, is like the control center of the body, responsible for thought, sensory perception, emotions, and movements. The movie *Inside Out* (Pixar, 2015) captures this concept very well, with the characters of emotion in charge of the control panel that animates the main character, Riley's, life. The brain receives sensory information, processes it, and translates it into an appropriate action in the body in the form of electrical and chemical transmitters that communicate between the brain and the body via the spinal cord, like a neural super highway.

These parts of our nervous system keep our bodies balanced, in a state of homeostasis. When we are stressed, our nervous system can be thrown out of balance, which leads us to seek that regulated state of homeostasis. The various branches of our nervous system help us to create this balance, and we can assist our bodies in maintaining this regulation by understanding what is happening in our bodies and between these systems.

While the central nervous system is the control center, the **peripheral nervous system** is the communication network of nerves that transports electrical and chemical messages from the brain to the muscles and organs. Sensory nerves communicate information from the sensory organs (eyes, ears, nose, tongue, and skin) to the brain, and motor nerves convey information that moves the body. The peripheral nervous system also relays information about pain from the body to the brain (except in the case of reflexes), which processes the information to determine whether the body needs some attention and care.

One part of the peripheral nervous system is the **autonomic nervous system**, which helps regulate our automatic, or unconscious, functions; for example, heart rate, breathing, blood pressure, and consciousness. There are two distinct branches of the autonomic nervous system, which are what most people are referring to when they talk about "nervous system regulation." These branches work in opposition to each other and are the sympathetic nervous system, which prepares us for action during stress (all the Fs), and the parasympathetic nervous system, which helps us recover and restore balance after stress. This is where the "magic" happens when it comes to our emotions and how we handle the stress and trauma in our work as helpers, healers, and changemakers.

Our **sympathetic nervous system** is likened to the "gas pedal" or accelerator of our nervous system, as it elicits the fight-or-flight response when triggered by threats and by emotional distress. It readies the body for a response to danger by quickly increasing heart rate, blood pressure, and breathing, while slowing down digestion and diverting energy to the muscles to move our bodies into action. This puts us in a mode of self-protection, which also increases inflammation due to the release of adrenaline and cortisol. This process is automatic and involuntary, immediately activated to keep us safe and alive when triggered by certain stimuli. *It is our sympathetic nervous system that makes us survivors.*

Our **parasympathetic nervous system** is likened to the "brake" or decelerator of our nervous system, as it elicits the "rest and digest," "feed and breed," or "calm and connect" responses. After the threat or danger has passed, the parasympathetic nervous system acts to counter and reverse the sympathetic nervous system's fight-or-flight response, slowing heart rate, blood pressure, blood sugar levels, and breathing rate, helping the body conserve energy, and calming the body down. It helps promote relaxation, allowing us to rest our bodies and minds, and promotes digestion so our bodies can take in fuel for healing. *Our parasympathetic nervous system is key in our practice of radical self-care* and can buffer the impacts of burnout when we harness its power to safely come into a space of rest.

The sympathetic and parasympathetic nervous systems work in opposition to each other, like a seesaw: when one side is activated, or goes up, the other side gets deactivated, or goes down. The **vagus nerve**, or nerves (based on the Polyvagal Theory, proposed by Stephen Porges [Porges, 2011]), is the longest nerve in the body and acts as the switch between the sympathetic and parasympathetic nervous systems. This has been called the "wandering nerve" and the "soul nerve" because it connects our brain to every organ in our bodies, keeping us regulated physically and emotionally from moment to moment. It is the epicenter of both the triggering and the healing of trauma in our bodies. Like nervous system regulation, Polyvagal Theory is important for us to understand as helpers, healers, and changemakers, but is also outside of my scope of expertise. I will offer a basic summary here but encourage you to read Dr. Porges's work for deeper learning.

The Polyvagal Theory suggests that there are pathways within our nervous system that correspond with our threat/safety responses (all the Fs) and allow us to shift from calm connection to immobilized fear and back to a state of calm as necessary, based on each threat we encounter. These pathways operate in a hierarchical way, moving from **ventral vagal** (safety and social connection of flock), through the **sympathetic nervous system** (our threat responses of fight-or-flight), to **dorsal vagal** (shut down response of freeze or fawn) if our initial fight-or-flight response is not possible. The goal is to then get back to the ventral vagal state of safety and connection, or homeostasis, as quickly as possible.

As you might imagine, being in a state of dysregulated fight, flight, or freeze can make intimacy challenging, and this is especially true for helpers, healers, and changemakers, who may get stuck in a threat response state due to the nature of our work. This makes it difficult for us to shift our arousal state into intimacy mode when we get home from work (role-swapping). If we want to maintain intimate relationships with those we love, we must notice when our work is keeping us dysregulated, engage in radical self-care to help us mediate the stress response, and learn to activate a state of calm connection.

ADAPTING TO DYSREGULATION

With our widespread collective tendency toward overworked, sleep-deprived, and stressed lives, our whole society tends toward a dysregulated baseline.

—Elizabeth A. Stanley, PhD, *Widen The Window*

Helping, healing, and change-making professions and movements depend on a prolonged and sometimes chronic level of emotional activation which provides a sense of urgency and motivates us toward action. This emotional charge is sometimes called the "helpers high," a state of arousal that we experience when we engage in altruistic work that serves a purpose. We may get a rush of serotonin, dopamine, or oxytocin, the feel-good hormones, and we become addicted to the feeling of accomplishment and accolades. This natural reward system in our brains gives us a sense of meaning and keeps us in a cycle of caring for others that can be a helpful motivation in our work. However, when the emotional hijacking is manipulated "for the greater good," we can experience the triggering of vicarious trauma or we may find ourselves in a state of hyperarousal or hypervigilance fed by the sense of urgency in our work. We can easily become addicted to this high, being unable to turn it off and even seeking an intense level of activation when we are away from work.

The baseline nervous system regulation for many helpers, healers, and changemakers tends to be hyperarousal. We are comfortable in crisis and thrive in chaos. We know how to survive. We are always assessing threats. When we walk into a room, we immediately look for the exits and the AED/Fire extinguishers or determine the location of the nearest hospital, etc. We are always aware of and paying stark attention to our peripheral vision. We see and hear more than one conversation at a time. We can tell when someone or something is out of place. When we do this work for years, even decades with no reprieve or relief from the stress of the work, we can become "adapted to dysregulation." Chronic stress arousal keeps our sympathetic nervous system constantly active, stuck in a hyperarousal cycle of cortisol release, adrenaline rushes, and dopamine crashes that produce our new baseline.

I became aware of this dysregulation in graduate school while on a research trip with a professor and fellow MSW student. As we drove, we passed a few garbage bags on the side of the highway, and we all noticed. Then we passed an abandoned foam cooler, and we all took a deep breath. I noticed my heart racing, my body tense up, and I felt a sense of uncertainty. I asked if I was the only one who assumed there's a body or body parts in garbage bags and coolers when I see them on the side of the highway. They both agreed that they, too, made that assumption, and we all laughed about how that's our reality as social workers who have seen some things. What I experienced was the hyperarousal of my nervous system which had been acclimated to my work and past experiences as a social worker, always in threat/alert mode. Being alert and aware of our surroundings is good for general safety, and being hyperalert and hyperaware may make us really good at our work. It's a comfortable place for so many of us because we've been in it for so long, we've adapted, or habituated, ourselves to a new baseline of dysregulation.

EXPLOITATION OF LIVED EXPERIENCE

I don't think we should say that someone has to experience with their bodies a particular form of oppression before they'll stand up and fight back against it.

—Angela Davis, *Angela Davis in Conversation With Joyce McMillan*

When our own traumatic experiences move us toward a helping, healing, or change-making profession, we may not be working with the exact same kinds of traumatic material we experienced. Sometimes, however, our organizations seek folks with "lived experience," those who have survived the specific traumas or adverse experiences our organizations seek to heal. While this is a phenomenal practice that comes from a place of shared liberation and collective action, I find many organizations lack a trauma-informed lens on this aspect of recent primary trauma experiences being triggered by the intensity of work-related trauma. I've seen this personally in organizations that hire former foster youth or survivors of domestic violence.

It makes sense to pull in those who have recently experienced oppression, as there are nuances to surviving certain challenges. Their wisdom and input is vital as we work to make changes that will impact others with the same or similar experiences. They are hired with the best intentions, but they are not given explicit warnings about the exposure to more trauma and the heaviness of the work. The organization often has no awareness of how to care for someone who might develop PTSD from the work they are passionate about, and when an employee expresses distress from the heaviness of the work, they may be confronted with more stigma than the victims they serve. They may be viewed as "too weak" for the work rather than being seen and having their secondary or vicarious trauma acknowledged and taken seriously.

This happens often in activist and nonprofit spaces. Those with "lived experience" are sometimes repeatedly pushed to the front to tell their stories to gain sympathy for the cause, or their stories are showcased at fundraisers and galas that they may not even be able to afford to attend. Often these are Black, Brown, and feminine bodies who are also the first targets of those who oppose change and who violently confront any actions toward progress . . . and the last to get the funds or accolades for the work. For example, the parents of murdered children, or the families of those killed by police fundraising for money they'll never see. Like Erica Garner, daughter of Eric Garner, who was killed by police after being put in a chokehold in 2014. Erica became an activist after her father's death, telling his story over and over again until she died of a heart attack at age 27. While her cause of death was ruled as from natural causes, I'm sure having her father's death on video played repeatedly and being asked to speak about her trauma had a literally heartbreaking impact.

This triggering of past traumas can also occur in our education and training programs, for those who are just joining the helping, healing, and change-making professions. You will be exposed to content that may break your heart or at least cause a reaction in you, especially if the content is similar to any trauma(s) you have survived yourself—an assignment on intimate partner violence when you have just recently gotten out of an abusive relationship; a reading about child sexual abuse that mirrors your own; a residency placement or an internship assignment in a space that is similar to that of a past traumatic event.

Sometimes the impact is from the assignment itself and other times it can come from the comments and questions of classmates or colleagues who may seem insensitive or indifferent to the impacts of those traumatic experiences. If you are new to this work or know someone entering these fields, *please take your radical self-care seriously during your education and training.* While it is absolutely the responsibility of our training and education programs to be aware of this and be more trauma-informed, we may have to take matters into our own hands. Creating a solid foundation of radical self-care and support is a nonnegotiable to hold you and sustain you through your certification or education program and as you begin your work.

DUTY OF CARE: SELF-REGULATION

When therapists fail to practice adequate self care they reinforce the idea that one should allow oneself to be abused. Such a model may invalidate the help a therapist can offer. The therapist who fails to take lunch breaks, doesn't go on vacations, and works too much overtime to help clients, may in fact be damaging them. . . . They are tuned to what we model and whether we practice what we preach. If we are modeling for our clients, then therapists have an ethical duty to actively demonstrate good self care.

—B. Hudnall Stamm, PhD, *Secondary Traumatic Stress*

We know the reality of our work and the impact it has on those we serve, and because we know how important our work is in the world, *it is our responsibility to show up more resourced and more regulated than those we serve.* Duty of care is used as a legal and ethical mandate in the helping professions. It is the responsibility that we take care not to harm others while we look after their safety, health, and well-being. Duty of care is toward those we serve but also must be considered for ourselves and our colleagues. This is where self-regulation comes in as part of our duty of care, to minimize the harm our work does to us. Self-regulation is our *duty of radial self-care.*

I recognize this may be a loaded statement, but in her book *Radical Healership*, Laura Mae Northrup articulates clearly what it takes from us to do this work of helping. "Whether your work is to support people to live or to die (such as death doulas and hospice workers do), whether it is medical, spiritual, or psychological—being a healer will also require you to heal" (2022, p. 166). She goes on to say, "It might even mean that you struggle with an addiction as you become a healer and as you practice. You do not need to be totally healed to do this work. What you need to be is a human, with a heart and a commitment to growth" (p. 167).

The goal of self-regulation, as an act of radical self-care, is to be able to maintain balanced emotional reality in the face of the trauma and stress of our work. The ability to regulate our own emotions, and thus our nervous system, allows us to serve others without being dysregulated by them. And lest we assume self-regulation is a selfish focus, we must acknowledge that because *we are the intervention* and folks come to us for help and healing, our regulation isn't just for us; it is also for those we interact with and serve. Our power lies in our ability to self-regulate.

Our ability to regulate our own emotions, thoughts, and behaviors is formed early in life in relationship to our caregivers and family members. Self-regulation is at the root of our attachment styles (see Chapter 2), which can impact our nervous system's responses. Who we are and how we present to the world are the result of our self-regulation. Signs of being able to keep ourselves in a state of balanced awareness are the ability to experience and regulate strong emotions and the ability to adapt our threat responses, which allow us to have strong interpersonal relationships and positive social interactions. Not surprisingly, connection with others, whether family or coworkers, can strengthen our ability to regulate ourselves. And after a long day of helping, spending time with people and in places that feed our souls can be rejuvenating.

It takes courage to self-regulate in the face of constant dysregulation. Also, regulating the self doesn't have to be a solo endeavor. Being with others helps us learn to regulate, and our self-regulation is constantly mediating the nervous systems around us. When we are deeply regulated, our nervous system is better able to coregulate with others. Self-regulation is the foundation of coregulation, and coregulation encourages self-regulation. It's a beautiful visual of how interdependent we truly are and why, as helpers, healers, and changemakers, we need to see self-regulation as our duty of care.

FALSE CURES AND PSEUDO-REGULATORS

Stress reaction cycle habits are pseudo-regulators—soothing in the short term, while actually making our stress load worse. We're usually drawn to pseudo-regulators, rather than true regulating activities, when we're depleted or dysregulated.

—Elizabeth A. Stanley, PhD, *Widen The Window*

We attempt to hold the weight of our work the best we can. We find ways to deny and dismiss the pain we are in so we can continue with the work; and when that doesn't help, we seek ways to soothe the uneasiness within our bodies, to numb the discomfort within our hearts, and it's easy to overindulge in "feel good" activities to counter the overwhelm of our work. We seek connection and comfort because we want to feel better, but our attempts to feel better are often self-soothing practices that have become an automated, conditioned response to stress. They may work in the moment but have longer-term impacts that can lead to burnout or at least make us more susceptible to it. When we do this, we succumb to what Freudenberger and North call "false cures"—actions that feel good in the moment and provide short-term relief but that can have longer term consequences.

> You may turn to a "false cure" to change your inner environment, to make it livable and to temporarily mask the symptoms. You're then able to return to your burnout path with renewed vigor, unaware that the "false cure" has camouflaged and exacerbated your underlying condition. By going along with the "false cure" solutions, you may be blinding yourself to the fact that you're propelling yourself deeper into the Burnout Cycle and becoming further alienated from that which is really needed. (Freudenberger & North, 1985, p. 18)

Understanding the root causes of our rush toward false cures is the start of being able to better identify why we are drawn to them and to notice when we are camouflaging the underlying condition of burnout. In her book *Widen the Window* (2019), Dr. Stanley calls them pseudo-regulators, or activities we seek out to sooth our unease or overwhelm that truly provide relief within our nervous systems, but in the long term have the opposite effect and keeping us in a loop of habitually seeking soothing outlets rather than addressing the root causes of our discomfort or overwhelm. There are many false cures we can use to disguise what we are feeling by overindulging or restricting ourselves; comfort food, retail therapy, and happy hour are a few common ways we try to reconnect and self-soothe.

Comfort food can be a great way to nourish our bodies and maintain our health. However, if we fall into overindulging in comfort food (or any kind of food) to ease discomfort, we may accidentally find ourselves locked into disordered eating habits. In the TV show *The Closer*, Kyra Sedgwick's character, Detective Brenda Johnson, has a candy drawer in her desk, and she stress eats chocolate while she solves murder cases. I found myself drawn into a similar food-reward related habit when I started doing home visits as a social worker. I was often scared out of my mind (which *just now, as I write this*, I am realizing was probably a secondary trauma response to the death of a social worker, which I shared in Chapter 1), so I would sit outside the home in my car and hype myself up by reminding myself that there was a scared child who had to live in that house . . . all I had to do was visit. Audre Lorde's quote about daring to be powerful was my mantra: *it became less and less important whether I was afraid*, I still had to do the home visit.

To ease my fear and soothe my nerves after a home visit, I would treat myself to a chocolate milkshake and fries, using the dopamine hit and serotonin boost as a reward. This worked fine when I was doing one home visit every few weeks. But eventually I started doing one home visit a week, then multiple visits each week, and then sometimes multiple visits each day. Every time, I would get myself a milkshake and fries—sometimes more than once a day. As you can imagine, self-soothing with sugary, salty, fast food didn't serve me well for long. My skin started to break out and I gained weight. Gaining weight isn't bad (no toxic diet culture here), but gaining weight from unhealthy eating habits negatively impacted my health. As a result, my joints ached, and I had trouble sleeping. Many helpers, healers, and change-makers become prediabetic and/or have high blood pressure or high cholesterol from using comfort food to ease their stress. It was a true false cure, in that it worked in the moment to make me feel good and give me a nice little dopamine boost, but over time it had negative impacts that made my burnout worse.

Retail therapy is like comfort food, in that it gives us the same endorphin rush of pleasure. I would buy things that made me feel good, and I loved the adrenaline rush of a bargain, finding the perfect planner or mug, or finding a gem among racks of clothes. The challenge was, once I got the thing home, it lost the luster it had in the store, and I was left with stuff I didn't really need and a feeling of guilt for spending money I didn't need to spend. And you better believe I got defensive if anyone questioned my spending habits, because I *deserved* those things. A girl can never have too many mugs (or plants or books or planners), right?

Buying things to feel better in the moment often leads to clutter or hoarding—tendencies that can put us in a financial crisis of our own making. My retail therapy habit ended in $23,000 in credit card debt (accumulated over five years) that I ignored until it became a burden in my life and in my relationships. Poverty and living paycheck-to-paycheck creates a certain energy in our bodies, and I didn't like the way it felt, let alone the realization that my attempt at self-care was actually hurting me and negatively impacting my financial future. This false cure supports a continuous cycle of mindless capitalism, which is especially hurtful when we are already underpaid for our work. Retail therapy not only failed to truly relieve my work stress, it also created more personal stress. I'm happy to share that I consolidated that debt, paid it off, and have been debt free ever since. Financial stability is possible if we don't fall into the trap of retail therapy as a false cure for the stress in our work.

Happy hour after work can be a fun way to connect with colleagues in a different environment and allow us to relax a bit outside of our professional roles. This is often the space where folks feel safe to role-swap or unmask. One of the domestic violence agencies I worked with often had happy hour on Fridays after work. Soon, they went to happy hour on Thursdays and Fridays. Then they added Wednesday because, why not? Some folks even went on Tuesdays—but never

Mondays (because, solid boundaries. . .). After a while, drinking became the only way they could find peace from the heaviness of their work. While drinking with colleagues discharged some of the stress of the work, eventually some of them fell into addiction, and a culture of alcoholism grew in the organization. It also created a division among the staff who joined in and those who didn't, which became a breeding ground for rumors about what certain folks did when they were drinking, which caused tension and disrupted staff cohesion.

The raw truth is that happy hours after work can lead to addiction and isolation from colleagues who may try to separate themselves. Addiction can also eventually lead to divorce or family discord. What starts as a socially acceptable way to hold the weight of our work, and one that is encouraged by colleagues and society, can end up being a false cure, causing disconnections that spread beyond work into our personal relationships. I once met a woman who shared that the year she won Teacher of the Year for her county—she was putting down a bottle of wine every night. It had become the only way she could hold the heaviness of her work as an middle school teacher. I also know a veteran police officer who won a local hero award while in the throes of addiction and risked losing his wife and children because of it. Luckily both of these helpers were able to seek help, find recovery, and keep their jobs and families intact.

> *Being a first responder was tough. But being a sober first responder was a thousand-layer cake of pain.*
>
> —Jennifer Murphy, *first responder*

For some folks, alcohol isn't the drug of choice, and food or shopping isn't their vice. Some use cannabis, psychedelics, opioids, or other drugs (prescribed and street) to numb out from the pain of our work. Others enjoy gambling, adrenaline sports, or body modification to distract from their work. These latter coping strategies are common in high-stress, public-facing roles, such as lawyers, politicians, and first responders. Destructive patterns can emerge and create addictions, eating disorders, and accumulation of debt. Again, these things "work" in the moment to distract us but can have long-term negative effects if we're not conscious of our engagement in them or we don't understand *why* we're engaging in them. The key is to allow ourselves opportunities to actually feel and process the pain and unease we feel in our work as helpers, healers, and changemakers rather than trade our discomfort for false cures that keep us stuck in that frustrating burnout cycle, like the churning of a washing machine.

REBALANCE WITH BOUNDARIES

> *The root of self-care is setting boundaries: It's saying no to something in order to say yes to your own emotional, physical, and mental well-being.*
>
> —Nedra Glover Tawwab, *Set Boundaries, Find Peace*

Part of our self-regulation is learning how to balance the stress in our work as helpers, healers, and changemakers. The term *work/life balance* is annoying because it's simply not possible. Work/life balance suggests that they are on equal footing, but work is simply one part of our whole life picture and our life (family, friends, community, self, etc.) should be highly prioritized over our work. When we are out of balance, one aspect of our lives (usually our work) can take over. Once we put work in its proper place in the larger perspective of our lives, the challenges we face in our work become more manageable and no longer have the power to negatively impact who we are and how we move in the world.

As helpers, we may have weak boundaries because our desire to help overrides our ability to see the benefit of having solid delineations. This can leave an opening for aspects of our work (strong emotions, traumatic content, etc.) to bleed into our personal lives. Creating solid boundaries (professional/personal) is one way we can rebalance our work when things get out of hand and our work takes over our lives. I often share with my students that boundaries are the way we communicate to others how to engage with us and how we want to be treated. They are not brick walls, but fences that can be changed and moved whenever the boundary is no longer serving its purpose. What you hold as a boundary today might be different than the boundary you held last year or the one you will need next year. A boundary you have at work might be different from one you have at home. Boundaries you hold with coworkers might be different than the ones you have with clients, which will be different from the ones you hold with family.

When we are regulated, we can know what we need and create meaningful boundaries that keep us balanced and healthy. When setting boundaries, we need to be clear and direct about our expectations and the actions we will take if our boundaries are violated. To do that, we have to know ourselves and understand our needs so we can set helpful, meaningful boundaries that allow us to preserve our time, energy, and attention. This means we have to rid ourselves of our people-pleasing and self-sacrificing tendencies and have the courage to hold our boundaries when they are tested. That said, we need to be firm and consistent in enforcing our boundaries. "No" is a complete sentence, and we never have to justify it. There are several types of boundaries to consider if we want to rebalance our time, energy, and attention.

Physical boundaries dictate the physical contact we have with others and include personal space, touch, and privacy, which impact our relationships with others. **Emotional** boundaries include limits on how much time and energy we give to certain people or situations, helping us to say "no" and to avoid taking on other's emotional states. **Intellectual/cognitive**, boundaries protect our thoughts, beliefs, and opinions by limiting how much personal information we share about ourselves and keeping us from feeling like we have to agree with others or justify ourselves to others. **Material** boundaries set limits on our money and belongings, allowing us to choose to whom we lend money, how we spend, and what we share with others. **Time** boundaries can help us manage our time and avoid overwhelm by setting limits on our work time and personal time and can help us prioritize our self-care. **Sexual** boundaries are limits around our sexual engagement, needs, and desires that include consent, our ability to explore safely, and taking ownership of our sexual fulfillment. While we may not see how sexual boundaries apply to our work, having strong sexual boundaries keeps us from inappropriate engagement with those we serve. **Energetic** and **spiritual** boundaries help us keep our peace and stay regulated by protecting our empathy from being exploited and giving us the space and protection to stay open and vulnerable rather than closing off and hardening. Creating boundaries around our care is a vital radical self-care practice that can protect us from burnout.

Over my years of engaging in radical self-care, I have found ways to understand and implement boundaries that work for me, specifically personal, professional, energetic, and spiritual boundaries. For me, this includes understanding the window of tolerance, what we need to stay within our scope of practice, the difference between caring for others versus *carrying* for others, and what it means to protect ourselves by armoring up. The following four sections are examples of these categories of boundaries as they relate to our work as helpers, healers, and changemakers.

WINDOW OF TOLERANCE (PERSONAL BOUNDARIES)

> *This mind–body system we share with our ancestors was optimized for short bursts of energy expenditure for immediate survival followed by longer periods of recovery, for longer-term tasks like healing, reproduction, and growth.*
>
> —Elizabeth Stanley, *Widen the Window*

Each of us has a threshold of emotional arousal, an optimal zone in which we don't feel too under stimulated nor too overstimulated. This is our window of tolerance, and it helps us mediate our emotional energy, so we don't get too bored or too overwhelmed. The window of tolerance is a way to illustrate the limits of our nervous system to handle the high or low levels of activity or arousal we experience through the emotions and content we are exposed to in our work. Experiences of stress and trauma that cause dysregulation are considered to be outside of our window of tolerance.

Our brains and bodies can handle quite a bit of fluctuation in and out of our window of tolerance, if we are able to return to the optimal zone of regulation within a reasonable time. We can experience something very arousing or activating and then come back to homeostasis, back within our window. Or we can experience something that shuts us down or immobilizes us for a period, then we come back to a state within our window (Siegel, 1999). The wider the window, the more choices we have for regulating our emotional states, buffering us from the negative impacts of stress and trauma. The key to self-regulation and having helpful personal boundaries is knowing our window of tolerance; this can significantly help us to manage challenges and mediate the impacts of stress and trauma. There is a visual description of "zones" that can help us understand how the window of tolerance affects us:

Below the window (understimulation/hypoarousal): We feel disengaged, bored, tired, and unmotivated. Learning, remembering, or making decisions can be challenging when we are feeling sluggish and can't stay focused. When we're below our window of tolerance, minor stressors can easily trigger us, and we become irritable or withdrawn, which makes us avoid challenges but also closes us off to new experiences and new ideas.

Above the window (overstimulation/hyperarousal): We feel flooded with emotions and easily overwhelmed. Fear, panic, or rage can show up quickly and we often feel driven by these strong emotions rather than being in control of them. Similarly to being understimulated, we may have difficulty thinking clearly or making decisions. Instead of shutting down, we may act impulsively, do or say things we don't mean, and find ourselves in a shame spiral that keeps us disconnected from others.

Inside the window (optimal arousal): We are calm and focused. We think clearly and stay alert and engaged. We are in a space where we can learn, problem-solve, and interact with others most effectively. We are resilient and able to handle stress and challenges without feeling overwhelmed, we can bounce back from setbacks within a reasonable time frame and we can adapt to change. When we are inside our window of tolerance, we are emotionally regulated, able to experience and express emotions in a healthy way; we can self-regulate to calm ourselves when we're feeling anxious, angry, stressed, or upset.

Our window can be narrowed by some of the life experiences we endure, like childhood trauma (ACEs), shock trauma in adulthood (traumatic individual or communal experiences), and chronic stress and relational trauma in daily life via our lifestyle and the occupational choices we make (Stanley, 2019). We have already discussed the impact of ACEs and acute trauma as well as the impacts of chronic stress in our lives, and our window of tolerance is created based on these experiences. But our window can be widened using our attention, by noticing when we are outside our window and actively engaging in the recovery process to bring ourselves back into our window. Ways our bodies can discharge the weighted energy of dysregulation are by shaking, swaying, crying, laughing, yawning, or taking deep belly breaths.

The premise of the window of tolerance is not to subject ourselves to more BS or bureaucracy, but the more arousal states we are aware of (stress, trauma and triggering) and the more experiences we can handle within our window (self-regulation), the better able we are to focus our work in a way that won't cause harm to ourselves, our loved ones, or those we serve. When we can remain within our window of tolerance, the stress and trauma we come across in our work has a boundary and is kept in its proper place. The goal is to widen the window because, as Elizabeth Stanley, PhD, shares, "the wider our window, the easier it is to find agency, function effectively during stress, and recover afterward" (Stanley, 2019, p. 23). Radical self-care practices help us widen our window so our work does not take over our lives and we have a sense of agency to keep clear boundaries between work and home, minimizing disruptions to both and keeping burnout at bay.

SCOPE OF PRACTICE (PROFESSIONAL BOUNDARIES)

All our will, all our work, all our competence will sometimes not be enough. This means that, in time, the practitioner must develop the capacity to accept lack of success—normative failure—as a component of the work.

—Thomas M. Skovolt and Michelle Trotter-Mathison, *The Resilient Practitioner*

One way to stay within our window of tolerance and buffer ourselves from emotional dysregulation is to stay within our scope of practice as helpers, healers, and changemakers. Our scope of practice is a professional boundary that delineates what work is ours to engage, encourages us to keep things in perspective, and helps us to prevent overwhelm. The urgency of our work can trick us into thinking we have to be everything and do everything for those we serve, which can lead us well out of our scope of service. While we may initially be able to get more done this way, eventually we realize that we are well beyond our scope of service or our scope of competence (i.e., the additional skills we have that may be complementary to our work but outside of our professional scope), and that can either frustrate us or cause real harm to those we serve. It can feel good to be able to find solutions and reach certain outcomes by doing more than we should, but it will also ensure an eventual burnout.

By knowing the boundaries of my work, I know when to release matters that are outside of my locus of control, my scope. For example, as a social worker, I do not give medical or legal advice. I refer clients/students to the professionals in those areas, and I stay in my lane. This keeps me safe from professional liability, but it also keeps me from taking on too much work or stress that simply isn't mine to hold. My work with families experiencing homelessness can be challenging because the needs are so vast and go beyond safe housing, but if they need help with fighting an eviction or accessing medical care, I will exhaust myself trying to extend beyond my professional ability. This is a perfect opportunity for collaboration with other helpers, healers, and changemakers. It is vital for us to remember that *we did not create all the trauma and suffering in the world, and it is not our job to fix it all.*

Staying within our scope of practice can also save us a bit from the heartache or lack of success we face in our work. A doctor may experience the death of a patient even after applying lifesaving treatments. A public defender may experience the conviction of a client even after putting forth a strong case for their innocence. A teacher may experience a student dropping out even after implementing several interventions. Once we've done all we can do within our scope of practice and competence, we must let it go and know that we have done all we could. Staying within the boundaries of our scope of practice removes the burden of feeling like we must do it all and allows us to accept the outcomes of our work and to begin again from a place of boundaried engagement. It also reminds us that *we are here not to save or rescue anyone but to encourage their agency and empowerment.* Knowing the parameters of our role and what falls under the purview of others can help reduce our sense of overload and overwhelm, helping us stay within our window of tolerance and buffering us from burnout. We always have the option to widen our scope of practice by engaging in ongoing education and learning new techniques, theories, and practices which help us grow in our work. This can be a form of radical self-care as well.

CARE WITHOUT CARRYING (ENERGETIC BOUNDARIES)

We may instinctively want to take away another's pain, but that's not healthy for us. I've learned to be present for my patients and workshop participants without shouldering their discomfort.

—Judith Orloff, MD, *The Empath's Survival Guide*

The energy we expend caregiving in our work as helpers, healers, and changemakers can exhaust us. We may be unable to disengage from the cycle of caring and empathic engagement in our work. We see and hear very difficult realities, and it is our job to show up to support those traversing oppression, injustice, and other systemic challenges. We hold both the macro system failures and the micro impacts of those failures as we engage, attune, and provide care to those we serve. This can cause us to hold a lot of other people's fear, hope, sadness, grief, terror, frustration, and other strong emotions that surround our work.

When we hold onto the emotions of others, we not only feel responsible for helping them, we also feel responsible for their lack of progress, relapse, recidivism, or failure to meet the outcomes of their treatment plans or goals. Holding on to those strong emotions of others can also impact our ability to truly help them, as Paul Bloom points out in his book, *Against Empathy*, "If I feel your pain but don't know that it's your pain—if I think it's *my* pain—then I'm not going to help you" (2016, p. 173). Energetic boundaries are one way we can balance our empathy and guard our hearts to protect us from the heaviness of our work. One such energetic boundary is the understanding that *we can care for others without carrying the weight of their struggles and trauma: we can care without carrying.*

In the summer of 2018, I attended a conference for educators at Stanford University put on by A Black Education Network (ABEN). Brother Wekesa Madzimoyo, cofounder (with his wife Afiya, MSW) of the AYA Educational Institute, spoke in a presentation about the weight Black women carry for others in the community. He reminded us that we can care for people without carrying the weight of their pain or challenges. When he said, "You can care without carrying," my whole body felt a relief that flowed from the top of my head to my toes, my face softened, and my shoulders released. This concept, that we can care for others without carrying their traumas, their stresses, their suffering, is one that shifted every cell in my body. At that moment, I realized that many of my episodes of burnout came when I was feeling too much and carrying the stress and trauma of others without recognizing that it was possible to care deeply for those I serve without carrying around those emotional burdens.

This is an invocation, a mantra, that we can speak out loud when the weight of our work is too heavy and we've been carrying too much. *We are still a good helper, healer, or changemaker when we engage our energetic boundaries and put down the work.* Whenever I begin to feel that I am carrying the weight of a student, parent, or coworker, I remind myself out loud that "I can care without carrying," and I instantly feel the weight lift and the protection of this energetic boundary in action. I invite you to do the same and notice what shifts, both in your work and in your well-being, when you acknowledge that you can care without carrying.

ARMORING UP (SPIRITUAL BOUNDARIES)

> *There is courage in witnessing someone else's pain without joining in and inhabiting it. You realize that your suffering is not their suffering and theirs is not yours.*
>
> —Omar Reda, MD, *The Wounded Healer*

When our work gets stressful and we're overwhelmed, we instinctively protect ourselves by physically and emotionally armoring up. Physical ways our body tries to protect itself when we experience stress include clenching our teeth (bruxing), breathing shallowly, panic attacks, muscle constriction, and constipation. We may also notice some emotional armoring, such as leaning into overwork, being critical of or correcting colleagues, or elevating ourselves above others as a form of protection. Sometimes the armor we put on is impenetrable, and it may also block off our ability to feel positive emotions, pushing us toward isolation and burnout. We may hold so tightly to armoring for so long that it impacts our health, and sometimes we don't notice the armoring has happened until the tension is released. What develops as a form of self-protection can become a pattern of self-destruction if we're not aware of it. This is the kind of armoring Dr. Brené Brown (2018) warns us against in her book *Dare to Lead*, suggesting that our armor can keep us from vulnerability but also from connecting with others and being strong leaders.

Rather than shielding ourselves from vulnerability, however, I suggest that by engaging a *spiritual boundary of intentional armoring*, we can protect our energy and put clear boundaries around our empathic engagement to guard our hearts from the heaviness in our work. Warriors wear armor to protect their vital organs. The very act of putting armor on is a sort of ritual; thus it acts also as spiritual preparation for the battles ahead. We can use armoring in the same way, donning items that make us feel safe and protected as we do our work as helpers, healers, and changemakers. These items might be a uniform or badge we wear for work that we imbue with a sense of responsibility to uphold our professional ethics and maintain our scope of practice (boundaries supporting boundaries). Maybe our armor comes in the form of jewelry, pins, or meaningful pieces that remind us of our mission.

I wear mala bead bracelets, hoop earrings, and rings that read "courage" and "love" as my armor every day, and I notice their absence if I forget to wear them. One of the bracelets I wear, with letter beads that spell out "GRATITUDE," was a gift from when I did an intervention with a group of girls in a North Carolina middle school. When I armor up with these pieces of jewelry and my sweater with "Social Worker" emblazoned on it, I feel a sense of power to do the work well and not be deterred by the challenges that come up.

Over the decades, I have met colleagues who wear a cross or other religious symbol around their necks, who place dream catchers, hamsa hands, or other religious symbols over their doorways, who burn candles, incense or palo santo between clients, and who wear their hair in a specific bun or braid pattern that brings a sense of confidence and courage. In one agency I worked at, one of the counselors had a small window that looked onto a brick wall, but she lined that windowsill with crystals that picked up the little rays of sunlight that would come through, illuminating her space with rainbows and flickering lights. Whatever you choose to put on as your armor, imbue it with the power to protect you from the stress and trauma you may absorb throughout your day. We can create a protective shield that allows us to navigate the challenges in our work as helpers, healers, and changemakers while staying connected to ourselves and others. In the next chapter, I will discuss rituals and ways to bring the sacred into our everyday lives, but for now, consider the pieces you might put on as your own intentional protective armor.

Knowing our window of tolerance, understanding our scope of practice, remembering that we can care without carrying, and armoring up can all help us create the boundaries we need to protect ourselves in our work. When we put these boundaries in place, we create a space to move beyond survival mode. These practices provide reinforcement to keep us regulated and balanced so we can thrive in our work.

RADICAL TENDENCIES: REGULATE AND REBALANCE

Since emotional regulation is the critical issue in managing the effects of trauma and neglect, it would make an enormous difference if teachers, army sergeants, foster parents, and mental health professionals were thoroughly schooled in emotional regulation techniques.

—Bessel van der Kolk, *The Body Keeps The Score*

A radical self-care practice can prevent and buffer us from the full impacts of traumatic events we may be exposed to in our work as helpers, healers, and changemakers. We can engage in radical self-care practices to lessen and learn how to navigate the impacts of trauma on our nervous system. Stress management, emotional regulation, regular exercise, healthy sleep habits, social connection, and a healthy diet can all help promote balance in our sympathetic and parasympathetic nervous systems and enhance our overall health and resilience.

THE POWER OF BREATH

You're going to take a breath anyway: use it to your advantage.

—William E. Dorman, *Restoring the Healer*

When you're in the middle of a crisis and someone tells you to take a deep breath, you want to punch them in the face. Understandable. But . . . have you tried taking a deep breath? I've read many articles and books about change that suggest telling someone to breathe when they are dealing with oppressive systems is "self-righteous bullshit," but those of us involved in the fight for liberation know how vital the breath is to resistance and to reclaiming our power.

We can't speak, shout, chant, or sing without the breath. Our breath is something we take for granted until it's impaired or taken from us. Anyone who has asthma or has had a panic attack knows this well. Given the recent past, those who have had COVID-19 might also know this well. Our breath is impacted by our work, so it must also be something we take seriously in our healing. Yes, there are real system issues, oppression is real and is breathtaking in its impacts, but when we are doing our work, our role is to be present and hold space in that moment with intention for change. Sometimes our breath is all we have. My breath was all I could take with me into the jails and prisons I've worked in and visited. My breath is all I have when I take a family to a homeless shelter. My breath helps me show up to serve others, and it acts as a protection for my nervous system.

The breath is also the most powerful way to regulate the nervous system, making it important that we respect and care for the breath. Our breath can shift our nervous system from fight/flight/freeze to rest/digest/express, stimulating the vagus nerve and promoting relaxation. Our breath gives us the power to respond, rather than react, to situations of injustice. Our breath allows us to slow down and clearly see the manipulations and lies of capitalism. Our breath is the most radical tool we have to combat the challenges we face and to realize the radical change we desire. When we practice these breathwork techniques regularly, even just 2 minutes daily, we create a nervous system resource that we can call upon in times of crisis. No, the breath doesn't immediately change the challenge before us, but having the ability to regulate our breathing does change how we show up for the challenge before us. Everything starts with the breath.

Deep belly breathing can help reduce stress and improve focus and attention. It can also lower blood pressure and improve sleep. This is just what it sounds like; take a deep breath from the belly and move it through the body. Here is a simple way to access deep belly breathing:

- Find a comfortable position and close your eyes or soften your gaze so that you are not looking directly at anything.
- Place one hand on your belly or abdomen, just below your rib cage, and the other on your chest.
- Take a slow, deep breath in through your nose, feeling your belly expand and your chest rise.
- Exhale slowly and completely through your mouth, with your lips slightly open, feeling your belly sink and your chest lower.
- Repeat as many times as needed until you feel a state of calm come over you or you notice a bit of clearing in your mind. By focusing on the rise of the inhale and the drop of the exhale, you can bring your nervous system into a state of calm regulation.

YOGA FOR REGULATION

> *Trauma-informed yoga supports survivors in activating their parasympathetic nervous system and creates more space for safety, rest, growth, and abundant joy.*
>
> —Zahabiyah A. Yamasaki, *Trauma-Informed Yoga for Survivors Of Sexual Assault*

The Art of Yoga Project is a nonprofit founded by Mary Lynn Fitton, a former nurse, after she witnessed the amount of dysregulation her young patients often carried. I have had the honor of working for AYP for more than a decade, facilitating yoga and radical self-care practices with young girls involved in the juvenile justice system (Harris & Fitton, 2010). These young women had very traumatic life experiences, but despite their dysregulation, or maybe because of it, they loved essential oils, guided meditations, and yoga. More specifically, they found regulation and balance in postures that challenged them, whether balancing poses, inversions, or the ability to find stillness during Savasana.

Yoga is one of eight limbs of contemplative practice as shared in Chapter 2. As Gail Parker points out in her book *Transforming Ethnic and Race-Based Traumatic Stress with Yoga*, "Yoga seeks to harmonize all systems of the body, mind, and spirit to attain clarity of mind, inner peace, and freedom from emotional pain and suffering" (2022, p. 25). The regulating and rebalancing power of yoga cannot be understated. Yoga is the practice of blending physical movements with our breath, shifting our nervous system balance from more "fight or flight" sympathetic activation to more "calm and connect" parasympathetic activation. When we practice yoga, it takes us away from the stress of our work and the busyness of our lives, and our nervous system encodes the sense of calm and control, bringing us back to regulation and balance even when we are away from our yoga mats. This is why the practice of yoga is a radical self-care practice.

Here are some ways we can regulate and rebalance with yoga:

Balancing Poses: Balancing poses in yoga can activate the vagus nerve, shifting our nervous system into the rest/digest mode, engaging our muscles, and focusing our attention so we don't topple over. When we practice a balancing pose, we create a space to experience physical balance. When we combine these poses with a calming breath, our nervous system imprints on this balance, and we can call upon it during times of stress. Tree Pose, Boat Pose, and Warrior Poses I, II, and III are examples of balancing poses we can do to experience physical balance and bring that sense of balance into our emotional experiences as well.

Inversions: Getting upside down can seem like a daunting task, especially as we get older. But inversions include more than just handstands, headstands, and forearm stands, fun as those may be. Child's Pose and Legs-Up-the-Wall Pose (also known by its Sanskrit name Viparita Karani) are also considered inversions because our head is slightly below our hearts when we practice these poses. By situating our bodies with our heads below our hearts, we activate the rest and digest mode of the parasympathetic nervous system, relax the muscles, and stimulate the lymphatic system, keeping our immune systems functioning well. I highly recommend using this pose at home at the end of a long workday or right before you go to sleep.

Savasana/Resting Pose: Meditation, lying in Savasana (the resting pose at the end of a yoga class), and guided imagery are all ways to experience full-body stillness, bringing us into a state of calm connection. Once we have this experience and our nervous system is used to it, we can engage that sense of calm connection anywhere we are by recalling the full body response. If lying down is not comfortable, we can give ourselves lots of pillows and bolsters for comfort or do Savasana sitting upright. Allow yourself to sink into the floor or the mat under you, feeling the ground support your weight, knowing that you are supported by the earth beneath you.

CUTTING CORDS FOR BOUNDARY SETTING

Cutting cords is a regular practice of releasing the connections, or "cords," we have that connect us with others (i.e., people, places, situations, or beliefs) that no longer serve us or them. In our work as helpers, healers, and changemakers, we often engage with and connect with those we serve to provide effective care. This is the beauty of our work, but if we are not creating clear boundaries, we may carry these ties and energetic connections with us long after the helping relationship is over. This can drain our energy and invade our emotional space, so regularly clearing them can keep us open and receptive. Here's a simple cord cutting meditation we can do to clear these old connections, helping us *care without carrying* and making space for new connections:

- Find a comfortable position and get into a relaxed state. Begin deep belly breathing as described on page 148.
- Visualize the person, place, situation, or belief you want to release. Visualize the cord connecting you to them. It might be a thick and heavy rope, symbolizing the strength of the attachment, or it might be a thin and wispy string, signifying a weaker connection.
- Now, imagine taking a powerful tool and decisively severing the cord. As you cut the cord, feel the weight lifting off you as the connection is severed. You can visualize the cord dissolving, being washed away, floating away, or returning to the other person/place/situation with love and compassion.
- Take another deep breath and as you begin to open your eyes, take a moment to express gratitude for the experience(s) you had with the other person, place, situation, or belief and gratitude for the release you've achieved.
- Gently bring your attention back to your body and physical surroundings, reconnecting with the present moment.

BALANCING NATURE CURES

During everyday life, a feeling of comfort can be achieved if our rhythms are synchronized with those of the environment.

—Florence Williams, *Nature Fix*

You don't even need a forest [to forest bathe]. Once you have learned how to do it, you can do shinrin-yoku anywhere—in a nearby park or in your garden.

—Dr. Qing Li, *Forest Bathing**

Many of us intuitively know that nature heals. We may be instinctively called to go outside and notice that when we do, we feel better. Nature creates a safe container to help us protect our energy. Fresh air, sunlight, and the sounds of nature shift our nervous system, allowing us to release stress and recharge our batteries.

Forest bathing: Known as *shinrin-yoku*, this is an experience of being fully immersed in nature. The goal is to immerse your senses in nature, taking in the sights, smells, sounds, and feelings of the forest around you. This can be a walking meditation that can help regulate the body and bring calm.* (*Dr. Li's book has beautiful visuals of what forest bathing can look like, if you need another book in your collection.*)

Earthing: There is science behind the idea that when our bare feet are on the ground, we tap into the electromagnetic energy of the Earth, and that helps ground our nervous system. We pick up the electromagnetic frequencies from the Earth and they can sync with the frequencies in our body. This is what creates the sense of grounding and connection when we have our feet firmly planted on the Earth. We can do this very simply by placing our bare feet on grass. Whether in a forest or in a small patch of grass in our yard or in a local park, we can begin to feel the energy of the earth and take advantage of the regulating pulse of the earth beneath us.

Blue therapy: Being in, on, near, or listening to water has beautifully positive impacts on our nervous systems and can create new neural pathways in the brain. The gentle rhythm of waves crashing on the shore can activate the calm state of the parasympathetic nervous system, as can the rush of a waterfall. Wallace Nichols came up with the term *blue mind* (which is also the title of his book), which, he claims, is a "mildly meditative state characterized by calm, peacefulness, unity, and a sense of general happiness and satisfaction with life in the moment" (Nichols, 2014, p. 6).

ARMORING UP

As a kid I watched *Mr. Rogers' Neighborhood* and found myself drawn to the opening, where he comes into his home and changes his sweater and shoes. His shift between being out in the neighborhood to being in his home, the simple practice of changing clothes, was a way of creating a boundary between work (assuming he was coming home from work) and home. As we consider our own pieces of armor, let's think about the pieces we would want to put on in our work as helpers, healers, and changemakers, and that we can take off when we get home.

Creating rituals can provide an energetic or spiritual shield of protection before going into spaces we know will challenge us or bring trauma. In the next chapter, we will look at ways to ritualize our armoring up. But for now, consider what you will put on that can have a protective effect while you're at work? Try one or all of these suggestions as your armor, and see if it helps mitigate some of the stress in your work.

Clothing: If you wear a uniform to work, is there a way to imbue it with a scent? Or can you add pins, ribbons, or other adornments that would feel protective? If you don't have to wear a uniform, consider other articles of clothing that make you feel safe and protected in your work. This can include shoes and other items of clothing. Maybe a formal suit or a specific set of cufflinks puts you in your power; maybe a comfortable sweatshirt works because it keeps you cozy; maybe what works for you is a well-fitted undergarment that makes you feel invincible. Be creative here but stay within your professional boundaries.

Jewelry: As mentioned before, religious jewelry can give us a sense of divine protection in our work, but we can also use common jewelry items to give us this same sense. Rings, earrings, necklaces, bracelets, belts, and body jewelry can become pieces of armor that, when we wear them, bring a sense of safety and protection when we work. Please be sure that wearing jewelry is safe for your work environment before wearing any—having a necklace or earring pulled off by a precocious child or angry client can be very painful.

Hair: In many cultures, hair has spiritual significance and is cared for with various rituals. How we wash, detangle, style, and care for our hair is done with intention. Hair is very personal and part of our image. It can also be protective and a source of pride, so how we wear it when we work is important. I know many women who wear their hair in protective styles like buns or braids when at work for safety and logistical reasons, but also as a way of armoring up for the work. Then, when we are home and in our own space, we can figuratively and literally let our hair down. During weekend rituals, I use wash day to deep condition my hair and apply protective oils in preparation for my work week. When I wash my hair during the week, I imagine the water cleansing the stress of the work day as I watch the bubbles go down the drain.

Name tags or badges: If you wear a badge or name tag on a lanyard, maybe decorating it with meaningful pins and ribbons would give you a sense of protection. My husband used to tease me about the number if "cause ribbons" I collected (blue for child abuse, purple for domestic violence, teal for sexual assault prevention, etc.), but they truly were my armor. Maybe your armor is a pin given to you by an organization or a family member, or a pretty lanyard someone made for you. If you're a first responder or work in a secure building, maybe the badge itself gives you a sense of power and protection.

GROUNDING THROUGH DRUMMING

Grounding our bodies can be done with rhythm and beats, as our nervous system naturally responds to external vibrations. We will explore this more in Chapter 4, but for now it is important to remember that our internal regulation is a rhythm that can be supported from outside of our bodies through drumming. Many ancient cultures and indigenous tribes use drumming to begin ceremonies, invoke community, and give a sense of grounding and calm. In modern music, drums are used to keep the beat and bring us into a trance-like state when we listen to them. This is why we unconsciously respond to our favorite songs by bobbing our heads, tapping our toes, and feeling a sense of calm connection.

Drumming can be a solo activity or a communal one, the latter also engaging our need for social connection. Slower, steady rhythms with deep tones tend to be more calming, while faster, complex rhythms can be more stimulating and energizing. We may notice our bodies seeking rhythm by tapping our fingers, tapping a pen or pencil on the table, or tapping our feet. This may be a sign that our body is craving some level of regulation or rebalancing. These rhythmic, steady sounds downregulate our sympathetic nervous system and activate our parasympathetic nervous system and bring us that calm we seek.

REFLECTIONS

- Where, when, or with whom do you notice yourself becoming emotionally dysregulated? Reflect on this over a period

of days, weeks, or months to see if there are specific people, places, or situations that dysregulate you more than others.
  - Write down your observations and review them after some time to see if you can find any patterns to your dysregulation.
- When have you found yourself in survival mode, and how did you know?
  - How does being in a state of hypervigilance impact your nervous system (and your physical/mental/emotional health, relationships)?
  - What can you do to rebalance/bring yourself back to a well-functioning regulated state and stay there?
- Can you identify your threat/trauma response stages (flock, fight, flight, freeze and fawn)?
  - Do you have one strong response or a few different responses?
  - Can you identify where this/these response(s) originated?
  - How do these responses show up for you today?
  - How do they show up in your work?

Consider what boundaries you need to put in place to balance your time, energy, and attention, using these boundary categories: physical, emotional, intellectual/cognitive, material, time, sexual, energetic, and spiritual:

- What boundaries do you currently have that are strong and should be kept?
- What boundaries do you currently have that are weak and should be strengthened?

4

RHYTHM AND RITUAL

Creating a container for challenges and change

> Ritual helps us remember and reestablish our inner rhythms and to place them once again in accord with the deeper cadence of our soul.
>
> —Francis Weller, *The Wild Edge of Sorrow*

The deeply rooted power of rhythm and ritual in our work cannot be understated. Whether it's the rhythmic cadence of each school year or the ritual of welcoming your students to the classroom; the rhythmic chant at a demonstration or the ritual of a restorative circle; the rhythmic beeping of medical machines or the sanitization ritual of the operating room. Our work often creates rhythms and rituals, sometimes called policies and procedures, that provide a sense of familiar repetition to help us hold the weight of the work.

The intention of this chapter is to bring your awareness to already present rhythms and to offer new ritual practices, both of which may guide you to that deeper cadence and to reconnect with your underlying passion for helping, healing, and change-making. These rhythms and rituals can serve as additional protection in our work. I will first share a few ways conscious rhythms and rituals show up in our work and then invite you to bring more rhythm and rituals into your practices of radical self-care.

THE POWER OF RHYTHM

A lot of my work in schools has been in doing interventions with and for students who need a little extra love. Many of them come to my attention when their circumstances and needs are known, and sometimes they make their needs known through their behavior (as we all do). One student came to my attention after refusing to give his cell phone to his teacher. There was an interaction that turned hostile, and the student left the classroom with some choice words. Not uncommon in secondary education.

The student was brought to my office and we started talking. I introduced myself and got to know him a bit. There's always a story, always a function to the behavior, and this kid had one. After a few visits and sussing me out, as all teenagers do, he shared his story. One parent died and the student came to live with another family member. The other parent was never in the picture, or at least wasn't someone this young man cared to mention. He expressed having mixed emotions about his parent's death, as there was a protracted illness and there was a lot of abuse, from what I could piece together. And the cell phone had that parent's case on it, which is why he didn't want to give it up.

The student kept coming to my office during passing periods and spent lunch in my office for weeks, often grabbing a cup of noodles and a bag of chips. We kept the conversation light, often about his classes or if he was making any friends. I keep a crystal sound bowl in my office (shocking, I know) and one day this student went right for the bowl. He asked if he could play it, so I took it out and showed him how to play it. He placed it on his palm, struck the bowl and played it until it resonated. He let the sound of the bowl fade out, slowly lowered it, and looked up at me with tears in his eyes.

"Ms. Nicole, why do I feel like I want to cry? I didn't even cry at the funeral and now I feel all the tears."

He said he felt a vibration through his body that "zapped" his heart, but he was worried that if he started crying he might never stop. I told him he was allowed to cry and that the bowl he rang was an F note, said to resonate with the heart chakra. We had a great talk about his conflicting feelings about not being sad over his parent's death and being almost happy that this parent was dead. I gave him space to express these emotions without judgment and he was able to begin to process his loss. Over the course of the school year, he eventually stopped coming to my office for lunch.

The experience with this student and the sound bowl is an example of how rhythm and vibration can affect our emotional state. Vibrations are used for healing in the medical field to break up kidney stones, dissolve tumors, and jumpstart parts of the brain, but vibrations and rhythm can also be used for healing in our work as helpers, healers, and changemakers. Rhythm can bring us together, create social connection, encourage a sense of belonging, and connect us despite any language or culture differences. Sometimes the power of rhythm can be obvious and sometimes it is a subtle vibration that we may not even notice until it is disrupted or stopped. When we can connect to rhythmic patterns or resonate with vibrations in our environment, we can impact our physical and emotional well-being.

RHYTHM AS REGULATION

All of life has a rhythm. Did you look at cells under a microscope in school? Every cell is in motion, vibrating with life. There is a frequency and cadence to life down to the cells in our bodies, which make up the organs and organ systems that keep us alive. Consider all the different vibrations in our bodies: our heartbeat, our breath, the blood pulsing through our veins. Each of our biological systems and the organs within them have their own vibrations and are interrelated and interdependent, creating our whole being. We also have circadian rhythms, reproductive rhythms, and digestive rhythms. Like a symphony, the rhythms in our bodies generally stay in sync, and if one aspect is off, causing disharmony or dysrhythmia in our bodies, we notice. This is the root of illness and disease.

Nature has a rhythm too. There are solar and lunar cycles that, for us, create the changing rhythms of the seasons, the tides, the blooming of flora and fauna. Even cities, suburbs, and rural areas have rhythms that are different from each other. There's a vibrational quality to the relationships we have with each other, such as a vibration of excitement at seeing one person but a vibration of irritation at seeing another. Stress produces a different vibration from hope. There's a notable difference between the energy we feel in our body when we're on vacation versus the energy we feel when doing our taxes. Our nervous system regulation and staying within our window of tolerance is also a rhythm of shifting in and out of the fight/flight and the rest/digest. All of these vibrations form the frequencies of our lives, and the rhythms regulate us as individuals and communities.

These vibrations are impacted by who we work with, how we work, and even where we work. I was presenting radical self-care to a group of teachers in a local jail. Many of them were hearing about vicarious trauma for the first time. After the presentation, one of them pulled me aside and shared, "I can't believe I've never heard of this vicarious trauma, but now all my random illnesses make sense. . . . I work all day in a locked facility, and I never even thought about how it changes everything in my body."

Those of us who work within physical systems of oppression (e.g., jails, prisons, juvenile detention centers, residential facilities, group homes, and even some schools) are often the most oblivious to the ways our workplaces shift our vibrations. We may notice how differently we feel when we're in the office during the work week versus how we feel on the weekends at home, but the nuance of small shifts in our vibrations throughout the workday are often invisible to us. This lack of awareness is not an accident. I think it's what these systems intend, and I also think it's part of our caregiving trauma adaptations to feel obligated to show up for the work no matter how horrible it makes us feel sometimes. The dysregulated rhythm of the work we do and where we do our work can become insidious and ultimately show up in our lives as burnout. Being aware of and harnessing the power of rhythm can help us stay regulated and feel safe as we work and can help us mitigate burnout.

There is also a protective rhythm and cadence to our work. If we work 9 to 5 (or any 8-hour shift), have weekends off (thank your unions), get summers off (for students and some educators), or have the option to take a sabbatical, we can use these times "off" to enjoy some relaxation and recover from the stress of our work. We can use that time to engage in hobbies, connect with family or friends, spend time in nature, or be by ourselves. This allows our bodies to recalibrate to a rhythm of calm or rest that we can take with us into our work when we return.

TRANSFERENCE AND COUNTERTRANSFERENCE

Shamanistic cultures view illness and trauma as a problem for the entire community, not just for the individual or individuals who manifest the symptoms. Consequently, people in these societies seek healing as much for the good of the whole as for themselves.

—Peter Levine, *Waking the Tiger: Healing Trauma*

Transference is often used to describe the emotional energy exchange in professional relationships between therapists and clients, but it can also be applied to the work of helpers, healers, and changemakers who are not therapists. Transference is the unconscious projection of thoughts, feelings, and attributes onto us by those we serve, seeing us through a distorted lens of their former traumatic experiences. Since we are human, we have an unconscious emotional response to the transference of those we serve, called countertransference. Basically, transference is their trauma residue, and countertransference is how we respond to their trauma residue based on our own trauma history. And since both are happening unconsciously, we can get into a cycle of constant triggering and dysregulation, unaware of what is happening. I experienced a situation of transference and countertransference between a teacher and student that perfectly illustrates this.

A student left class and was brought to my office by our campus supervisors. The teacher had asked students to put their phones away and the student refused. When the teacher came over to the desk and demanded the phone be put away, the student stood up, threw some books off the table, cursed the teacher out, and left the classroom. When I met with the student, she said, the teacher "just hates me for no reason" and told me that she found herself irritated by everything the teacher said and did. When I asked her if the subject matter of the class was challenging at all, she shared that she really liked English class and might want to become a writer someday but that this teacher was making the class unbearable. The teacher was equally irritated by the student and we all agreed to have the student stay in my office during that class period for the rest of the week, so I could help figure out the issue and how to get her back to class safely.

When I spoke with the teacher, he angrily shared that he had been teaching for more than a decade and "didn't deserve to be treated like that by anyone, let alone a student." His anger shifted to distress when he shared that the student's outburst had made him feel unsafe in his own classroom and that he felt disrespected by being cursed out in front of the whole class. He told me how hard he had worked on the lesson plan for that day and how excited he was for the work they were going to do and how this student's behavior shut it all down. I shared with him a little bit about this student's past challenges, and he shared that he had similar challenges as a youth. When I told him that the student really liked his class but felt like he hated her, he softened a little and said, "She does great work, but I just can't work with that attitude."

As I gathered a little more information from each of them, the signs of transference and countertransference became very clear. The day of the incident, the student had received a text message from her mother, with whom she had a strained relationship and interactions with whom the student described as mostly being "her standing over me and yelling about what I was doing wrong," I asked the teacher where he was standing during the original incident in the classroom and he said he was standing over the student's desk, pointing his finger and telling her what she was doing wrong . . . and I realized what was happening.

I offered the teacher and student a restorative mediation so she could get back to class and repair some of the harm created by the incident. During that mediation, the student was able to reflect that when the teacher stood over her, pointing his finger and raising his voice, she was triggered and projected those feelings about her mom onto the teacher. The student was able to share with the teacher that she really liked his class but that sometimes his behavior did remind him of how her mom treated her. Her transference caused her to react in a way that then caused the teacher to react from his own triggering.

The teacher shared with the student how much time and effort he put into the lesson plan that day and that when she stood up and cursed him out, it made him feel threatened. His countertransference caused him to kick the student out of class, reinforcing the student's feelings of abandonment and rejection. Ultimately, each was able to see where the other was coming from and made some agreements. The student agreed to keep her phone in her backpack during class, and the teacher agreed not to stand over her or raise his voice. Understanding each other's triggers and bringing awareness to the transference and countertransference that occurred made it possible for them to mend their relationship and come to a respectful agreement. The student was able to go back to class, ending the semester with a B+. Had they not been made aware of this dance of transference and countertransference, they would have continued to dysregulate each other, the school year would have been very challenging for the student, and the teacher would have been on a path to certain burnout (and possible early retirement).

CONSCIOUS COREGULATION

In fact, from the time you were very little, you've had people who have smiled you into smiling, people who have talked you into talking, sung you into singing, loved you into loving.

—Fred Rogers, *Won't You Be My Neighbor?*

In the previous chapter, emotional regulation and our duty of care in the form of self-regulation was discussed. We must take responsibility for our own regulation in our work as helpers, healers, and changemakers because of the prevalence of transference and the importance of coregulation in our work. Coregulation is the phenomenon wherein our nervous system manages our emotions through interaction and engagement with others. More specifically, coregulation is the process, or product, of interactions between two or more nervous systems causing a shift in the regulation of each individual's nervous system. This happens in relationships when one person's mood is contagious and pulls the other person into the same state of emotional regulation, like the Mr. Rogers quote, we are "smiled into smiling." We sync with those around us, catching the rhythm of their emotions.

One aspect of emotional coregulation can be called *emotional contagion*, when our emotional affect is spread to those closest to us or we "catch" the emotions of those we serve. This is how contagious laughter spreads among a group, but we may also experience this with strong, negative emotions. Catching the emotions of others isn't always bad, but because of the challenges in our work, we must guard ourselves enough to maintain a state of calm regulation. We may find ourselves in a dark mood after interacting with someone who is depressed, or we are irritated and realize it is because we just got out of a session with someone who was angry. This can be dangerous and, like compassion fatigue, can be a precursor to burnout (Rothschild & Rand, 2006).

Those we serve come to us in a state of dysregulation or may become dysregulated during the course of our work with them. Depending on the nature of our work, we may face hostility, angry outbursts, violent reactions, or negative emotional states in those we serve. In addition, our work is emotionally demanding when an intervention stops working, a client in recovery relapses, or we witness widespread recidivism. These circumstances require that we be even more calmly rooted and deeply settled in our nervous system, even more emotionally regulated, so they can regulate with us and gain some sort of grounding. The good news is that when we have well-regulated nervous systems, they are powerful enough to positively impact the nervous systems of those around us.

> *When one settled body encounters another, there can be a deeper settling of both bodies. But when one unsettled body encounters another, the unsettledness tends to compound in both bodies.*
>
> —Resmaa Menakem, *My Grandmother's Hands*

Regulation is a rhythm. Dysregulation is also a rhythm, albeit one that can cause long-term damage if it goes ignored or unchanged. Dysregulation is a form of altered vibration in our nervous system, and as mentioned previously, when we aren't paying attention or we've been in the work too long, these dysregulated vibrations can cause illness. If one bodily system is dysregulated, it impacts the other systems and can eventually cause our whole body to shut down. Our heartbeat can become dysregulated, our breath can become irregular, our blood vessels may become constricted causing our pulse to elevate, and even our skeletal muscles may cramp or twitch. Almost every helper, healer, or changemaker I know has felt their eyelid twitch uncontrollably after a stressful period at work. Dysregulation has a very real impact on our bodies and our health.

Because of the power of these interactions, we must be careful of how we seek regulation with others. Dysregulation in our work causes us to instinctively seek relief through coregulation, but as I cautioned that community care is healthy only if the individuals within that community are healthy, the same applies for coregulation. We must be sure we are coregulating in healthy ways so we can be the solid source of regulation for those we serve rather than being a source of dysregulation or being dysregulated by them.

Sometimes we find what feels like coregulation with our colleagues or family members in venting. Venting is cathartic, and sometimes it just feels good to rant about how bad the healthcare system or the state of public education is or about our micromanaging boss or our annoying coworker, but these rants can incubate cynicism.

> Cynical colleagues spread a highly infectious disease. This disease of negativity is easy to catch. It is also a seductive

> disease because, when one first gets it, he or she feels better. Some venting can be very helpful, yet when negativity faucet is fully open, hope fades. Cynicism, in the air, is especially dangerous in the relationship-intense helping fields. (Skovolt & Trotter-Mathison, 2016, p. 90)

Similarly, we can be so excited to find someone who shares the same struggles that we use trauma dumping and trauma bonding as an attempt to regulate ourselves. Trauma bonding, in this context, is a way of finding common connection with our colleagues through shared traumatic experiences, but this strategy can lead to codependency instead of coregulation, leaving us in a state of vulnerability. Codependency is the abandonment of the self for the other, whereas coregulation is the attunement to the self and to the other. By attuning to others, we can recognize their emotional states and notice when their trauma is being triggered and/or we are experiencing transference. This process requires a level of empathy sufficient to recognize the feelings of others, avoid emotional contagion, and defend against our own countertransference so we can deepen the settling in our nervous system, which will in turn help to settle theirs. The attunement and empathy of coregulation with others creates a rhythm that involves our nervous system and the concepts of resonance and entrainment. Ultimately, we must be conscious about our ability and responsibility when it comes to coregulation.

RESONANCE AND ENTRAINMENT

> *When we use sound to become entrained with our personal physiological rhythms—our heartbeat, pulse, brain waves—we also build a bridge that can transport us from a tranquil state to a deeper level of spiritual realization, one that links us with the infinite energy and spaciousness of the universe.*
>
> —Dr. Mitchel Gaynor, *The Healing Power of Sound*

Rhythm has the power to heal through two main mechanisms: resonance and entrainment. Resonance and entrainment are musical concepts, but they impact our physiology, biology, and emotions. Resonance speaks to the natural vibrations of objects, which have the ability to spark vibration in another object. When two tuning forks are placed near each other and one is activated, the vibrations from the activated tuning fork will activate the other one, causing both to vibrate even if the second tuning fork hasn't been touched. In the sense of regulation and coregulation, resonance speaks to the ability of an organism's vibrational frequency to match another external vibrational frequency, like an emotional contagion. Emotional contagion can be dysregulating, but we can engage this same resonance for healing and transformation by using sound to "change disharmonious frequencies of the body back to their normal, healthful vibrations" (Goldman, 2002, p. 14).

Entrainment is a synchronization (attunement) between two vibrating entities, like when two pendulums are engaged at different times but eventually begin to swing in sync; when everyone on the dance floor moves to the same time when the beat drops; and when women in the same household find their menstrual cycles sync after spending time together (though this is scientifically disputed). In terms of regulation via entrainment, the object that is vibrating at a stronger frequency pulls others of less powerful frequency into harmony with it so that both objects now vibrate to the rhythm of the stronger rhythmic frequency (Goldman, 2002).

When we experience dysregulation, we notice the disharmony in everything we do, and we begin to feel "out of sync" with those around us and with our work, making it hard to connect or create community. As Dr. Mitchell Gaynor explains in his book *The Healing Power of Sound*, "when we say we feel 'out of synch' [*sic*] or 'not on the same wavelength' with somebody, what we really mean is that we're not entrained with that person" (Gaynor, 1999, p. 71). It takes the courage of one strongly regulated nervous system to move us toward healing. We can coregulate this way when we show up to our work with a regulated nervous system so those we serve can then regulate to our frequency. "Just as it is possible to set an object into its own natural motion through resonance, so it is possible to restore the natural vibratory frequencies of an object that may be out of tune or harmony" (Goldman, 2002, p. 13).

Transformation and healing happen in the spaces where we feel resonance with others and can experience rhythmic synchronicity between our nervous systems. We do this by being conscious of our own needs and attuned to the needs of others. "The client cannot function psychologically at a higher level than the helper" (Skovolt & Trotter-Mathison, 2016, p. 91), making it imperative that we show up more regulated than those we serve. In our work as helpers, healers, and changemakers, entrainment helps us synchronize our breath and heartbeat with those we serve, which makes them more comfortable with us and better able to come into their own space of calm regulation. "Many psychotherapists already know that one way to calm a client's panic attack is to breathe slowly themselves. The panicked client will often, unconsciously, synchronize his breathing, slowing it and becoming calmer in the process" (Rothschild & Rand, 2006, p. 105).

When we show up grounded, present, and attuned to ourselves, it will show in our tone of voice, our posture, our affect, and how we engage with others. Being grounded, present, and attuned to ourselves empowers us to avoid the trap of transference and countertransference and to be able to stand in a state of calm that allows others to entrain or regulate. This is where healing happens in relationships, through the synchronicity, resonance, and entrainment of regulation. This is the essence, the rhythm, of coregulation, and where the supportive power of rituals has a role to play.

THE RHYTHM OF RITUAL

Ritual is not compatible with the rapid rhythm that industrialism has injected into life. So whenever ritual happens in a place commanded by or dominated by a machine, ritual becomes a statement against the very rhythm that feeds the needs of that machine. It makes no difference whether it is a political machine or otherwise.

—Malidoma Patrice Somé, *Ritual: Power, Healing, and Community*

Ritual elicits a certain vibration, a pitch, that enables us to individually or communally connect with the sacred.

—Frances Weller, *The Wild Edge of Sorrow*

Burnout from stress and overwhelm creates dysregulation that pulls us out of our natural rhythms, creating a dysrhythmia in our bodies, hearts, and work. When we are thrown off rhythm or things become overwhelming, turning to routines can give us a small sense of control, help us create a safe container for our lives, and bring us back into resonance with ourselves and our world. When we bring ritual into our routines, we include an aspect of meaning to the things we do in our lives. If we are to hold the space of being more regulated than those we serve, we need a foundation of routines and rituals that help us acknowledge and release the weight of compassion fatigue, vicarious trauma, and moral injury that we may experience in our work.

Routines are sets of actions we perform in a certain order. This may be our daily coffee run before work or our stop at the gym on the way home from work to release the stress of the day. The repetition of our routines give us a sense of safety and predictability that can act as a steady foundation when we have little control over other aspects of our work. Some of the routines in our work are called policies or protocols and act as boundaries for our work. These may be standardized intake forms, courtroom procedures, or bell schedules in a school. We may also have meeting norms or professional ethics that guide the work we do in a more contained and routine way. While we may not be able to easily change these aspects of work, we can bring intention to these practices to create more regulated states for ourselves as we engage in the more benign parts of our work. When we turn our routines into rituals, they have the power to deepen the care we give ourselves and they allow us to care for others without harming ourselves.

Rituals are intentional approaches to the routines in our lives that add an element of the sacred to our everyday activities. Some rituals require simple awareness and others require more elaborate ceremonies. By calling in the sacred aspects of the ways we bring meaning to our lives, we are participating in what brother Somé calls a "spirit-based activity performed by humans" (1997, p. 53). We can scan our lives for areas we can bring sacredness into our everyday actions. Rituals and routines can orient us to an aspect that exists beyond our work, beyond our roles and identities, and beyond our separateness or isolation.

There are three main kinds of rituals: communal rituals, family rituals, and individual rituals. Community rituals might be religious ceremonies, cultural celebrations like parades or festivals, civic events like town hall meetings or service projects, and shared community rituals like community gardens or neighborhood trick-or-treating for Halloween. Family rituals might be holiday traditions, milestone celebrations like birthdays and graduations, or weekly routines like family game nights or movie nights. Individual rituals might include morning or evening routines, spiritual practices like meditation or prayer, or finding focus in creative practices like journaling, sketching, or dancing.

We may also engage in rituals at work, bringing intention to the transitions or actions we engage in every day. These rituals help us clear stagnant or stuck energy in our spaces and can bring some containment with and for those we serve. Some examples of clearing or containment rituals:

- Washing hands before and after every patient.
- Taping the top of the doorway on the way into the classroom in the morning.
- Lighting some incense between each client (if it is safe to do so).
- Ringing a bell to open a session or have a bell on your door to announce arrivals.
- Changing pictures, pillows, or other decorations in your space (if you have them).
- Cleaning or clearing a space at specific times (first of the month, holidays, seasons, etc.).

These rituals are interdependent and each is as important as the others (Somé, 1997). Our individual rituals remind us that we are in constant coregulation with those in our communities and in our families. Our work rituals remind us that the work we do as helpers, healers, and changemakers is sacred. Rituals bring us comfort, certainty, order, and connection to something larger than ourselves, and they can alleviate pain and facilitate healing. There is no end to the power of ritual when we engage it consciously.

CREATING SAFE CONTAINERS

> *Ritual space needs containment. The better the container, the deeper the work. In short, a container is sort of like the overall effect of the emotional, physical, and spiritual boundaries around an event or space. Strong containment allows for big emotions.*
>
> —Laura Mae Northrup, *Radical Healership*

There is wisdom in these ritual practices that we can tap into: as we engage in radical self-care, we can shift our numbing routines into more aware, mindful rituals. This is how we use the power of rhythm to create safe containers as we face the challenges in our work as helpers, healers, and changemakers. The power of rituals requires that we keep the space and intention protected and sacred. "Safe containment means keeping the space away from any impurities, and unwanted intrusions" (Somé, 1993, p. 38). We do this by cleaning the physical space we intend to use in the ritual (this includes cleaning ourselves), protecting the space during the ritual, marking the timing of the ritual with an opening and closing, and providing space for processing after the ritual. We can also create containment internally, if we find ourselves in a place where we cannot find quiet or control the space we are in. This can be done by closing our senses off with headphones, like in a crowded café, or we can engage in a repetitive action with our body, like tapping our fingers, humming, or a craft like knitting or crocheting.

In 2003, I was a graduate student at the University of Connecticut studying social work administration. My internship included working with the local rape crisis coalition, which I would begin working for upon graduation. As part of this work, I was sent to attend a few conferences on sexual assault and domestic violence. At one of the conferences, I was in a session listening to a panel of defense attorneys share their "witness examination" techniques during rape trials (basically, how they put the victim on trial instead of the perpetrator). As I sat, attention rapt but also feeling a heaviness in the pit of my stomach, I turned to the back of the room and saw a group of four older women knitting. I immediately wrinkled my nose in disgust. "How can they be so rude!? These people are up here presenting, and those women are back there not even paying attention, just doing their own thing. . ." I will also admit that back then I would have described these women as "old," but now that I'm in my forties, I hilariously realize they were probably . . . my current age. Perspective, right?

During a break in the conference, I asked one of the women what she was making. She was making a scarf and hat for her grandchild. Without prompting, but demonstrating that she sensed some judgment on my part, she lovingly told me, "I've been coming to these conferences for a long time, and these sessions can be really heavy. I've found the best way for me to absorb the content they're sharing is to be doing something steady with my hands."

What I didn't know then, was those women were onto something radical. They may not have been aware of what they were doing at the neurological level, but they could sense their actions were creating a buffer to the vicarious trauma of the heavy content they were absorbing at the conference. By sitting comfortably, allowing their hands to be occupied in rhythmic mindful awareness as they listened to the presentation, *they created a safe container within their own nervous systems* where they could absorb the information that was shared without having to experience or hold onto the stress response the content may otherwise have created.

What these women did was an act of radical self-care, and those of us doing helping, healing, or change-making work can use techniques like this to prevent vicarious trauma. The *rhythm and ritual* of knitting created a *repetitive pattern of regulation* that allowed these women to *care without carrying* the weight of the work and *avoid dysregulation.* These women were veteran advocates and community organizers who met annually at these conferences to share this time together. They created what Babette Rothschild calls an oasis by engaging in an activity that demands some level of concentration and attention; a way to take a break from the traumatic content they were taking in (Rothschild, 2000). They figured out how not only to stay sustained in this work but also to create community and to engage healing rhythms as a way to bring safe internal containment to their traumatic environment.

RADICAL TENDENCIES: RHYTHM AND RITUAL

Our bodies and minds are very responsive to the rhythms of nature. Indigenous cultures knew this and expressed it through their rituals. They knew to stay close to nature and to listen to the rhythms and vibrations of the natural world. They turned routine activities into sacred rituals that held the needs of their communities. We have access to this same natural wisdom when we honor and incorporate these practices into our radical self-care.

SACRED PAUSE

> *Engaging the process of societal healing requires us to reach for individual moments of radical awakening, and to move those moments from the silence and stillness into the walk of our daily lives.*
>
> —Sherri Mitchell, *Sacred Instructions*

In the same way, there is power in these rhythms and vibrations, there is a power to stillness. Sometimes, the only way we can identify the vibrations or the dysregulation in our lives and in our work is to become still and pause. Becoming still and pausing were some of the more challenging aspects of the COVID-19 pandemic quarantine: we were forced to stop everything and stay home, creating an immediate stillness that many of us were not prepared for. Intentionally removing ourselves from the rush of work or the overwhelm of a busy schedule gives us the space to notice what isn't working and to make decisions from a place of calm instead of chaos.

We can take a pause between class periods, patients, meetings, or client calls to reclaim a bit of calm throughout the workday. I often take a deliberate pause before I start my workday, between calls to guardians or service agencies, before and after I meet with a student or family, and at the end of my workday before I turn off the lights and leave the office. You can create a more sacred pause in your day by starting or ending the day with a calming practice or finding intentional space during transitions within your work day.

SOUND HEALING

When we utilize singing bowls or practice toning, the fine, harmonious vibration instantly entrains us to the frequency of our own essence.

—Dr. Mitchel Gaynor, *The Healing Power of Sound*

When I think of rituals, music and sound come to mind as ways to create some form of containment. Religious rituals often include singing or hymns, family rituals might include singing the birthday song or including music during a graduation party or holiday gathering, and we may include music and sound into our individual rituals as well. Here are a few ways to bring sound healing into our radical self-care practices.

Crystal Bowl Sound Healing: When we think of "sound healing," many of us picture the white crystal sound bowls we see in yoga studios or online. These are bowls made of crystal, usually quartz, and are played in succession during a sound bath or sound healing session. This healing power is what my student felt when he played my F note crystal bowl in my office. Each bowl resonates at a specific frequency and plays a pure tone note that is said to be connected to an energy center in our bodies called chakras, or a spiritual system of guidance used in various religious traditions (Hinduism and Buddhism):

- C note = Root chakra; grounding, security, and connecting to the Earth; I am.
- D note = Sacral chakra; internal organ health, creativity, and pleasure; I feel.
- E note = Solar plexus chakra; personal power, self-esteem, and emotional life; I do.
- F note = Heart chakra; love, healing, compassion, and immune system strength; I love.
- G note = Throat chakra; truth, communication, and self-expression; I speak.
- A note = Third eye chakra; intuition, imagination, and the senses; I see.
- B note = Crown chakra; higher consciousness, spirituality, and connection; I understand.

If you don't have access to crystal sound bowls, you can attend a sound healing at a local yoga studio or access them on apps like YouTube, Insight Timer, Calm, and Spotify. Other ways we can tap into the healing power of sound and vibration: The vibrations of voice intonation can be another form of sound healing, making chanting and singing forms of voice intonation that have some amazing healing qualities. Chanting and singing protest songs has been a longtime tool of connection and revolution, used by Martin Luther King, Jr., Fannie Lou Hamer, Peter Seeger, and others. While it can be used to bring people together collectively, it can also be an individual healing modality. In the 2021 documentary *Tina*, Tina Turner shared that she used chanting to survive and heal from the well-known hardships she suffered during her life. Chanting, breathing, repetitions, and tones can ease pain and help us survive even the most daunting situations.

When we repeat a mantra, we engage the relaxation response and soothe our nervous system. If you don't have access to chanting, or if it feels a bit silly to you, try watching a video or listening to others chanting, which can have similar positive effects. There are recordings of chanting from various cultures and religious groups that can help you release stress. Our nervous system relaxes just from hearing it. Even plants respond when Gregorian chants are played for them.

- **Chanting:** Chanting is a practice and mantra is the tool used in the practice. Both can help us create containment during a ritual. Find a mantra that works for you. It can be something simple that you create, it can be something standard from an already established practice, or it may be given to you from a meditation community. Repeating a mantra for a specific period of time while seated comfortably can bring us into a tranquil mental state and help our nervous system rest.
- **Singing:** We all notice how we feel when a certain song comes on: we know the lyrics, and we feel compelled to belt it out. Singing can bring a sense of community when we engage in cultural songs, patriotic songs, protest songs, or gospel songs. I've never seen someone sing with a frown on their face, even if they were off key. We can all be Beyonce in the shower or in our car, so sing like no one's listening, and enjoy the state of calm it brings you.
- **Vocalizing/Humming:** Vocalizing the sound "voo" is a physical way to activate the vagus nerve and bring calm to our bodies. It can stimulate the pain-relieving chemicals in our nervous system to help us toward healing. I used this practice during my healing from a hysterectomy when my abdominal incision made it difficult to do much physically. The steady, gentle vibration of "voo" in my body gave me an immediate sense of relief and release. When we hum, the vibrations in our chest act to break up stuck energy and activate our parasympathetic nervous system, shifting us into a state of calm.

ALTARS

Consider creating an altar in your office or workplace as a ritual of containment. Creating a space like this in your classroom, office, or break room can allow members of your community to share items of significance to them, bringing a piece of their history or lineage into the space. This practice does not have to be religious in any way, simply a communal offering of engagement, awareness, and solidarity. The altar can represent the different people, cultures, or skills in the community and can bring focus and intention to the space.

In restorative practices, an altar is created in the center of the circle as a way to bring focus and intention to the circle. Participants can be asked to bring an object that has meaning to them and share it in the center of the circle. Then, when sharing occurs, those objects can be used as talking pieces to facilitate respectful communication and spark reflection. This is a beautiful way to bring the individuals into a sacred communal practice.

OPENING AND CLOSING RITUALS

Many of us have work rituals we may not even identify as such. Releasing the energy we pick up throughout the day is a good practice for staying regulated and rebalanced.

- **Opening:** Begin your day by setting an intention that prepares you for the work ahead. This may involve meditation, prayer, or simply taking a few moments to breathe deeply and connect with yourself. You might use a phrase, a quote, a song lyric, or even just a word. Put it on a Post-it note, and look at it throughout your day as a gentle reminder.
- **Closing:** Create a closing ritual to leave work behind and transition into your personal life. This might involve reflecting on the day's experiences, expressing gratitude, or writing down your thoughts and feelings in a journal. You could use

the time it takes to commute home to wind down and leave work at work, so when you show up at home, you are ready to connect with family and friends.

- **Opening:** Setting up our classroom or office space at the start of our work cycle (e.g., new school year). This allows you to create the space for your students to learn and for you to have access to the tools you need to teach. It can also allow you to create an oasis for yourself within your classroom.
- **Closing:** Deep cleaning our classroom or office space at the end of a work cycle (e.g., end of the year, graduation). This process can allow you to cleanse your space, purge old documents, and ensure you have what you need for the next group of students who will come through your classroom doors in the fall. It can also act as your closing ritual to the school year.

- **Opening:** Morning rituals, like listening to music, taking a walk, or preparing our breakfast/coffee/tea with intention. How we start our morning can impact the quality of the rest of the day, so be intentional here. Checking emails or listening to the news first thing in the morning might put you in a negative headspace, so opt for movement or positive content that can set you on the right track. Mantras can come in handy here too.
- **Closing:** Evening rituals include listening to calming music, taking a sunset walk, reading a book, or playing a game with family can help settle us at the end of the day. We might eat dinner with the family, find quiet in a personal hobby, or engage in sleep hygiene by winding down for the night in a way that helps promote sleep. This can help close our day and prepare us to be rested for whatever we may encounter the next day.

PAIN RELEASE RITUALS

When things are out of control, some seek rhythmic patterns to contain the pain and overwhelm we feel, bringing a sense of ease and release. When nothing we try can cut it or none of these efforts seems to rise to the level of activation our nervous system requires, some turn to body modification to ease the pain.

- **Tattoos:** In many cultures, there is a long history of tattooing with ritual body art to mark milestones. The power of having our skin marked by another is one that we can harness in our radical self-care practice. When we get a tattoo, we are in community—even in resonance—with the artist doing the work and the lineages of artists they learned from. The vibration of the tattoo gun on our skin causes a release of adrenaline and dopamine that can only be described by those who have experienced it. I have noticed that I crave tattoos when I'm feeling beyond overwhelmed. The experience of vulnerability and invincibility I feel when being tattooed are like a cathartic release of all the pent-up stress and energy from my work. I have been lucky to find amazing female tattoo artists at both New York Adorned (New York, NY) and State of Grace (Japantown, San Jose, CA). In a way, my tattoos have also served as protection, a way I've "armored up" to do the work of helping. If this is something that you want to try, first be sure you know about the physical risks of tattoos. If you're still sure you want one, be sure to use an experienced and qualified tattoo artist who wears gloves, uses sanitary disposable equipment, and sterilizes any reused equipment, and be sure to choose a design that you will love forever.
- **Piercings:** When I was in graduate school, after finishing finals and nearing graduation, a fellow student asked me to go with her for a piercing. At that point I had only my ears pierced but was interested in more. I ended up getting my nose pierced, and I was shocked by the release I felt in my body once the initial pain subsided. Maybe it was from reclaiming my body or just the adrenaline rush, but the shift I felt in my body was instantaneous, I felt more connected to my body and suddenly understood why some people get lots of piercings. My ear piercings and nose ring have been my only forays into body

modification (besides tattoos), but I've heard from other helpers, healers, and changemakers that the element of control of pain during a piercing, as well as the "armor" of it, has helped relieve their stress and depression. Maybe there's something to this. As with tattoos, inform yourself about the physical risks of piercings, and if you still want to proceed, be sure to use only to use an experienced and qualified piercing artist who wears gloves, uses sanitary disposable equipment, sterilizes any reused equipment, and uses only hypoallergenic jewelry.

FIRE AND WATER RITUALS

A fire ritual is a place where things that interfere with our connection with our soul's purpose can be surrendered, and where fire can serve as a point of focus. The result of this ritual is usually a sense of orientation and even calmness symptomatic of a certain level of harmony with Spirit.

—MALIDOMA PATRICE SOME, *The Healing Wisdom of Africa*

In the previous chapter, Regulate and Rebalance, we discussed the impact nature has on our nervous system. Natural elements are important to our healing process, and we can harness the elements in a more intentional way to create rituals with the elements. Fire and water are two natural elements we can use to balance our nervous systems and connect with the higher calling of our work as helpers, healers, and changemakers. These rituals have been used in Native American, Aboriginal, and other indigenous cultures for centuries and can be used separately or together, like engaging in a fire ritual that ends with water being used to extinguish the flames or to cool off the body. Some fire and water rituals include:

- Lighting a candle or burning sage, incense, or palo santo (fire and smoke).
- Building a bonfire to sit near while telling stories.

- Writing down limiting beliefs and burning that paper in a fire or immersing it in water.
- Sitting in a steam room or sauna as a purification ritual.
- Pouring libations to honor those who came before us.
- Crying when sadness or grief hits.
- Immersion in a large body of water, like a cold plunge or ceremonial swim.
- Chanting or speaking positive incantations into a glass of water.

Japanese scientist Masaru Emoto studied the way water molecules are impacted by our words, thoughts, and feelings. His book, *The Hidden Messages in Water*, shared his findings that where there is dysregulation and distress, when harsh words are spoken, or when pollution is present, water molecules become distorted. But in the presence of love, kind words, and clear intentions, water molecules form orderly and geometric shapes. For example, frozen water crystals from natural spring waters appear perfectly geometric while frozen water crystals from contaminated tap water appear deformed. Words, thoughts, pictures, and music have the power to transform the shape of each molecule. "Water exposed to the words 'thank you' formed beautiful geometric crystals, no matter what the language. But water exposed to 'you fool' and other degrading words resulted in obviously broken and deformed crystals" (Emoto, 2004, p. 45).

PLANTS AND GARDENING RITUALS

[T]he presence of plants reduces illness and stress and changes people's perceptions of their place of work, increasing comfort, satisfaction, and performance. These effects are increased further still if the windows open onto green spaces.

—Marco Mencagli and Marco Nieri, *The Secret Therapy of Trees*

Houseplants became all the rage during the pandemic, and for a very good reason. Caring for houseplants and tending a garden have known positive effects on our nervous systems. Plants help filter and oxygenate the air and absorb pollutants, while seeing green in our spaces can calm our nervous system. We can also get this effect by having fresh cut flowers in our work space if potted plants are inconvenient or unable to grow in our workspace. There is research that shows time spent in or viewing nature, "green time," counters the negative effects of screen time: "In general, high levels of screen time appeared to be associated with unfavourable psychological outcomes while green time appeared to be associated with favourable psychological outcomes" (Oswald et al., 2020). There is something to the directive: "Go touch grass."

My Friday after-work ritual is to water my plants. I light a candle, turn on some music, fill my watering can, and walk from plant to plant, feeding it and checking its growth. Coincidentally, by including music, fire, and water into my plant watering ritual, it becomes more sacred and more powerful. It's an amazing way to rebalance my day, and it slows down whatever may still be vibrating in my body. It allows me to shift from the work week into the slow rhythm of the weekend and creates that necessary boundary between work and home.

Solo: If you have houseplants already, consider making their maintenance part of a new ritual. Light a candle or incense, play some music or a podcast (plants respond to classical music and chanting), and as you move from plant to plant, slow your breathing and notice the details in the plants. I close out my work week by watering my office plants on Friday before I shut down for the weekend, and when I get home I water my houseplants as a way of easing into home for the weekend.

Communal: Bringing plants and flowers into our workspaces imbues those spaces with a sense of calm. You could propagate plants from cuttings already in your space to share with colleagues or bring flowers from your garden (or the store) to liven up the space. My office, adjacent to our Wellness Center, is full of plants, and students and staff always remark how calm the space feels. Occasionally I set out cuttings from my spider and monstera plants for students and staff to take for themselves. It creates a sense of community and coregulation.

RHYTHMIC HEALING

Learning to knit, crochet, sew, paint, or use your hands in a rhythmic fashion can help buffer us from the impacts of stress and trauma. As I shared in the conference story earlier in this chapter, using our hands in a rhythmic way shifts our nervous system into a space where traumatic content cannot settle. During her treatment for breast cancer, Audre Lorde used the practice of eurythmics, the synchronizing of body movements to rhythm for healing. During her battle with cancer, author Suleika Jaouad painted daily from her hospital bed. When we engage in something that requires a bit of attention but not too much strain, we allow our bodies to resonate with the frequency of regulation. Some activities to consider:

- knitting, crocheting, weaving, or sewing
- painting, drawing or doodling
- origami, collaging, vision-boarding, or other paper crafts
- puzzles or card games, like solitaire
- playing an instrument (i.e., one you already know how to play)

NATURE IMMERSION

Although we can't always do much to turn off the barrage of stressors in our lives, we can try harder to get the restorative reprieves- from quick nature doses to longer ones—that give our thinking brains a chance to recover.

—Florence Williams, *The Nature Fix*

Nature can help us shift from the stress and overwhelm to a calm, connected state of mind. When we immerse ourselves in the natural world by taking walks in the forest, meditating by a body of water, or simply sitting beneath a large tree, we absorb nature's calming and restorative frequencies and can find the inner peace we need to counter the frenetic pace of our work. We can ritualize our time in nature by engaging our senses, touching leaves or trees, getting our feet in the grass or sand, and taking in all the beauty that surrounds us. We can also do our other rituals in nature, being careful not to disturb the ecosystem or leave anything behind. *Please be especially mindful and careful when using smoke or fire in outdoor settings.* If you don't live near woods or forests, rest assured, you can still benefit from nature. "The good news for city dwellers is that just fifteen to forty-five minutes in a city park, even one with pavement, crowds and some street noise, were enough to improve mood, vitality, and feelings of restoration" (Williams, 2017, p. 140). Consider these options:

- Take a sunrise or sunset walk to start or end your day with nature.
- Find a local park or reservoir area to have lunch or host a work retreat.
- Hold a restorative circle, picnic, or other ritual gathering in the woods.
- Listen to audio of a thunderstorm, ocean waves, crickets at night, or other nature sounds.
- Go camping for three or more days to allow your body to rebalance to natures rhythms.

REFLECTIONS

- What are the common rhythms in your life?
- Where and with whom in your personal life do you feel most "resonant"?
- What are the common rhythms in your work?
- Where and with whom at work do you feel most "resonant"?

- What are some everyday routines you engage in at home or at work?
- What are the important rituals in your life (if different from above)?
- Are there rituals that are part of your work? If so, what are they? If not, what rituals could you develop to be part of your work?
- How can you bring music or sound into your routines and rituals?
- How can you bring nature into your routines and rituals?

5

REST AND RESTORE

Providing space for deep release and revolutionary rest

> So often, we therapists, activists, and allies are focused on the negative impacts of oppression but neglect to fully attend to the protective and resiliency factors in our work. Yet one might argue that focusing more on innovative and personalized ways to foster self-care and resiliency might be one of the most important things we can do for ourselves and each other in the face of daily traumas, microaggressions, and other forms of systemic, interpersonal, and ideological oppression.
>
> —Christine Caldwell and Lucia Bennett Leighton, *Oppression and the Body*

> We center rest as a means for healing and liberation.
>
> —Tricia Hersey, *Rest Is Resistance*

One very clear symptom of burnout is insomnia or the inability to rest. Lack of sleep is also linked to a host of diseases and an increased risk of suicidal behavior (Bernert & Joiner, 2008). Rest, as a vital, radical self-care practice, is beginning to become more obvious. Many of us in the helping, healing, and change-making fields sacrifice sleep as a badge of honor, starting in our schooling for the work. Those in the legal and medical fields almost compete to see who gets the least sleep, while those in the education, nonprofit, and social service sectors seem to compete to see who can send the latest or earliest email.

I was presenting at a conference, and I asked a group of educators about taking sick days. Everyone in the room laughed and moaned at the same time. Someone spoke up and said the only time she took any sick time was when she had a double mastectomy after a breast cancer diagnosis, and she *still* felt like she had to work from the hospital! Someone else shared that he had to work on a grant application while his child was in the hospital getting chemotherapy. Others added similar stories of waiting until severe illness or near-death before taking time off and still feeling responsible for the work left to be done.

We know that suffering and crisis take no days off, so neither, we think, can we. Or at least that is how we are made to feel. We pride ourselves in taking zero sick days or in being able to survive on very little sleep, to pull all-nighters, and to get things done. I love that we can do this when it is important and necessary, but it is becoming the status quo for people in helping professions, and we cannot become complacent to this fact. We tend to create workplace cultures that mimic this "always on/no days off" mentality. When we take a day off, even a sick day, we are made to feel bad about it. Sometimes this is a very stealthily implicit understanding that when one person takes a day off, the workload doesn't go away but rather gets shifted onto someone else's plate. We may hesitate to take any time off, lest our workload create a burden on our coworkers.

When people take time off, take sick days when they are sick, and maybe even take a few mental health days each year, they are more productive. And while productivity isn't necessarily the goal, taking sick days or vacation days (if we're lucky enough to have them) allows us the rest and time away from our work that we need. Taking this time for ourselves also helps prevent burnout and turnover in our professions. Seeking respite and rest, which can be done with intention, is a way to recover from our work. My intention in this chapter is to give helpers, healers, and changemakers permission to take a rest and to convince them that rest is not just okay but necessary if we want to make real, lasting change in this world.

THE STRESS/SLEEP DEPRIVATION CYCLE

Within the brain, sleep enriches a diversity of functions, including our ability to learn, memorize, and make logical decisions and choices. Benevolently servicing our psychological health, sleep recalibrates our emotional brain circuits, allowing us to navigate next-day social and psychological challenges with cool-headed composure.

—Matthew Walker, PhD, *Why We Sleep*

Sleep is crucial to a healthy life, and it impacts almost every aspect of how we show up as helpers, healers, and changemakers. Sleep moderates our energy, our ability to problem solve, focus, learn, remember, regulate our emotions, and make logical decisions. When we can access good, restful sleep, we can show up for our work more regulated and grounded, so we feel more in control of our thoughts and emotions throughout our day. This allows us to make wise decisions, contribute good ideas, and exercise compassion for ourselves and those we serve. Sleep also helps us consolidate what we learned throughout the day and recalibrates our immune system, keeping us healthy and allowing us to remember important information (Sapolsky, 2004).

As described in Chapter 3, our nervous systems are tuned to spot stressors and act if there is a real or perceived threat. Navigating the world and interacting with society in general can activate a level of threat perception in our nervous system but the levels of stress and trauma in helping, healing, and change-making work certainly increase the speed and duration of that activation and have an impact on our physical, mental, and emotional health.

The work we do to regulate ourselves, our coworkers, our family members, and those we serve throughout the day can be exhausting.

We go home after a long day of work and, hopefully, look forward to having some down time and getting a good night's sleep. When it comes to sleep, the National Sleep Foundation (Hirshkowitz et al., 2015) suggests that most adults get 7 to 9 hours of sleep per 24-hour cycle. Some of us need more sleep and others need less, depending on our age and a few other mitigating factors. I work with teenagers often and encourage them to get as much sleep as they can, especially as their brains are forming and they are experiencing so many hormonal changes. Many helpers, healers, and changemakers find lack of sleep commonplace in our professions.

Our work creates a rhythm that may directly counter our body's own rhythms. Specifically, our circadian rhythms that tell our body when to be awake and when to sleep can be disrupted directly and negatively by our jobs. Even if we are able to mediate the stress and trauma from the content of our work, we may find that the pace and timing of our work can impact us just as severely. Night shifts, and shift work in general, can impact our sleep, throwing off our circadian rhythm. Certainly, working long shifts of 10–24 hours can significantly impact sleep, as can being on call, even if you're not actively working. Never knowing when the alarm is going to go off, when the next patient is going to roll into the ER, or when the hotline phone may ring is a particular kind of stress, and it impacts the quality of sleep we get.

> We are not a nocturnal species and if a person works at night or works swing shifts, regardless of how many total hours of sleep she's getting, it's going against her biological nature. People who work those sorts of hours tend to over activate the stress-response, and there is little habituation that goes on . . . night work or shift work increases the risk of cardiovascular disease, gastrointestinal disorders, immune suppression, and fertility problems. (Sapolsky, 2004, p. 234)

Lack of sleep can impact the quality of our work, decreasing our motivation and productivity as well as our creativity and inspiration for the work. It also impacts our ability to make sound decisions, which can lead us to make less ethical decisions, subsequently compounding our sense of failure or moral injury. Exhausted medical professionals are more likely to make a medical error or a misdiagnosis that can lead to injury or death for the patient. We are more likely to have job-related accidents and injuries, contributing more to workplace fatalities. The Chernobyl nuclear disaster in 1986 and the Exxon Valdez oil spill in 1989 were caused by sleep deprived operators, creating lasting, devastating global impacts (Walker, 2017). When we are overworked and under-rested, our work suffers and, by default, those we serve suffer too.

Getting enough sleep is a nonnegotiable aspect of our well-being, but our sleep is compromised by the work we do. When our sleep is constantly interrupted or disrupted by work, or a form of sleep abuse, it can even lead to death. There is even a word for it: *karoshi,* a Japanese term meaning death by overwork (see Chapter 1)—a cost of caring. *Karoshi* can cause a myriad of health issues: organs shut down, immune systems weaken, and infections, and other diseases can develop, including strokes, heart attacks, chronic pain, diabetes, skin conditions, infertility, and anxiety and depression. Sleep deprivation is used as a torture technique for a reason.

In his classic *Why Zebras Don't Get Ulcers,* Robert Sapolsky (2004) shares the many reasons sleep is so vital to our well-being, the critical impact stress can have on our health, and the frustrating sleep deprivation/stress cycle. Not getting enough sleep can cause stress, and being stressed can cause us not to get enough sleep. We've all been caught in this cycle, being stressed from work and unable to sleep, but then finding that our lack of sleep is causing more stress. Sleep involves an aspect of letting go of our thoughts, or at least letting go of the traumatic content and material we have interacted with during the day. If we are not able to release our thoughts, we can get stuck in a state of insomnia, where our bodies and brains never get the rest needed to repair and restore. The two main factors that cause chronic insomnia, compromising the amount and quality of the sleep we get, are emotional concerns and emotional stress (Walker, 2017). Insomnia can happen to anyone in any profession, but when it happens for us as helpers, healers, and changemakers, it can have devastating effects.

There are some headlines that underscore the devastating impacts of sleep deprivation on our fellow helpers, healers, and changemakers. In the United Kingdom in 2019, a dedicated National Health Services nurse who had "nightmares about work" committed suicide after the stress of working 12-hour shifts left her unable to lead a life of her own and contributed to a "downward spiral" (Wheeler & King, 2019). A study of teachers in Japan found that each month, teachers were working an average of 123 hours of overtime, beyond teaching their students, making them "vulnerable to overwork deaths" (DW News, 2022). And in 2023, after the Los Angeles Police Department saw four suicides within a 48-hour window. The widow of a sheriff's deputy, who served for more than 21 years, said it was the constant overtime forced on her husband that caused him to make that tragic choice. In an interview, his widow shared, "I told him [the sheriff] in the hospital he killed my husband. Working him overtime, overtime, overtime. All the time. Walking like zombies, everywhere" (Tokumatsu, 2023).

So how do we shift out of this stress/sleep deprivation cycle and into a more stable state of rest? We start by expanding our idea of relaxation to include active resting practices that move us beyond sleep but also can help our brains and bodies truly find the restoration we need to continue as helpers, healers, and changemakers. While they are similar, sleep and rest are not the same thing, but each has their own benefits. Sleep is a specific type of rest, but rest doesn't necessarily have to be sleep. Not all rest is sleep and not all sleep is restful. Sleep has a specific "protocol," and we usually have some routines or rituals around sleep. We don't often think of rest in the same way as sleep, but my hope is that by engaging in a radical self-care practice, you will begin to bring some more routines and rituals to both your sleeping and your ability to rest so you can restore your well-being as you do the important work of helping others.

When we sleep, our sympathetic nervous system "shuts down in favor of that calm, vegetative parasympathetic nervous system" (Sapolsky, 2004, p. 233). Sleep is predominantly a time when the stress response is turned off. When we sleep, our stress hormones decrease, allowing a shift in our nervous system's regulation; but when we are deprived of sleep, the sleep-induced decline of those stress hormones doesn't happen. This shift in our nervous system is what helps us maintain our equilibrium, and sleep helps us to buffer the impacts of stress and trauma so we can access our healing and take back some of the control and predictability our nervous systems need to function optimally. By incorporating rest into our work, we can create a powerful buffer against the negative effects of stress and trauma. Two ways to do that are with the relaxation response and by keeping one day a week for ourselves, a sabbath.

THE HEALING POWER OF REST: THE RELAXATION RESPONSE

> *A major asset of the Relaxation Response and remembered wellness is that they are self-administered. Their power lies within each of us. In this way, self-care is revolutionary and quite different from the medicine commonly practiced in both traditional and nontraditional settings.*
>
> —Dr. Herbert Benson, *The Relaxation Response*

Dr. Herbert Benson developed a technique to calm the body and mind to create an environment of well-being for the patients he saw in his medical practice. His book, *The Relaxation Response*, originally published in 1975, became the most recommended self-care book by health professionals because in it, he shared his finding that "regular elicitation of the Relaxation Response can prevent, and compensate for, the damage incurred by frequent nervous reactions that pulse through our hearts and bodies" (Benson & Klipper, 1975/2000, p. xvii). He was one of the first people to declare that self-care is a multidisciplinary practice that can cure many of the stress-related diseases seen by medical professionals, and created a protocol that is accessible to all, regardless of economic status or ability to pay for treatment. Even in 1975, he was bewildered that health insurance companies did not reimburse for self-care treatments and vowed to continue his medical practice and research to see his understanding of mind/body-wellness change the medical world.

Dr. Benson's call for what he identifies as remembered wellness, is our natural potential for self-healing predicated on his belief that our stress responses are the primary catalyst for disease and that "each of us possesses a natural and innate protective mechanism against 'over-stress,' which allows us to turn off harmful bodily effects, to counter the effects of the fight-or-flight response. This is the Relaxation Response" (Benson, 2000, p. 10). Ultimately the relaxation response reduces the activity of our sympathetic nervous system's fight-or-flight and shifts us into the rest-and-digest and care-and-connect aspects of our parasympathetic nervous system. In this way, it directly counters the involuntary stress responses that gets triggered in our work as helpers, healers, and changemakers.

Intentionally employing the relaxation response in our daily lives and in our work routines is vital for our well-being. The protocol for the relaxation response is straightforward. We need a quiet environment, a word or phrase we can repeat over and over again (rhythm of repetition), a passive/receptive attitude, and a comfortable position that we can stay in for 10 to 20 minutes up to twice daily. In a way, it is a form of meditation but with a very specific focus on the repeated word or phrase.

1. ***A quiet environment:*** Find a space with as few distractions as possible, including electronic devices. It is easier to remove distracting thoughts if we are starting from a quiet place.
2. ***A mental device:*** Have a word or phrase to repeat; this keeps us alert during the practice of relaxation. We can also focus on an object instead of a spoken word; both methods will help keep the mind from wandering during the practice.
3. ***A passive/receptive attitude:*** This is the "letting go" aspect of relaxation, allowing the mind to release any thoughts that come up (through repetition of the mental device) and releasing worry about doing the practice the right way. In a way, this is a form of self-compassion and care.

4. *A comfortable position:* The goal is to release any muscular tension and remain comfortable but relaxed. Laying down is not advised because it is conducive to falling asleep—the goal is to stay alert and awake while in a restful and relaxed state.

By practicing the relaxation response intentionally, maybe when we are away from our work and able to find that quiet place, we are better able to engage that same state when we are busy at work. We can incorporate this practice into our rituals of commuting to and from work, when walking or spending time in nature, or even when we are sitting in a contentious staff meeting at work and feel our stress level creeping up. The power of this practice cannot be understated and truly can help us find some rest as we continue our work of helping and healing. Rest is not a luxury; it is a necessity. When we prioritize rest, we are better able to cope with the challenges of life and to thrive in our work and personal relationships. By incorporating these strategies, we can create a powerful buffer against the impacts of stress and trauma.

SABBATH AS A RITUAL FOR REST

The Sabbath it is not for the sake of the weekday; the weekdays are for the sake of the sabbath.

—Casper ter Kuile, *The Power of Rituals*

In his book *The Power of Rituals*, Casper ter Kuile shares many rituals that can help guide our lives and help us create a sense of well-being. One ritual that applies well to our need for rest is that of taking sabbath: a day each week on which we remove ourselves from the "collective busyness" of life and work. Intentionally taking time to counter the stress of our daily lives and work is a common practice in most religions. Saturday or Sunday is seen as a day of rest, when most people of faith focus on traditions and family as a way of celebrating in communion with others. It causes us to slow down and take stock of our lives in a more meaningful way.

By taking a day to intentionally separate ourselves from our work, we are able to engage in hobbies, to explore play, and to be vulnerable in a different way than our work allows When we take a day to focus on our own well-being and that of our family or community, we are engaging in self-compassion and a fully engaged, calm-focused vulnerability that stokes wellness within our bodies and minds. When I was a teenager, I volunteered at hospitals as a candy striper on Sundays as my service to my community. When I was a Court Appointed Special Advocate for teens in the foster care system, I used Sundays to visit one of my kids at the Boys Ranch, a local juvenile detention facility, for the nine months he was there. Now I use my Sundays as a day of radical self-care to help me decompress from my work and prepare for the coming week. While this works for me, I appreciate ter Kuile's warning that the Sabbath "isn't a time to catch up on tasks. Nor is it simply a time of rest to prepare for a busy week. It is a time to revel in the beauty and delight of simply being" (ter Kuile, 2020, p. 72).

By intentionally marking one day a week for a Sabbath-type rest, we can come back to ourselves, remember who we are and why we are so passionate about our work as helpers, healers, and changemakers, and use the time to engage in the radical self-care practices that sustain us.

RADICAL TENDENCIES: REST AND RESTORE

Creating space for deep release and revolutionary rest is necessary for our individual and collective well-being. It invites us to move beyond superficial solutions (false cures) and explore deeper levels of healing and transformation. We can approach this concept by creating physical space, cultivating mental space, revolutionizing how we see rest, and engaging collective restoration.

REST AS REFUGE

> *Rest can save, sustain, and prop us up when we feel weak and our backs are against the wall. Our greatest hope to thrive and disrupt is to rest deeply and intentionally. The rest is the work. It is how the portal for liberation and a reckoning will emerge and remain open. May the portal of rest be our refuge. May we go there often.*
>
> —Tricia Hersey, *Rest is Resistance*

Our culture is one of hustle, busyness, and productivity at all costs. Our work as helpers, healers, and changemakers mimics this with a layered sense of urgency to address the many challenges in the world. It is vital to remember that rest is not a luxury and we are entitled to it. It also might be helpful to know that our ancestors valued rest and many cultures still include a midday siesta. Rest can include active practices, like yoga nidra, which will be explained in a few pages, or it can be less active practices like napping and sleeping.

Napping for ten to thirty minutes is all we need to give our bodies time to rest, restore, and reset. While it is important to note that naps are not a way to make up for sleep deprivation, this form of shallow sleep allows us to turn off our thoughts, creating the space for rest. If you are one of those people who thinks naps are for toddlers, consider the idea that Dr. Rubin R. Naiman shares in his book *Healing Night* (2014): "Napping is a social statement. It asserts that rest and sleep are important, equally important to wakefulness and productivity. One's willingness and ability to sleep by day is also a reflection of one's valuation of sleep by night. Napping is also a psychological statement. It is essential to balance the day's powerful call to extraversion with a remembrance of our inner self" (pp. 156–157).

There are a few ways we can approach napping and sleep that can give us a more restful experience. Dr. Naiman offers three aspects to consider as we approach sleep:

1. ***Intentionally "deluminate," or dim the lights, as we begin to slow down.*** This includes electronics and screens, but also dimming other lights in the home can help induce a calm atmosphere and prepare our bodies for sleep. This period of dusk can be used to bring us together with family as we shut down distractions and focus inward toward rest. We can set an alarm to remind us to start winding down or we can set our lights to dim at a specific time, if that technology is available to us.
2. ***Use an evening ritual to prepare ourselves for sleep*** and help us handle the natural anxieties that may arise as we move toward resting. Sometimes the transition between day and night can be unsettling or can make us worry about what is to come. By creating an evening ritual, as described in Chapter 4, we create a structure that can see us off to sleep, like taking a bath, having a cup of warm milk or tea, saying a bedtime prayer, or playing a bedtime lullaby. "Evening ritual and prayer simply help us invoke sleep" (Naiman, 2014, p. 63).
3. ***Learn to surrender to sleep.*** Naiman suggests that we don't "go" to sleep so much as we *surrender* to sleep. In order to fall into sleep, we must be able to let go of the day, our worries, and our anxieties. Learning to surrender our control every night can be challenging, but there are ways to create a space for sleep (consider light, temperature, and sound). Meditation and visualizations, as well as music or nature sounds, can help us with the releasing process each night.

YOGA NIDRA FOR CONSCIOUS REST

Yoga nidra gives us the direct experience that our inner core is stress-free and that unshakable inner peace and joy really exist within rather than outside ourselves. We learn firsthand about the temporary nature of our thoughts, feelings, and emotions, and this changes our perspective on stress and on ourselves.

—Julie Lusk, *Yoga Nidra for Complete Relaxation & Stress Relief*

There are practices that help bring the body into a state of relaxation and focus without necessarily putting us to sleep. Yoga nidra is one of those practices. Yoga nidra is a form of yoga that means "yogic sleep" and it allows us to control the relaxation state of our nervous system. It is a progressive form of deep relaxation that can give us space between the thinking and decision making we do in our work by slowing the pace of our breath and our thoughts, moving us toward deeper brain states of relaxation without putting us fully to sleep. Similarly to the relaxation response, yoga nidra allows us to experience a self-induce a state of calm as the basis of our self-regulation. Conscious rest can become a foundational part of our radical self-care that we can engage in to buffer the intensity of our work.

Yoga nidra includes breathwork and guided relaxation to help us reduce stress and shift out of a stress response into a state of relaxed receptivity. Through a process of progressive muscle relaxation, tension and stress can be released from our bodies. By engaging our body, breath, and conscious awareness, yoga nidra moves us through the various states of the brain that can put us into a state of deep, but conscious relaxation. "Yoga nidra gives us the practical means for quieting the mental ruckus and opening our heart for this to happen" (Lusk, 2015, p. 44). It is claimed that an hour of yoga nidra is equivalent to hours of sleep, but it is not a replacement for a good night's sleep. Books about yoga nidra offer scripts but if this is a new practice for you, consider finding a yoga nidra class near you or finding a guided yoga nidra video.

CREATING SPACES FOR REST

Mindfulness-based programs have been shown to improve well-being among several types of caregivers. . . . Mindfulness also improves mental health among teachers and nurses. The general benefits of mindfulness practice, such as stress reduction, may explain how it is helpful to these populations. However, mindfulness practice also requires tuning in to our own experiences. This may assist those of us in caregiving roles to remember to balance our own needs with those of others.

—Rachel Goldsmith Turow, *Mindfulness Skills for Trauma and PTSD*

Since we live in a culture that is still hostile to rest, there may not be many spaces where we can practice it. Some schools have wellness centers or calm corners that allow space for intentional rest and mindfulness practices. Some offices offer nap pods and hospitals offer rooms for employees to rest in the middle of the day, but the most of us may have to create those spaces more intentionally and on our own. Creating a designated space for rest, being immersed in nature, and engaging in mindfulness practices are a few ways to create some spaces for rest. Some things to consider:

- **Dedicated rest area/calm space:** Designate a specific area in your home or at work solely for relaxation and rejuvenation. This could be a cozy corner in your bedroom filled with soft pillows and blankets, a hammock strung between trees in your backyard, or even a quiet nook in a public space, like a local library or neighborhood coffee shop. Creating a calm corner in your classroom or a wellness center at your school or organization gives both clients and colleagues a place to take a moment of respite until they are ready to engage again. One could engage the relaxation response, yoga nidra, or meditation in this space as well.
- **Nature immersion:** If you've gotten this far in the book, you've noticed nature is a mainstay in our radical self-care practice. When it comes to finding space to rest and restore, nature works its magic here as well. In addition to the nature practices in previous chapters, here are a few ways to engage in rest through nature.
  - **Morning sunlight:** Getting sunlight in our eyes within the

first hour or two we are awake can help our circadian rhythm stay on track and prime our bodies for better rest. Sunlight in the morning induces better sleep patterns by letting our brains know we should be awake and setting our circadian rhythm into a balanced cadence with the rest of our day. This can be a challenge if we wake in the middle of the night for a work shift, but there are some artificial ways to get similar benefits through lights that mimic sunlight.

- **Sunset walk:** In the same way that getting sunlight in the morning helps our brain and body to know it's time to wake up, looking at an evening horizon signals to our brain that it is time to slow down and prepare for sleep. Taking a walk when the sun is setting helps with digestion, can bring us connection with community and nature, and activates our parasympathetic nervous system of rest-and-digest, setting us up for a good night's sleep.
- **Natural sensory deprivation:** One way to get some rest is through sensory deprivation. Simply being in nature, away from emails, screens, traffic, and maybe even our cell phones, can allow all our senses, and thus our nervous system, a deep rest and reset. Being in water—a bath, pool, or a float tank—can give us a sense of weightlessness as well as silence and darkness when we're submerged. More and more, float tanks, hot springs, and other water-based therapeutic spaces are available to us, but we can also create this environment at home by turning off lights and electronic devices.

• **Mindfulness practices:** Engaging in mindfulness meditation or other contemplative techniques cultivates awareness of your inner world. By observing your thoughts and feelings, in the present moment and without judgment, you can create space for them to release and dissolve naturally. "Mindfulness cultivates balance. Rather than feeling all of our overwhelming emotions at once, we can carefully titrate our approach to them" (Turow, 2017, p. 2). A warning about mindfulness is that when you start practicing being in the present moment, you may become mindful of things that are not working for you. This can be a bit discouraging, but this is where the wisdom comes in. When we can notice the things that are not working for us, whether behaviors, habits, or our interactions with others, we have the power to change them. This is also why the "without judgment" part is so important. Mindfulness techniques include the relaxation response or a more formal mindfulness practice, but whatever the technique, it elicits the same changes in your nervous system and overall well-being.

- **Journaling or reading:** Express your emotions and thoughts freely through journaling. This cathartic process can help you gain clarity and release pent-up emotions and the emotional stress you may carry throughout our day. Journaling doesn't have to be an intense or time-consuming practice. You can do a bullet journal or minute journal that allows you to jot down a brief note about your day or what you're grateful for in that moment. Reading allows you to escape into a space of imagination, a form of safer dissociation that can help you see your connections to others and yourself in new and different ways. This can also be a part of your evening/sleep routines and rituals.
- **Creative expression:** Explore artistic endeavors like painting, music, or dance as a means of releasing emotional tension and accessing deeper levels of self-awareness. While creative expression can be done individually, collective experiences like sip and paint parties, gaming groups, or vision board gatherings work too. Don't let perfectionism stop you here, you don't have to be good to enjoy the benefits of creative expression.

COLLECTIVE RESTORATION

By engaging in radical self-care that actively creates space for deep release and revolutionary rest in our lives, we pave the way for greater individual and collective well-being. We can cultivate a workplace that values inner peace and sustainable living over the relentless pursuit of hustle culture and burnout. This revolutionary shift can help us thrive and flourish as helpers, healers, and changemakers.

- **Rest-supportive policies:** Each of us can work toward creating policies that promote healthy work balance, such as paid leave, flexible work hours, or adequate time between shifts. Some schools promote perfect attendance (because most schools are funded through Average Daily Attendance or warm bodies in the seats), and while I understand the idea of having all kids in school every day, this is an example of an unhealthy goal. It may be uncomfortable to question these types of policies or practices in our work, but we can use our authority, especially those of us in positions of power, to advocate for a workplace that prioritizes radical self-care.
- **Challenge the cult of productivity:** Question professional norms that equate busyness and constant activity with productivity or success. Instead, we can promote the importance of taking time for rest and rejuvenation as essential for individual and collective well-being. Encouraging staff to take mental health days (without guilt) is one way our agencies and organizations can support rest and challenge the cult of productivity. When our organizations, agencies and professional membership organizations take rest seriously, we can revolutionize the ways future helpers, healers, and changemakers will engage with their work—without the constant threat of burnout.
- **Create supportive communities:** We all thrive in environments where open communication and vulnerability are encouraged. If we want this kind of community, we can be the ones to initiate the change by being an example of good radical self-care practices, encouraging others to engage in their own practices, allowing us to feel safe and supported as we engage in deep release and transformative rest.

6

RECLAIM AND REPLENISH

How we move forward from here

> Too often in the helping fields, we focus on the immediate tasks at hand and the intense human needs before us, rather than thinking of how we must take care of ourselves if ourself, the healing agent, is to thrive for the decades of our work.
>
> —Thomas M. Skovholt and Michelle Trotter-Mathison, *Resilient Practitioner*

> When we allow, accept, and integrate the gifts of every individual, we create a radical opportunity for the advancement of the whole. . . . When we willingly embrace the miraculous beauty of who each of us is individually, we open fully to the possibility of who we can become collectively.
>
> —Sherri Mitchell, *Sacred Instructions*

There is darkness in the world, but it is our job as helpers, healers, and changemakers to bring the light and be the light. This requires us to show up for our work in a way that protects us, empowers those we serve, and changes the systems we work within. We can only do this with a commitment to change and deep reserves of resilience. But resilience runs out. This is the reality for helpers, healers, and changemakers. We can only work so hard for so long before we use up our reserves and hit the wall. Then the body says "NO." We must be able to reclaim our resilience and replenish it, using the radical self-care practices shared throughout this book.

In summary, our work as helpers, healers, and changemakers is undeniably dysregulating. We show up when things don't go according to plan (or when it hits the fan) and have to hold space for suffering while seeking to eliminate it in a world that is mostly indifferent to the suffering we witness. The dysregulation in our systems and institutions keeps us separate and often fighting each other rather than communicating and collaborating across systems and silos. As long as we are all just surviving our work, bracing ourselves for the next tragedy or crisis to hit, we will never see the thorough or systemic change we need.

But it doesn't have to be this way. The beauty is that we are resilient. We have an amazing opportunity to reclaim our professions and move into a state of radical historical and social change in the coming years and decades. In the face of dysregulation, we can commit, to ourselves and to each other, to move forward as helpers, healers, and changemakers who practice radical self-care and thrive in our work. We can't have growth without curiosity, and we cannot have liberation without imagination, but if we are stuck in survival mode or burdened by the weight of the trauma in our work or in denial about it all, we will not have the energy nor the stamina to keep pushing for collective action toward change.

If we are serious about real change in the world and in our work as helpers, healers, and changemakers, we must engage in radical self-care. We can cultivate the ability to stay in jobs that we love by identifying when stress, vicarious trauma, or moral injury are creeping in and acting on our curated wisdom and collective practices. There are questions we must ask ourselves and changes we must make within the organizations we serve to make practicing radical self-care standard operating procedure.

RADICAL RESILIENCE

Resilience helps us stay grounded and settled, no matter what happens to us. It enables us to sustain and protect ourselves—and each other—over time. It's a way for our body to access possibility and coherence, regardless of the circumstances.

—Resmaa Menakem, *My Grandmother's Hands*

Resilient strength is the opposite of helplessness. The tree is made strong and resilient by its grounded root system. These roots take nourishment from the ground and grow strong. Grounding also allows the tree to be resilient so that it can yield to the winds of change and not be uprooted.

—Peter Levine, *Waking the Tiger: Healing Trauma*

Just as the stress and trauma in our work can be passed on from coworker to coworker and through generations, so too can resilience. When we learn ways to care for and nurture ourselves toward wholeness, we transmit those healing actions to those around us, including future generations. This is why our self-care is so vital to our ability to make real change in the world. "We know our well-being is dependent on the well-being of others; we know each person flourishes when we are all flourishing together. In this regard, justice-minded people have a head start on resilience" (Cheng-Tozun, 2023, p. 45).

Resilience is about how we show up rather than what we do. How we show up matters for ourselves, our colleagues, those we serve, and those we call family. Resilience, generally, is our ability to bounce back after a challenging situation. Relative to our nervous system, resilience is the ability of our system to regain regulation, baseline, homeostasis. In our work, resilience is the ability to face the stress and trauma in our work without being changed by it and the ability to get back to our baseline of regulation fairly quickly.

Regaining our footing, so to speak, is vital in our work, as we may have to adjust ourselves between patients, classes, or cases. Without some level of resilience, we just get further and further from our regulated state of calm, and we can get stuck back in survival mode. What makes our resilience radical is our ability to be firmly rooted in our deliberate sense of well-being and to engage our radical self-care practices in a way that provides us a deep well of strength to handle whatever comes our way. Beyond just handling the stress in our work, radical resilience gives us the foundation from which to move beyond our work and to challenge the systems and structures that no longer serve our well-being.

RECLAIMING OUR EMPATHY

> *Radical empathy is a call for action that requires a sense of self and an understanding of why the fight for social justice is the most important thing we can do for future generations.*
>
> —Terri E. Givens, *Radical Empathy*

> *Compassion is not a relationship between the healer and the wounded. It's a relationship between equals. Only when we know our own darkness well can we be present with the darkness of others. Compassion becomes real when we recognize our shared humanity.*
>
> —Pema Chödrön, *Comfortable with Uncertainty*

Empathy is our ability to understand the struggles of others and to see things from their perspective; it is a form of entrainment with others. Our empathy is constantly engaged in our work as helpers, healers, and changemakers, and we must guard and reclaim our empathy so we don't sacrifice our wellness for those we serve. Empathy can be a superpower if it is employed in a thoughtful way, but it can also drain our life energy if it is exploited or overused. To avoid this, we have to guard against **unconscious empathy**, which can lead to "unmanageable countertransference, projective identification, compassion fatigue, vicarious trauma, and burnout" (Rothschild & Rand, 2006, p. 11). We bring awareness to our empathy by recognizing its impact on our bodies and to our ability to care for ourselves.

Somatic empathy (Rothschild & Rand, 2006) engages our brains and bodies (cognitive and somatic) in our interactions with those we serve, and if we are not fully aware of our own regulation or dysregulation, it can put us on a path to burnout. Knowing when we are fully grounded and present gives us the ability to make choices about the support we need to safely engage in our work so we don't absorb too much of the stress and trauma we may come upon. "Empaths are more prone to take on the emotional or physical pain that they haven't worked out in themselves. The more you heal issues that trigger you, the less likely you will be to absorb such symptoms from others. You might still sense them, but they won't impact you as deeply or drain you" (Orloff, 2018, p. 43).

Our empathy can also be used to create real change in our professions and in our larger world. If we want to reclaim our empathic engagement, we might consider radical empathy (Givens, 2022). **Radical empathy** moves us beyond the interactions between ourselves and those we serve to the larger global community. Radical empathy "encourages each of us . . . to be motivated to create the change that will allow all of us to benefit from economic prosperity and develop the social relationships that are beneficial to our emotional well-being" (Givens, 2022, p. 1).

Bringing compassion, conscious awareness, and a larger, macro perspective to our practice of empathy protects us from the negative impacts of our work. When we are fully present, we are able to do our work as helpers, healers, and changemakers without becoming overwhelmed, drawn into hypercaregiving, or codependent on colleagues or clients. We also bring a level of self-compassion to our work, so we honor our boundaries and know when it is time to take a break or get some support ourselves. This allows us to maintain a strong rhythm of regulation for others to oscillate with and entrain to, bringing a sense of calm and clarity to our work. When we reclaim our empathy, we will see long-lasting positive benefits for our health and well-being and the change we bring can last for generations to come. "What makes empathy radical is the focus on *taking action and creating change*" (Givens, 2022, p. 152).

COLLECTIVE HEALING ENERGY

> *Regardless of what work we do, part of our work is to help bring about a collective healing, transformation, and awakening for our own well-being and for the sake of our planet.*
>
> —Thich Nhat Hanh, *Work*

> *Healing is political and is an act of resistance. In my opinion, the end goal of healing is not to make us better able to function within a capitalist system; it is to liberate us from that system. Let history remind us of how powerful healers actually are. Your work is extremely important.*
>
> —Laura Mae Northrup, *Radical Healership*

We need collective solutions and collective energies to make the radical changes we seek in our work as helpers, healers, and changemakers. Hopefully you agree that our individual radical self-care is not just for us, but for those we serve and the world in which we serve. There is no separation of the individual and the collective, but rather an intricate dance of interdependence, when we are caring for ourselves as caregivers for others. When we each prioritize our self-care and we show up grounded, regulated, attuned, and resourced, we have the power to see the realities of our work and to identify what changes would make our work more equitable and just. This, in turn, leads to more transformative relationships among ourselves, others, and the planet. By engaging regularly in radical self-care practices, we create a healing energy that transcends our work and ripples out beyond our individual selves toward those we serve, those we are in community with, and those who are or will become our colleagues.

"Becoming a healing practitioner is a commitment to being awake, to turn toward, to live through the pain, so that we may have the strength and the vision to witness and love others as they travel their own path of healing. If being a healer is the work you have been called to do: *do it by healing yourself*" (Northrup, 2022, p. 166). Change can happen only if those of us who see the suffering in the world have the commitment to our own healing and the energy to stay with the work when things get hard and the courage to demand the changes we know are possible. Then we must share our knowledge and resources with each other and those who come after us.

One way to harness and share our collective healing energy is for some of those who have been in this work longer to become mentors, coaches, or guides for those who are just coming into our professions. Our schools of training need the healing energy of wisdom and years of practice that can be transmitted only from those of us who have been doing this work for decades and have seen some things, good and bad. We are aware of what works and what doesn't—whether policies, legislation, or direct practice—and we can impart that awareness and knowledge to others as they learn to become helpers, healers, and changemakers. We need those with experience in our professions to share their skills and to pass down their wisdom to future generations to help stem the tide of turnover.

One of the collective commitments we can make to each other is to support and grow our professional communities to ensure our professional education is current and compassionate. Experienced folks may fulfill this commitment in various ways, such as by becoming a mentor to those new to the profession, a supervisor for those seeking licensure, a professor in a college or university training program, or a professional coach. Another method would be sharing your wisdom through a podcast, a video series, an online training platform, a book, etc. We can also reach across and between helping professions to bridge gaps in our understanding of each other's roles and how we can be more interdependent and interconnected for the greater good. Knowing there are folks who can apply their skills in a variety of contexts can help lift us out of any ruts we may find ourselves in after working in the same profession for years. This interconnection also creates a nice segue to a career change if we begin to feel too overwhelmed by the work we are currently doing; for example, a social worker moving into the education field, a medical professional shifting into legislative work, or an educator opening a yoga studio. The skills we gain as helpers, healers, and changemakers can be used widely to create more healing in the world beyond our respective professions.

Harnessing our collective energy, we can move toward a more healed way of working in the world. Rather than allowing burnout and turnover to decimate our professions, we can call on the strength of our radical self-care practices and deepen the well of knowledge from which all of us can be replenished. While radical self-care can help you balance the difficult aspects of our work, if I'm honest, I hope that some of you will be inspired to quit your day job as a helper, healer, or changemaker to do the larger work of systems change from the outside with insider knowledge. We need former educators and former social workers and former medical professionals, etc. to work upstream, creating policy on state and national levels and speaking to the needs of our professions, in place of the folks currently working there, who have never once spent time with a client, student, or patient. *If you ever needed a nudge to run for a political office or to step into local service, consider yourself nudged.*

TOWARD A LOVE ETHIC

> *Activism is not just about what we do; it is also about who we are and how we show up in the world.*
>
> —Resmaa Menakem, *My Grandmother's Hands*

All our professions have foundational ethical imperatives that keep us in line with the scope of our work and that protect us from liability.

There is no shortage of serious work ethic among helpers, healers, and changemakers. What we need, now more than ever, is a softening of this work ethic, the one that pushes us beyond our physical, mental, and emotional limits and almost guarantees a one-way ticket to burnout. Rather than allowing the stress and trauma of our work to consume and dysregulate us, we can create a more conscious way to work. Rather than moving deeper into a work ethic that no longer serves us, we can bring change to our work in a more conscious, communal, and caring way.

Martin Luther King, Jr. understood this reality to his core, knowingly stating, "It will be power infused with love and justice that will change dark yesterdays into bright tomorrows, and lift us from the fatigue of despair to the buoyancy of hope" (King, 1968). He understood very clearly the immediate need to move toward love. It can seem like a silly notion, or one that is overly emotional and failing to meet the harsh demands of the moment. On the contrary, I believe we will never see real social change if we do not prioritize love. Love is strength, it takes courage and demands action. One powerful way we can take action toward love is to adopt a love ethic in our work as helpers, healers, and changemakers.

bell hooks defines a love ethic as a way to affirm our interconnectedness and says that, "Embracing a love ethic means that we utilize all the dimensions of love—'care, commitment, trust, responsibility, respect, and knowledge'—in our everyday lives" (hooks, 2000, p. 94). She deeply believed that our current circumstances demand radical change and that the only thing holding us back from that radical change is fear. Love conquers fear, and a love ethic can move us closer to radical change. A love ethic disrupts our current models of professional work and can bring more support and resources to our work in a way that stokes our passions and expands our purpose. A love ethic reminds us that we must be courageous in the face of the challenges that we will continue to see in our helping, healing, and change-making professions for years to come. With a consistent, foundational practice of radical self-care, we can meet these challenges with love and courage.

RECLAIMING OUR RESILIENCE

> *In our bones we sense that this is no ordinary time. It is a time of deep change, not just of social structure and economy but also of ourselves. If we want to see change in our lives, we have to change things ourselves.*
>
> —GRACE LEE BOGGS AND SCOTT KURASHIGE, *The Next American Revolution*

Reclaiming our resilience as a helper is crucial for the effectiveness of our work and our well-being. Just saying we are resilient but then continuing to pile on work and expectations is exploitation. We have to reclaim our resilience and use the power we have to readjust after stress or trauma to hold space for our own well-being by refusing to let it be used to keep us in cycles of stress, overwork, or overwhelm. If we want change, we must change things ourselves, so here are some key strategies we can use to replenish our stores of resilience as we move toward change:

- **Acknowledge the reality of our work and honor our burnout:**
  - Be aware of the trauma that shows up in your work and be honest about how it impacts you, your organization, and the outcomes you're trying to achieve.
  - Recognize the signs of burnout (in yourself and your colleagues), such as emotional exhaustion, cynicism, and reduced efficacy.
  - Be honest with yourself and others about your limitations and your need for support. Ask for support when you need it.
- **Practice compassion and gratitude:**
  - Remember why you came to this work and cultivate self-compassion to acknowledge your strengths and contributions to your profession.
  - Express gratitude for the positive aspects of your work and the

people you help; find moments of gratitude for the small wins in your work.
    - Remember that your work makes a difference, even if it isn't always visible. We are the light in the storm, and it is important that we remember how necessary we are in our communities.
- **Seek support and community:**
    - Find mentors or advisors in your profession to learn from.
    - Connect with other helpers who understand your experiences and challenges. Find your "emotional support" coworkers, allies, and accomplices.
    - Seek professional help from a therapist or counselor when needed, and remember that this is best practice in our work.
- **Prioritize self-care:**
    - Engage in activities that nourish our physical, mental, and emotional well-being, such as exercise, healthy eating, meditation, mindfulness practices, spending time in nature, pursuing hobbies, or connecting with loved ones.
    - Ensure you get enough sleep and prioritize rest and relaxation.
    - Stay in connection with others, as isolation and loneliness lead to burnout.
- **Set boundaries and cultivate saying "no":**
    - Learn to say "no" when you feel overwhelmed. You do not have to explain yourself or why you may not have the bandwidth for additional work.
    - Communicate boundaries clearly and respectfully to prevent misunderstandings.
    - Be open to shifting boundaries when needed, but don't hesitate to enforce them.
- **Advocate for change:**
    - Raise awareness of the challenges faced by helpers, and advocate for radical systemic changes. This might involve lobbying for more comprehensive legislation, better work conditions, more funding and resources, and support for helpers across professions.
    - Consider offering trainings and education to those who are

new to the helping professions. Share your expertise and passion with others through mentoring, coaching, or creating cooperative learning environments that embrace continuous learning and professional development to enhance our skills and effectiveness. We always need veteran helpers, healers, and changemakers to share their wisdom and to make our education and training/licensing programs as radical as possible.
- Contribute to creating a culture in your own organization or agency that values and prioritizes the well-being of helpers, especially if you are a supervisor, director, manager, superintendent, or serve in another leadership capacity.

These are steps we can take right now to begin to create the change we know is possible in our professions.

RADICAL TENDENCIES: RECLAIM AND REPLENISH

> *Those of us who wish to see a truly, radically different world must demand of ourselves the possibility that we are called to lead not from the right to left, or from minority to majority, but from spirit towards liberation.*
>
> —ADRIENNE MARIE BROWN, *Emergent Strategy*

When I consider how we move forward in our work as helpers, healers, and changemakers, I look to our ancestors, those who came before us and met the struggles of their time. Many of them understood the need to be sustained and replenished in the work. Ella Baker leaned into the support of friends and allies, Fannie Lou Hamer and Martin Luther King, Jr. leaned on their spiritual beliefs, Rosa Parks practiced yoga, and Audre Lorde leaned into rest as their respective radical self-care practices. One of my favorite photos is of Audre Lorde, laid out on a lawn chair, resting, with a book in her hands and a stack of books nearby. It is the visual representation of her famous quote, "Caring for myself is not self-indulgence, it is self-preservation, and that is an act of political warfare."

REFUELING STATIONS AND GREENHOUSES OF CARE

She [Ella Baker] was committed to the struggle for the long haul, having devoted thirty years to progressive causes. . . . One way she sustained herself physically during times of intense struggle, and psychologically and emotionally during lulls, was by reconnecting with old friends and comrades. They took care of her and provided her with refueling stations and respite from battle as she continued her itinerant insurgency across the South.

—Barbara Ransby, *Ella Baker and the Black Freedom Movement*

In my office at home I have created a space that is very special to me. It is simple and quiet, with beautiful things about, and a ray of sunlight cascading through a low window on the best of days. It is here that I write whenever I am home, and where I retreat to center myself, to rest and recharge at regular intervals.

—Audre Lorde, "A Burst of Light" in *I Am Your Sister*

Organizational factors can contribute greatly to our burnout; however, we shouldn't wait for our place of employment to provide the care we need. We can create oases and designated spaces at work that also serve our well-being. Refueling stations can be spaces we create that allow us to rest and refuel. This can be a room in our home, a space in a community center or local park, or a regular gathering of loved ones who help us recharge. We can also create a refueling station at work, or what Skovholt and Trotter-Mathison call a "professional greenhouse. . . . A learning environment where practitioners growth is encourage; leadership that promotes a healthy other-care vs. self-care balance; social support from peers; receiving other-care from mentors; mentoring others; an emotional environment of respect, playfulness, humor, and joy" (2016, p. 149) to help us stay focused and replenished.

It is important to remember that we are the individuals who make up these organizations and agencies, and we can make real change if we begin with ourselves. Being intentional and explicit about the support we need at work and away from work is vital to our well-being and the well-being of our communities and organizations. Our activist ancestors knew this well, and it is something we can bring to our fellow helpers, healers, and changemakers. When our coworkers see how we show up for our work and how we are resourced and regulated for the work, they will become curious. Modeling the change we want to see gives us the opportunity to share our vision of radical self-care for our profession.

In 2018, I was invited to share radical self-care at a yoga studio called Be Replenished, in Columbus, Ohio. During the question and answer period, a young woman from the back of the room raised her hand and asked, "So when are you writing your book?" Her question caught me off guard and made my heart race. I was just beginning to talk about radical self-care and doing workshops with fellow helpers, and while I always got positive feedback, I wasn't sure if my message was landing. The intention of being of service to those who serve kept me going, and I wondered if self-care would ever catch on as an ethical imperative in our work. Maybe I was wasting my time, and nothing could change the burnout and vicarious trauma in the helping professions.

Then I took a deep breath and took in the space where I was standing. The studio where that workshop was held, The Yoga Carriage, was created by three amazing Black women, one who had been a social worker for years and left after facing burnout. They built this beautiful space of refuge, restoration, and replenishment specifically for those who care for others; a refueling station, a respite from battle. I was in a room, in community, with others who shared their vulnerabilities. I was in a room *created by healers for helpers.* I was in a space to create change and shift how we approach our radical responsibility.

This is the energy and the kind of spaces that we can create for each other when we engage our radical self-care. We don't have to wait for others to create these spaces for us. So what or who are we waiting for?

In the spirit of Ella Baker, Rosa Parks, Fannie Lou Hamer, Audre Lorde, and all those who came before us in the struggle, I urge you to find your own refueling stations. As we do the challenging work of helping, healing, and making change, we will need places, spaces, and people who promote calm and ease in our lives. Engaging a few radical self-care practices while spending time with ancestors, allies, and accomplices can be our respite and our acts of political warfare. Whether it's a group of friends who take your mind off work, a retreat you can get away to for some much-needed solace, or maybe just an activity that allows you to release some stress, finding and using these refueling stations can replenish and fuel you for the days and times when your work is too much.

A FINAL WORD: RADICAL HOPE AND OUR RADICAL RESPONSIBILITY

> *What makes this hope radical is that it is directed toward a future goodness that transcends the current ability to understand what it is. Radical hope anticipates a good for which those who have the hopes as yet lack the appropriate concepts with which to understand it.*
>
> —Jonathan Lear, *Radical Hope*

Given the reality of our work, it is easy to despair and become hopeless. As helpers, healers, and changemakers, we must stand strong in the face of helplessness. In her book *Teaching Community*, bell hooks shares that we can lose hope in the healing power of justice, become cynical, and move into a space of learned helplessness, which only serves to cultivate despair in our culture. "Despair is the greatest threat. When despair prevails, we cannot create life-sustaining communities of resistance" (hooks, 2003, p. 12). She wrote this book after taking a break from teaching due to burnout and suggested that every teacher needs some time away from the classroom. We serve people and communities that come to us for help, and while we are human and need to experience the reality of our work, we also need to be the bearers of hope. We need to be the light, the anchor, or the possibility for those we serve, and we cannot do this from a place of despair.

Radical change requires that we push back against despair. That we hope in things we have not yet seen or experienced, want better for those who come after us, and have the courage to imagine new ways of being and working in the world, especially as helpers, healers, and changemakers. Chief Plenty Coups of the Crow nation responded to the collapse of his civilization by turning to radical hope, insisting that how we live—with courage and in connection with each other and nature—determines the survival of our cultures and civilizations (Lear, 2006). To move forward toward liberation, we must have hope and courage for the journey. Not hope as self-deception or as being naïve to the real challenges ahead of us, but hope that we *can* get to real change if we sow the necessary seeds for future generations.

"Critical hope demands a committed and active struggle . . . audacious hope demands that we reconnect to the collective by struggling alongside on another, sharing in the victories *and* the pain" (Duncan-Andrade, 2009, pp. 185, 190). Many will complain about the conditions in the system, but few will commit to doing the work of abolishing what is no longer working and reimagining something new. Radical change requires revolutionary hope, radical imaginations, and restorative healing, all of which require action and collective struggle. But we cannot do this work if we are exhausted, demoralized, and burned-out. We cannot do this if we are losing colleagues to turnover, illness, and death. And we can't do this work if we just gripe about the challenges without working toward the solutions. Instead, as we commit to radical self-care as part of our radical healing, we will move bravely and boldly toward individual well-being, community health, and broader social justice (Naiman, 2014).

Sitting in my county's Child Death Review Team meeting recently, I was reminded of the need for radical hope in our work. First, let me address the obvious. The Child Death Review Team is exactly what it sounds like: a team of professionals who review the untimely deaths of children and youth to identify trends or patterns of harm and to use their shared power to alert the community to these risks through public health campaigns. Under the leadership of our county's medical examiner, the team reviews the autopsy reports and scene photos and provides a records review, sharing any system involvement of the youth or family so we can get a picture of the child's life and the circumstances surrounding their death. Using all the information available to us, we, as a team, identify adverse childhood experiences and classify the death. We also use the meetings to find gaps in services or systems, and we seek actionable remedies to prevent future child fatalities.

The members of this team are representatives from major county agencies, including social workers, nurses, pediatricians, neonatologists, therapists, schools, EMT/ambulance services, juvenile and family court advocates, probation officers, homicide detectives, and death investigators from the coroner's office. We meet once a month for three hours and deal directly with cases of death. Every case is heartbreaking, but many of the members have been there for ten years or longer, including myself, so we are used to the work. That said, occasionally we review a case that truly shatters our hearts and brings out some emotions among this group of veteran helpers, healers, and changemakers.

There is a sense of deep respect and compassion in the room and an acknowledgment that we are doing good, necessary work, as challenging as it is. Being in the same space with other professionals who perform this hard work and being able to openly discuss our systems where we are all seen and heard is so powerful, creating a safe environment and solidarity with the other folks in that room. When I leave CDRT meetings, I take some deep breaths in the car to reset my nervous system before getting on with the rest of my workday. It is a living reminder of why we need radical self-care to hold and manage the reality of our work. It is also a stark reminder that when we come together, across helping professions and with care for each other, we can make a larger impact toward real change with our common goal of preventing childhood deaths.

Hope is vital to our very existence and necessary for us to even begin the struggle for change, both individual and communal. "I am hopeful, not out of mere stubbornness, but out of an existential, concrete imperative" (Friere, 1995, p. 8). We need radical hope and courage as we engage in our work as helpers, healers, and changemakers. Our professions need to come back to their roots of service, people over profit, and impactful outcomes. We are far too intelligent, capable, and committed to still be dealing with these challenges. We MUST care for ourselves, create communal cultures of care, and strengthen our collective courage to imagine a new way forward. **Radical self-care is our radical responsibility.**

So now it's your turn. How will you engage your radical self-care and create a culture of care in your life and work?

REFERENCES

Alexander, C. (2021). *Year of the nurse: A covid-19 2020 pandemic memoir.* Caskara Press.

Associated Press. (2023a, March 13). California "teacher of the year" accused of child sex abuse. *AP News*. Retrieved April 23, 2023 from https://apnews.com/article/national-city-teacher-of-year-sex-abuse-charges-not-guilty-california-lincoln-acres-elementary-be62d80718e25b046f86897dd40c7f64

Associated Press. (2023b, April 13). Nurse pleads guilty to replacing fentanyl with saline. *AP News*. Retrieved April 23, 2023 from https://apnews.com/article/nurse-fentanyl-theft-florida-a2c55a1a64fffb6a661d74a69a4a9761

Bailey, R., & Brake, M. (1975). *Radical social work*. Edward Arnold.

Barks, C. (2004). *The essential Rumi* (New expanded edition). Harper Collins.

Benson, H., & Klipper, M. Z. (1975). *The relaxation response.* HarperCollins.

Bernert, R. A., & Joiner, T. E. (2008). Sleep disturbances and suicide risk: A review of the literature. *Neuropsychiatric Disease and Treatment*, *Volume 3*(6), 735–743. https://doi.org/10.2147/ndt.s1248

Bethell, C., Jones, J., Gombojav, N., Linkenbach, J., & Sege, R. (2019). Positive childhood experiences and adult mental and relational health in a statewide sample. *JAMA Pediatrics*, *173*(11), e193007. https://doi.org/10.1001/jamapediatrics.2019.3007

Blackstone, J. (2018). *Trauma and the unbound body: The healing power of fundamental consciousness*. Sounds True.

Bleiberg, J., & Stengle, J. (2022, October 24). Police: Boyfriend at Texas hospital for baby's birth kills 2. *AP News*. Retrieved November 10, 2022, from https://apnews.com/article/health-dallas-shootings-588b62b3e2420075247482b2e31c1b14

Bloom, P. (2016). *Against empathy: The case for rational compassion.* Ecco.

Boggs, G. L., & Kurashige, S. (2012). *The next American revolution: Sustainable activism for the twenty-first century*. University Of California Press.

brown, a. m. (2017). *Emergent strategy: Shaping change, changing worlds*. AK Press.

brown, a. m. (2019). *Pleasure activism: The politics of feeling good.* AK Press.

Burke Harris, N. (2018). *The deepest well: healing the long-term effects of childhood adversity.* Houghton Mifflin Harcourt.

Caldwell, C. (1996). *Getting our bodies back: Recovery, healing, and transformation through body-centered psychotherapy.* Shambahala.

Caldwell, C., & Bennett Leighton, L. (2018). *Oppression and the body: Roots, resistance, and resolutions.* North Atlantic Books.

Care Collective. (2020). *The care manifesto: The politics of interdependence.* Verso.

CBS News. (2023, April 7). Homeless woman kills shelter coordinator with ax in front of staff, Vermont police say. *CBS News.* Retrieved August 29, 2023, from https://www.cbsnews.com/news/leah-rosin-pritchard-killed-ax-morningside-house-homeless-shelter-vermont/

Chapman, C., & Withers, A. J. (2019). *A violent history of benevolence: Interlocking oppression in the moral economies of social working.* University of Toronto Press.

Cheng-Tozun, D. (2023). *Social justice for the sensitive soul: How to change the world in quiet ways.* Broadleaf Books.

Chödrön, P. (2002). *Comfortable with uncertainty.* Shambhala.

Chödrön, P. (2019). *Welcoming the unwelcome.* Shambhala.

Colegrove, K. (2020) *Mindfulness for warriors: Empowering first responders to reduce stress and build resilience.* Mango.

Cronholm, P. F., Forke, C. M., Wade, R., Bair-Merritt, M. H., Davis, M., Harkins-Schwarz, M., Pachter, L. M., & Fein, J. A. (2015). Adverse childhood experiences: Expanding the concept of adversity. *American Journal of Preventive Medicine, 49*(3), 354–361. https://doi.org/10.1016/j.amepre.2015.02.001

Curtice, K. B. (2023). *Living resistance: An indigenous vision for seeking wholeness every day.* Brazos Press.

Dass, R., & Gorman, P. (1985). *How can I help? Stories and reflections on service.* Alfred A. Knopf.

Dorman, W. E. (2016). *Restoring the healer: Spiritual self-care for health care professionals.* Templeton Press.

Duncan-Andrade, J. (2009). Note to educators: Hope required when growing roses in concrete. *Harvard Educational Review, 79*(2), 181–194, 399. Retrieved from https://www.proquest.com/scholarly-journals/note-educators-hope-required-when-growing-roses/docview/212262732/se-2DW News. (2022, December 20). *Japan's teachers vulnerable to overwork deaths* [Video]. YouTube. https://www.youtube.com/watch?v=YSMV2H8u9As

Edwards, J. (2018, February 17). Lauryn Hill's Impromptu Speech Steals the Show at Los Angeles Event. [Video]. YouTube. https://www.youtube.com/watch?v=-fDELNhTeZM

Emoto, M. (2004). *The hidden messages in water.* Atria Books.

Felitti, V. J., Anda, R. F., Nordenberg, D., Williamson, D. F., Spitz, A. M., Edwards, V., Koss, M.P., Marks, J. S. (1998). Relationship of childhood abuse and household dysfunction to many of the leading causes of death in adults. *American Journal of Preventive Medicine, 14*(4), 245–258. https://doi.org/10.1016/s0749-3797(98)00017-8

Figley, C. R. (1995). *Compassion fatigue: Coping with secondary traumatic stress disorder in those who treat the traumatized.* Routledge.

Flaherty, J. (2016). *No more heroes: Grassroots challenges to the savior mentality.* AK Press.

Freire, P. (1995). *Pedagogy of hope: Reliving pedagogy of the oppressed.* The Continuum Publishing Company.

Freudenberger, H. J., & North, G. (1985). *Women's burnout: How to spot it, how to reverse it, and how to prevent it.* Penguin Books.

Frewen, P., & Lanius, R. A. (2015). *Healing the traumatized self: Consciousness, neuroscience, treatment.* Norton.

Gaynor, M. L. (1999). *The healing power of sound: Recovery from life-threatening illness using sound, voice, and music.* Shambhala Publications.

Gillespie, C. (2001, October 18). Devoted Ohio caseworker killed during interview with parent. *Seattle Times.* Retrieved October 29, 2022, from https://archive.seattletimes.com/archive/?date=20011018&slug=case18

Givens, T. (2022). *Radical empathy: Finding a path to bridging racial divides.* Policy Press, University of Bristol.

Glover Tawwab, N. (2021). *Set boundaries, find peace: A guide to reclaiming yourself.* Penguin Publishing Group.

Golden, M. B. (2023, July 23). I had my dream job as a death investigator. Then it morphed into a nightmare. *Huffington Post.* Retrieved August 5, 2023 from https://www.huffpost.com/entry/death-investigator-covid-pandemic-nightmare_n_64986492e4b08f753c2cb43a

Goldman, J. (2002). *Healing sounds: The power of harmonics.* Healing Arts Press.

Gould, D. B. (2009). *Moving politics: Emotion and ACT UP's fight against AIDS.* University Of Chicago Press.

Guggenbühl-Craig, A. (2021). *Power in the helping professions* (3rd ed., rev.). Spring Publications.

Hamer, F. L., Parker Brooks, M., & Houck, D. W. (2011). *The speeches of Fannie Lou Hamer: To tell it like it is.* Jackson: University Press of Mississippi.

Hanh, T. N. (2012). *Work: How to find joy and meaning each hour of the day.* Parallax Press.

Harris, D. A,. & Fitton, M. L. (2010). The art of yoga project: A gender-responsive yoga and creative arts curriculum for girls in the California Juvenile Justice System. *International Journal of Yoga Therapy,* 20, 110–118. https://doi.org/10.17761/ijyt.20.1.w33375003846vt18

Herman, J. (1997). *Trauma and recovery.* Basic Books.

Hersey, T. (2022). *Rest is resistance: A manifesto.* Little, Brown Spark.

Hillert, A., Albrecht, A., & Voderholzer, U. (2020). The burnout phenomenon: A résumé after more than 15,000 scientific publications. *Frontiers in Psychiatry, 11*. https://doi.org/10.3389/fpsyt.2020.519237

Hirshkowitz, M., Whiton, K., Albert, S. M., Alessi, C., Bruni, O., DonCarlos, L., Hazen, N., Herman, J., Katz, E. S., Kheirandish-Gozal, L., Neubauer, D. N., O'Donnell, A. E., Ohayon, M., Peever, J., Rawding, R., Sachdeva, R. C., Setters, B., Vitiello, M. V., Ware, J. C., & Adams Hillard, P. J. (2015). National Sleep Foundation's sleep time duration recommendations: Methodology and results summary. *Sleep Health, 1*(1), 40–43. https://doi.org/10.1016/j.sleh.2014.12.010

hooks, bell. (2000). *All about love: New visions*. Harper Perennial.

hooks, bell. (2003). *Teaching community: A pedagogy of hope*. Routledge.

Hundsdorfer, B. (2022, January 5). DCFS worker fatally stabbed during home visit. *Capitol News Illinois*. Retrieved April 29, 2023, from https://capitolnewsillinois.com/NEWS/dcfs-worker-fatally-stabbed-during-home-visit

Hunter, E. M. (2004). *Little book of big emotions: How five feelings affect everything you do (and don't do)*. Hazeldon.

Jaffe, S. (2021). *Work won't love you back*. Bold Type Books.

Jameton, A. (1984). *Nursing practice: The ethical issues*. Prentice-Hall.

Jany, L., & Winton, R. (2023, November 8). Four current and former L.A. Sheriff's Department employees died by suicide in a 24-hour span. *LA Times*. Retrieved November 15, 2023 from https://www.latimes.com/california/story/2023-11-07/four-current-and-former-l-a-sheriffs-department-employees-died-of-suicide-in-a-24-hour-span

Johnson, M. C. (2023). *We heal together: Rituals and practices for building community and connection*. Shambhala.

Joseph, R. (2018). Getting to the guts of physician burnout: A resident's perspective. *Medical Economics, 95*(15). Retrieved January 13, 2022 from https://www.medicaleconomics.com/view/getting-guts-physician-burnout-residents-perspective

Khan, L. (2021). *Deep liberation: Shamanic tools for reclaiming wholeness in a culture of trauma*. North Atlantic Books.

King, N. (2016, Dec 8). When a psychologist succumbed to stress, he coined the term "burnout." *NPR*. Retrieved April 23, 2023 from https://www.npr.org/2016/12/08/504864961/when-a-psychologist-succumbed-to-stress-he-coined-the-term-burnout

Kivel, P. (2020). Social service or social change? Who benefits from our work. Retrieved June 24, 2022 from https://paulkivel.com/wp-content/uploads/2011/07/Social-Service-or-Social-Change-2020-Update.pdf

Knoll, C., Watkins, A., & Rothfeld, M. (2020, July 11). "I couldn't do anything": The virus and an ER doctor's suicide. *New York Times*. Retrieved

January 13, 2022 from https://www.nytimes.com/2020/07/11/nyregion/lorna-breen-suicide-coronavirus.html

Kress, T. M., Emdin, C., & Lake, R. (2022). *Critical pedagogy for healing: Paths beyond "wellness," toward a soul revival of teaching and learning.* Bloomsbury Academic.

Kyodo williams, a., Owens, L. R., & Syedullah, J. (2016). *Radical dharma: Talking race, love, and liberation.* North Atlantic Books.

Law, T. (2019, October 16). New York City police officer dies by suicide— the 10th NYPD suicide in 2019. *TIME.* Retrieved January 13, 2022 from https://time.com/5702036/10th-police-suicide-nypd-new-york-city/

Lear, J. (2006). *Radical hope: Ethics in the face of cultural devastation.* Harvard University Press.

Lennon, R. P., Parascando, J., Talbot, S. G., Zhou, S., Wasserman, E., Mantri, S., Day, P.G., Liu, R., Lagerman, M., Appiah, A, Rabago, D., Dean, W. (2023). Prevalence of moral injury, burnout, anxiety, and depression in healthcare workers 2 years in to the COVID-19 pandemic. *The Journal of Nervous and Mental Disease, 211*(12), 981–984. https://doi.org/10.1097/nmd.0000000000001705

Levine, P. A. (1997). *Waking the tiger: Healing trauma.* North Atlantic Books.

Levine, P. A. (2024). *An autobiography of trauma: A healing journey.* Park Street Press.

Li, Q. (2018). *Forest bathing: How trees can help you find health and happiness.* Viking.

Lorde, A., Byrd, R. P., Cole, J. B., & Guy-Sheftall, B. (2009). *I am your sister: Collected and unpublished writings of Audre Lorde.* Oxford University Press.

Lowell, H. (2021, August 3). Fourth officer who responded to US Capitol attack dies by suicide. *The Guardian.* Retrieved January 13, 2022 from https://www.theguardian.com/us-news/2021/aug/03/kyle-defreytag-us-capitol-attack-police-officer-dies

Lowery, W., & Stankiewicz, K. (2016, February 15). "My demons won today": Ohio activist's suicide spotlights depression among Black Lives Matter leaders. *Washington Post.* Retrieved January 13, 2022 from https://www.washingtonpost.com/news/post-nation/wp/2016/02/15/my-demons-won-today-ohio-activists-suicide-spotlights-depression-among-black-lives-matter-leaders/

Lusk, J. (2015). *Yoga nidra for complete relaxation and stress relief.* New Harbinger Publications.

Maté, G. (2011) *When the body says no: Exploring the stress-disease connection.* Trade Paper Press.

Maté, G. (2022). *The myth of normal: Trauma, illness, and healing in a toxic culture.* Avery.

Margolfo, K. (2022, August 14). Social worker arrested for helping child sex trafficker. *WDTN*. Retrieved September 3, 2022 from https://www.wdtn.com/news/social-worker-arrested-for-helping-child-sex-trafficker/

Martínez, N., Connelly, C. D., Pérez, A., & Calero, P. (2021). Self-care: A concept analysis. *International Journal of Nursing Sciences, 8*(4), 418–425. https://doi.org/10.1016/j.ijnss.2021.08.007

Mascarenhas, L. (2023, August 8). New York doctor is charged with drugging and assaulting patients. *CNN*. Retrieved October 20, 2023 from https://www.cnn.com/2023/08/08/us/queens-doctor-charged-sexual-assault/index.html

Maslach, C., & Leiter, M. P. (1997). *The truth about burnout: How organizations cause personal stress and what to do about it.* Jossey-Bass.

Mathieu, F. (2012). *The compassion fatigue workbook*. Routledge.

Meko, H. (2023, March 31). Court clerk and defense lawyer are charged in a cash-for-clients scheme. *The New York Times*. Retrieved May 5, 2023 from https://www.nytimes.com/2023/03/31/nyregion/defense-lawyer-bribe-sdny.html

Menakem, R. (2017). *My grandmother's hands: Racialized trauma and the pathway to mending our hearts and bodies*. Central Recovery Press.

Mencagli, M., & Nieri, M. (2019). *The secret therapy of trees: Harness the healing energy of forest bathing and natural landscapes* (J. Richards, Trans.). Rodale Books.

Mills, K. (2007). *This little light of mine: The life of Fannie Lou Hamer*. University Press of Kentucky.

Mitchell, S. (2018). *Sacred instructions: Indigenous wisdom for living spirit-based change*. North Atlantic Books.

Morales, A.L. (2019) *Medicine stories: Essays for radicals*. Duke University Press Books.

Mother Teresa. (2012). *Where there is love, there is god: A path to closer union with god and greater love for others*, edited by Brian Kolodiejchuk . Doubleday Religion.

Murphy, J. (2021). *First responder: A memoir of life, death, and love on New York City's front lines*. Pegasus Books.

Myers, M. F. (2017). *Why physicians die by suicide: Lessons learned from their families and others who cared*. Michael F. Myers.

Naiman, R. R. (2014). *Healing night: The science and spirit of sleeping, dreaming, and awakening*. New Moon Media.

Nichols, W. J. (2014). *Blue mind: The surprising science that shows how being near, in, on, or under water can make you happier, healthier, most connected, and better at what you do*. Little, Brown and Company.

Nicol, D. J., & Yee, J. A. (2017). "Reclaiming our time": Women of color faculty and radical self-care in the academy. *Feminist Teacher, 27*(2), 133–156. Retrieved August 5, 2022 from https://www.muse.jhu.edu/article/715993

Northrup, L. M. (2022). *Radical healership: How to build a values-driven healing practice in a profit-driven world.* North Atlantic Books.

Olfson, M., Cosgrove, C. M., Wall, M. M., & Blanco, C. (2023). Suicide risks of health care workers in the US. *JAMA, 330*(12), 1161–1166. https://doi.org/10.1001/jama.2023.15787

Oswald, T. K., Rumbold, A. R., Kedzior, S. G. E., & Moore, V. M. (2020). Psychological impacts of "screen time" and "green time" for children and adolescents: A systematic scoping review. *PLoS ONE, 15*(9), e0237725. https://doi.org/10.1371/journal.pone.0237725

Orloff, J. (2018). *The empath's survival guide.* Sounds True.

Owens, L. R. (2020). *Love and rage: The path of liberation through anger.* North Atlantic Books.

Oxford Languages. (n.d.). *Oxford languages English dictionary.* Retrieved January 13, 2022, from https://languages.oup.com/google-dictionary-en/

Page, C. & Woodland, E. (2023). *Healing justice lineages: Dreaming at the crossroads of liberation, collective care, and safety.* North Atlantic Books.

Parker, G. (2022). *Transforming ethnic and race-based traumatic stress with yoga.* Singing Dragon.

Pearlman, L. A., & Saakvitne, K. W. (1995). *Trauma and the therapist: Countertransference and vicarious traumatization in psychotherapy with incest survivors.* Norton.

Perry, B. D., & Winfrey, O. (2021). *What happened to you? Conversations on trauma, resilience, and healing.* Flatiron Books.

Porges, S. W. (2011). *The polyvagal theory: Neurophysiological foundations of emotions, attachment, communication, and self-regulation.* Norton.

Raffo, S. (2022). *Liberated to the bone: Histories. bodies. futures.* AK Press.

Ransby, B. (2003). *Ella Baker and the black freedom movement: A radical democratic vision.* University of North Carolina Press.

Raphael, K. (2016, August 23). Why do so many activists commit suicide? *Medium.* Retrieved January 13, 2022 from https://medium.com/@KateInOakland/suicide-and-the-left-bf24a5eafcd

Reda, O. (2022). *The wounded hero: The pain and joy of caregiving.* Norton.

Roberts, N. F. (2023, March 19). Sounding The Alarm: Firefighters Remain More Likely To Die By Suicide Than On Duty. *Forbes.* https://www.forbes.com/sites/nicoleroberts/2023/03/19/sounding-the-alarm-firefighters-remain-more-likely-to-die-by-suicide-than-on-duty/?sh=3729b3a42353

Rosenberg, S. (2017). *Accessing the healing power of the vagus nerve: Self-exercises for anxiety, depression, trauma, and autism.* North Atlantic Books.

Rothschild, B. (2000). *The body remembers: The psychophysiology of trauma and trauma treatment.* Norton.

Rothschild, B., & Rand, M. L. (2006). *Help for the helper: The psychophysiology of compassion fatigue and vicarious trauma.* Norton.

Sainato, M. (2022, May 27). “It’s all preventable”: Tackling America’s workplace suicide epidemic. *The Guardian.* Retrieved June 8, 2023 from https://www.theguardian.com/us-news/2022/may/27/us-workplace-suicide-rates-pandemic

Salzberg, S. (1995). *Lovingkindness: The revolutionary art of happiness.* Shambhala.

Sanders, C. (2021). *Black magic: What black leaders learned from trauma and triumph.* Simon & Schuster.

Sapolsky, R. M. (2004). *Why zebras don’t get ulcers* (3rd ed.). St. Martin’s Press.

Shatz , R., & Barash, A. (Directors). (2020). *Lenox hill* [Film]. Netflix Original.

Shay, J. (2014). Moral Injury. *Psychoanalytic Psychology, 31*(2), 182–191. https://doi.org/10.1353/itx.2012.0000

Siegel, D. J. (1999). *The developing mind: How relationships and the brain interact to shape who we are.* Guilford Press.

Skovholt, T. M. (2005). The cycle of caring: A model of expertise in the helping professions. *Journal of Mental Health Counseling, 27*(1), 82–94. Retrieved June 28, 2022 from https://link.gale.com/apps/doc/A127977274/AONE?u=anon~a4e1fbcb&sid=googleScholar&xid=52595ef1

Skovholt, T. M., & Trotter-Mathison, M. (2016). *The resilient practitioner: Burnout prevention and self-care strategies for counselors, therapists, teachers, and health professionals.* Routledge.

Somé, M. P. (1994). *Of water and the spirit: Ritual, magic, and initiation in the life of an African shaman.* Penguin.

Somé, M. P. (1997). *Ritual: Power, healing, and community.* Penguin Compass.

Somé, M. P. (1998). *The healing wisdom of Africa: Finding life purpose through nature, ritual, and community.* Jeremy P. Tarcher/Putnam.

Song, Y. K., Mantri, S., Lawson, J. M., Berger, E. J., & Koenig, H. G. (2021). Morally injurious experiences and emotions of health care professionals during the COVID-19 pandemic before vaccine availability. *JAMA Network Open, 4*(11), e2136150. https://doi.org/10.1001/jamanetworkopen.2021.36150

SSEXBBOX. (2017, May 22). *On inequality: Angela Davis and Judith Butler in conversation.* Oakland Book Festival 2017. [Video]. YouTube. https://www.youtube.com/watch?v=-MzmifPGk94

Stamm, B. H. (1999). *Secondary traumatic stress: Self-care issues for clinicians, researchers, and educators* (Second). Sidran Press.

Stanley, E. (2019). *Widen the window: Training your brain and body to thrive during stress and recover from trauma.* Avery.

Sugrue, E. P. (2020). Moral injury among professionals in K–12 education. *American Educational Research Journal, 57*(1), 43–68. https://doi.org/10.3102/0002831219848690

Tawwab, N. G. (2021). *Set boundaries, find peace: A guide to reclaiming yourself.* Penguin.

ter Kuile, C. (2020). *The power of ritual: Turning everyday activities into soulful practices.* HarperCollins.

Tokumatsu, G. (2023, December 9). *Widow of sheriff's deputy who died by suicide says constant overtime pushed him to tragic choice.* NBC Los Angeles. Retrieved December 15, 2023, from https://www.nbclosangeles.com/news/local/widow-of-sheriffs-deputy-who-died-by-suicide-says-constant-overtime-pushed-him-to-tragic-choice/3287347/

Turow, R. G. (2017). *Mindfulness skills for trauma and PTSD: Practices for recovery and resilience.* Norton.

upEND Movement. (2022, October 19). *Angela Davis in conversation with Joyce McMillan | How We endUP 2022* [Video]. YouTube. https://www.youtube.com/watch?v=5xDmaQyni4M

Vainshtein, A. (2022, January 20). *Searchers find body of missing Stanford nurse.* San Francisco Chronicle. Retrieved February 6, 2022 from https://www.sfchronicle.com/bayarea/article/Search-continues-near-Dumbarton-Bridge-for-16791246.php

van der Kolk, B. (2014). *The body keeps the score: Brain, mind, and body in the healing of trauma.* Penguin Books.

van Dernoot Lipsky, L., & Burk, C. (2009). *Trauma stewardship: An everyday guide to caring for self while caring for others.* Berrett-Koehler Publishers.

Vielmetti, B. (2021, December 22). *Former children's court judge sentenced to 9 years for child porn.* Milwaukee Journal Sentinel. Retrieved January 13, 2022 from https://www.jsonline.com/story/news/crime/2021/12/22/ex-wisconsin-childrens-court-judge-gets-9-years-child-porn-case/8975934002/#

Walker, M. P. (2017). *Why we sleep: Unlocking the power of sleep and dreams.* Scribner.

Weinberg, M. (2009). Moral distress: A missing but relevant concept for ethics in social work. *Canadian Social Work Review / Revue Canadienne de Service Social, 26*(2), 139–151. http://www.jstor.org/stable/41669909

Weller, F. (2015). *The wild edge of sorrow: Rituals of renewal and the sacred work of grief*. North Atlantic Books.

Wheeler, S., & King, L. (2019, November 20). *NHS nurse stressed over 12-hour shifts killed herself after "downward spiral."* Mirror. Retrieved April 23, 2023, from https://www.mirror.co.uk/news/uk-news/nhs-nurse-stressed-after-working-20922721

Wible, P. (2016). *Physician suicide letters answered.* Pamela Wible, MD.

Williams, F. (2017). *The nature fix: Why nature makes us happier, healthier, and more creative.* Norton.

Wohlleben, P. (2021). *The heartbeat of trees: Embracing our ancient bond with forests and nature* (J. Billinghurst, Trans.). Greystone Books.

World Health Organization. (2019). *Burn-out an "occupational phenomenon": International classification of diseases.* World Health Organization. Retrieved 20 August, 2022 from https://www.who.int/news/item/28-05-2019-burn-out-an-occupational-phenomenon-international-classification-of-diseases

Wright Glenn, A. (2017). *Holding space: On loving, dying, and letting go*. Parallax Press.

Yamasaki, Z. A. (2022). *Trauma-informed yoga for survivors of sexual assault: Practices for healing and teaching with compassion*. Norton.

Zannoni, J. (2023). *Drowning in hats: How to thrive in the madcap business of nonprofit leadership.* Platypus Publishing.

INDEX

ABOUT THE AUTHOR

Nicole M. Steward has been a social worker for over two decades. A strong advocate for youth experiencing homelessness and those caught in the child welfare/juvenile justice systems, she has been a rape crisis counselor, CASA, foster parent, and is a past chair of the Santa Clara County Child Abuse Prevention Council. Nicole is currently a McKinney-Vento/Foster Youth Liaison in the San Francisco Bay Area, and is the president of the Board for the National Association for the Education of Homeless Children and Youth (NAEHCY). She is also a yoga teacher and sound healer with a focus on trauma-informed practices, and offers self-care workshops and retreats. A quote that drives her forward in her work is by Lilla Watson: "If you have come to help me, you are wasting your time. But if you have come because your liberation is bound up with mine, then let us work together."